My Four Homes

My Four Homes

A MEMOIR

Manisha Roy

CHIRON PUBLICATIONS
ASHEVILLE, NORTH CAROLINA

Also by Manisha Roy

NONFICTION

The Reckoning Heart: An Anthropologist Looks at Her Worlds
Bengali Women

COEDITOR

Liber Amicorum: A Festschrift for Jyoti and Minakshi Datta
Lekhoni: An Anthology of Immigrant Bengali Writings
Cast the First Stone: Ethics in Analytic Practice

FICTION AND MEMOIR

"Ei Akashe . . ."
Professor Hamilton's Passage to India
Sulatar Proshna ebong Annyanya Golpa
Amaar Chaar Baari

Book and cover design by Marianne Jankowski.
Printed in the United States of America.

ISBN 978-1-63051-212-5 paperback
ISBN 978-1-63051-213-2 hardcover
ISBN 978-1-63051-214-9 ebook

Library of Congress Cataloging-in-Publication Data
Roy, Manisha, 1936-
    My four homes : a memoir / Manisha Roy.
      pages cm
    Includes bibliographical references and index.
    ISBN 978-1-63051-212-5 (pbk. : alk. paper) -- ISBN 978-1-63051-213-2
(hardcover : alk. paper) -- ISBN 978-1-63051-214-9 (e-book)
    1. Roy, Manisha, 1936- 2. Roy, Manisha, 1936---Homes and haunts. 3.
Women anthropologists--Biography. 4. Jungian psychology. I. Title.
GN21.R67A3 2015
301.092--dc23
[B]

2015003485

*This book is dedicated to the women and men
of the next generations in my family on both sides,
so they can learn the story of one of their elders.*

My life is a necklace studded with various precious and semiprecious stones. Each one tells a story I remember— some bright and dazzling, others not so bright, some dull and ordinary—but all unforgettable. I chose these stories because they shaped my life and they want to be told. New stories are still being born— but at a different pace in my seventh decade.

CONTENTS

Grandmother's Home

Parents' Home

My Home

A gallery of photographs follows page 166.

FOREWORD

In *Bengali Women*, a fascinating book published in 1976, Manisha Roy subtly shed light on the associations and inconsistencies existing between the traditional ideal of feminine life and its deep reality in Bengal, a region in the eastern part of India, an ancient civilization. Here, Roy recounts, in the first person, the life of a woman grappling deep inside with contradiction. She is groomed by tradition and breeding to honor her family, her social class, and her gods in her behavior and life choices. However, she can meet such expectations only by giving up her personal goals.

In this story, unfolding over seven decades, Roy creates a poignant drama in which we see first a child, then a young woman, and finally a woman, transcended by an inner force as she opposes the collective law. But at what price ? The price of her mother's shame and a daughter's rejection, with the daughter fleeing to exile and subjecting herself to immense suffering. Like the great goddesses who are the guardians of tradition, such a mother punishes any transgression by repudiating and banishing the rebel, condemned either to die within her deepest being or to leave the maternal paradise forever.

Long before she had a PhD in anthropology, Manisha, at the ripe age of four and with her eyes wide open to the world around her, applied her keen intelligence to understanding and seeing the link between the way people behave and the social world they inhabit.

In *Bengali Women*, Roy used examples from daily life—sometimes personal memories—to explain the culture and mores of Bengal. Here she shows us how language, ethnic identity, religion, customs, rituals, and more dictate the major turning points in anyone's life, from birth to death. Based on her own personal history, she reveals the power of the cultural conditioning she presented in her first book.

Indeed this is the story of a woman, of a thrilling life, that goes far beyond autobiography. The subject travels from continent to continent, from India to America to Europe and back again. But perhaps, above all, it is the story of the self-realization of the unconscious, to borrow from the opening of Jung's *Memories, Dreams, Reflections*.

In this book, a Bengali woman describes her life honestly. If we tend to be charmed, in most cases, by her observations and descriptions, we also can't help being overwhelmed by how—tradition—in the names of Durga, Krishna, Shiva, Kamakhya, and other gods—grinds down the individual, particularly women, who are taught that they owe their being to these powers and have no right to set a different course for their life.

Over the years, from the foothills of the Himalayas to the fertile plains of undivided Bengal, we follow Roy to her various homes. First the home of her parents near the border with Nepal, China, and Burma, where she was born. Then the homes of her paternal grandparents, in what is now Bangladesh, and her maternal grandparents, where the whole family was forced to flee the Japanese in the Second World War.

From tea plantations on the slopes of the Himalayan foothills to the fertile valley of the Brahmaputra and the Ganges River, lined with rice paddies and villages carved out of the jungle, Roy guides us on an amazing journey through the India of the past, describing an Assam worthy of the *Mahabharata*. From the aroma of sandalwood, the tang of the spices, the color of the saris, the damp heat of the rice paddies, the harvest festival, the sound of the conches, the sacrifice of the bull, and all the other rituals that punctuate life from moment to moment. Her descriptions enchant the heart and senses, so lively are they with humor, written in a vivid style sustained by a rich vocabulary.

Just as we are most enchanted, the spell is broken by the collapse of British rule. An unending series of fratricidal riots abates only when India is partitioned on the basis of religion. Tragedy strikes those who must leave, abandoning land and belongings that had been handed down for generations. This is where personal history mingles with the history of the subcontinent. According to a Sanskrit proverb, "Mother and motherland are greater than heaven." What can be more dreadful than being expelled and rejected by Mother Earth, by the Goddess, by the Mother? Roy shows us this maternal wound with strength and modesty. It has exacted much suffering from both her soul and her body. Yet it defined her path.

In fact, Manisha Roy always knew that the only deity she could really trust lived deep within herself, in the same place as her one and only true home. This god is what C. G. Jung called the Self. From earliest childhood, her whole life is a living example of the manifestation of the Self in an individual.

Although she survived her long journey into the night, it took a heavy toll. Indeed we all have to embark alone on our inner journey in search of our own destiny, in order "to become what we are," as Nietzsche said. But, as this book shows, this necessity leaves a deep wound, which heals only slowly, "for the relation to the mother . . . *must die, which itself almost causes man's death*" (C. G. Jung, *Symbols of Transformation*, par. 480).

Viviane Thibaudier
Paris
September 2014

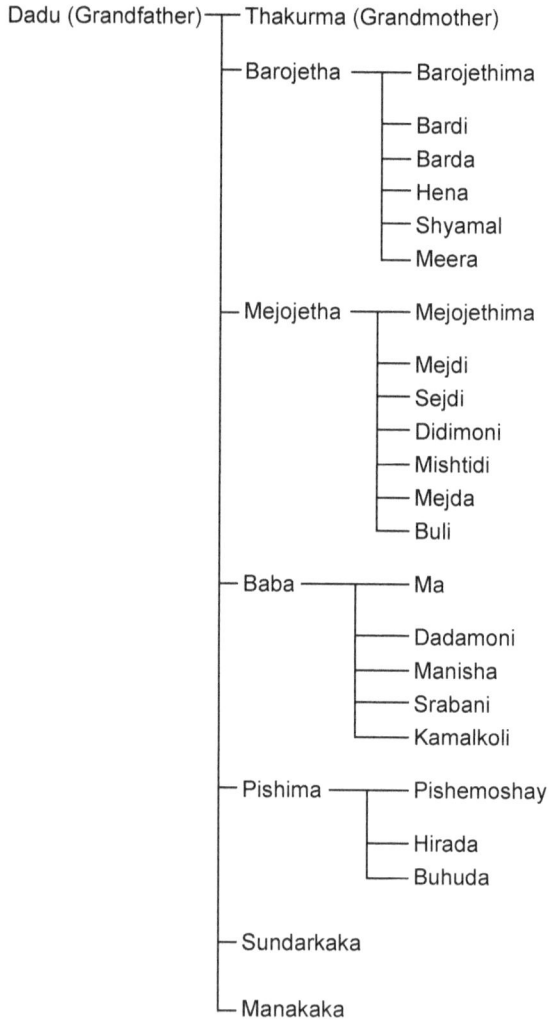

FATHER'S FAMILY

This chart gives the kinship terms for my family members as referred to in "Grandfather's Home" from my point of view. In the Bengali language, different terms are used to describe family relationships on the father's side and on the mother's, and the same term is used to address and to refer to a relative.

Within a generation words often take on a suffix such as *didi* (or the shorter form *di*, feminine) or *dada* (*da*, masculine) when referring to siblings and cousins who are older than oneself. Hirada and Budhuda are two male cousins—my father's sister's sons. I used their given names with the suffixes *da* to mean that they were older than I am. First cousins on both sides of the family are considered like siblings. For the younger siblings we use their given names. Sometimes a prefix is added which signals to the listener that the person referred to is older or to denote some special attribute, such as "handsome" (*Sundar*) or "sweet" (*Mishti*). For example, Barojetha is my oldest uncle on my father's side, and Mejojetha is the middle one.

Across generations, *jetha* refers to the father's older brothers and *kaka* refers to his younger brothers. *Pishima* refers to all the father's sisters, both older and younger. Jetha's wife is called Jethima and Kaka's wife is Kakima. The suffix *ma*, which means "mother," is added to these women relatives by marriage to put them in the category of mothers. In family life, they act as surrogate mothers, or even as adopted mothers if needed.

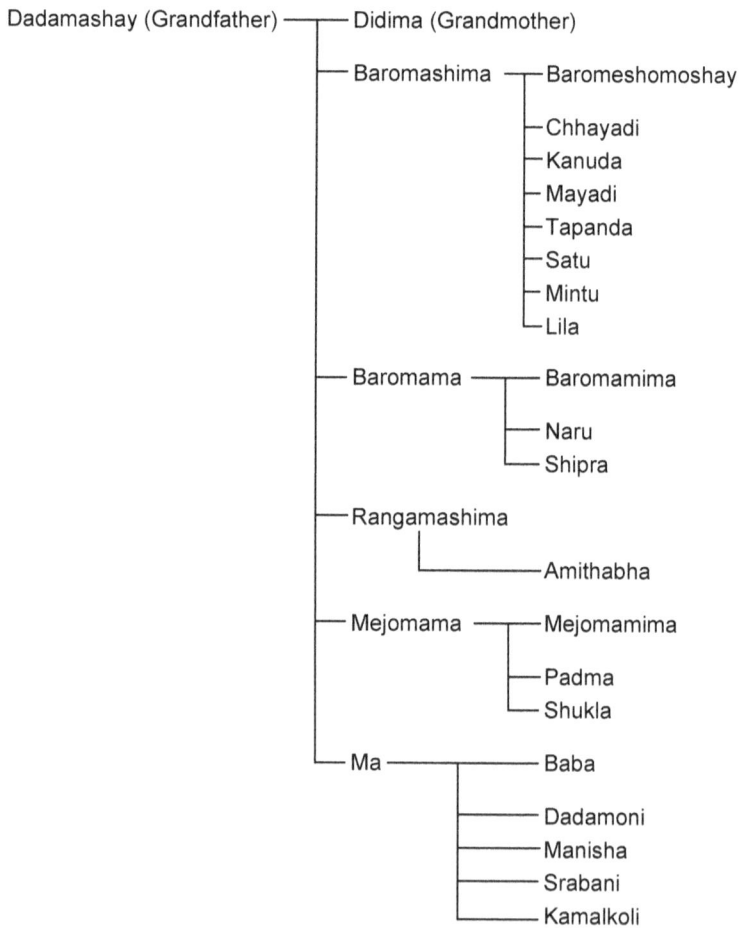

MOTHER'S FAMILY

In this chart I mention only those relatives I refer to in "Grand-mother's House." My mother had two older sisters, whom I addressed as Baromashima and Rangamashima. The mother's sisters are called *mashima*, and their husbands are *meshomoshay*. Baromashima is my older aunt, *baro* referring to big or old and Rangamashima is so called because of her fair complexion—the Bengali word for which is *ranga*. The mother's brothers are called *mama*.

My mother had three brothers, the youngest was away studying in the city at the time. I knew only her two older brothers, and I addressed them as Baromama and Mejomama (*mejo* meaning the middle) and their wives as Baromamima and Mejomamima, respectively. In this chart Rangamashima's husband is not mentioned because she was a widow. My cousins on this side included the seven children of Baromashima and her husband, one son and a daughter of Baromama and Baromamima, and Rangamashima's only son; Mejomama and his wife had two daughters at the time. When my story starts, I had one older brother, Subhas, who I called Dadamoni, and a sister, Srabani, whose nickname is Debi. My two younger siblings were born later.

My Four Homes

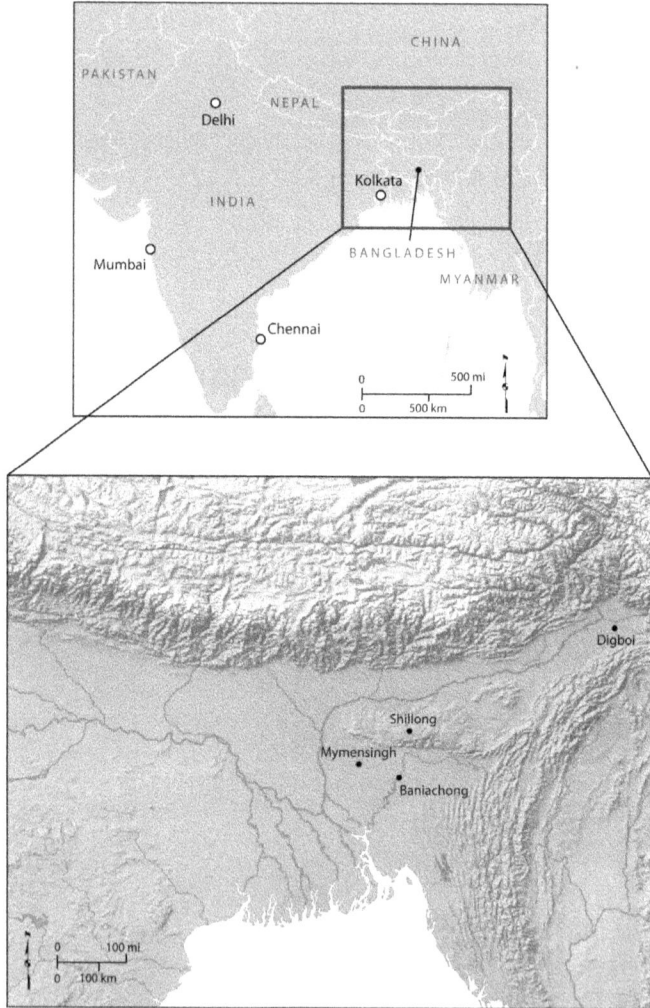

*Map of undivided India before independence in 1947
showing my birthplace, Digboi, in the state of Assam, and Shillong,
Mymensingh (mother's family home), Baniachong (father's family home),
and Kolkata, where I went to college before coming to America*

The year was 1951. It had been four years since India's independence after nearly three hundred years of British rule. The price of freedom from foreign rule was more than Indian politicians had bargained for. Millions of Hindus and Muslims of Bengal and the Punjab were uprooted, losing close family members in riots and becoming refugees on either side of the border of the newly divided country. Calcutta, a city of several million, had to accommodate additional millions of refugees overnight, spilling out of the railway stations and putting enormous pressure on its infrastructure. The emotional cost to these families was beyond measure. Indians did not have to fight their foreign rulers to gain freedom, but the pages of history books were forever stained with the blood of neighbors and friends who had lived side by side for generations worshipping different gods until independence. All this happened because the political partition of the country was mostly based on religion.

When independence came, my family was in Digboi, a small oil town in the northeastern corner of India near the borders of Tibet and Burma. We shuddered from a safe distance without any comprehension of the suffering of these people. But in a way my personal life paralleled the country's history. I for one never imagined the price I would pay for my own independence as I grew into adolescence in a nuclear family dominated by a conservative albeit loving mother.

My brother—older by nearly two years—and I were idle, waiting for the results of our final exams after four months of very hard work preparing for the set of eight tests that would determine our academic futures. Being studious and disciplined, I had spent most of my high school years totally buried in my books. I had already discovered deep satisfaction and peace in concentrating on work. I found that the printed word was able to transport me to an uplifted world in a way that nothing else could. Now suddenly I was without that engrossing commitment and did not know what to do with myself for the next three months.

Mother, an attentive student in her adolescence and still a voracious reader, understood the situation and decided to avert the possibility of my idle brain turning to something devilish. She came up with devices of her own, a plan she had been concocting for some time. One afternoon as I was weaving a fantasy about a story I had just finished reading, Ma appeared with a sewing basket. She said, "A girl needs to learn other skills besides reading fat books," and picked up the book from my lap and put it aside. She wanted me to learn some technique of embroidery or other. A few days into it, I began to enjoy this newfound skill of sewing with colorful silk threads and a needle, sketching pretty designs on cloth.

A few days later Mother approached me with a set of four squares cut from the finest white cotton and said, "Here, let's see how much you have learned. You'll embroider these handkerchiefs with the designs I shall draw for you." She used carbon paper to apply some designs to one corner of each square and chose different colored threads. One of them was called "flying swan"—a round picture divided by water and sky where three swans stretched their wings and feet. Another was a bouquet of flowers—red, blue, yellow, and purple—held by a hand. A butterfly sat on the bouquet. Stretching the cloth in a round bamboo frame, I began to fill in the blue pencil lines with colorful silk threads and was delighted to see the slow transformation of the pencil drawings into water, sky, birds, and flowers. I'd had no idea that I would enjoy such an activity. In school I'd been totally bored with the domestic science class where we learned how to sew patches and do blanket stitch. After finishing the four handkerchiefs I said to my mother, "Baba will really be surprised when you give these to him. He has no idea that I could do something like this."

"These are not for your father. By the way, what do you think of Subrata? Don't you think he is nice?" Avoiding my eyes, she folded the handkerchiefs neatly.

"Who? Roasted Eggplant? You mean to tell me that I have done all this painstaking work for Roasted Eggplant?" I was about to explode.

"What do you mean by 'roasted eggplant'? What an awful name for a nice young man! Shame on you! He is such a nice gentleman. Besides, he has a good job. Your father is very pleased with his work, and I'm sure he will have a very successful career in the future. I'm going to talk to him soon and then write to his parents with a proposal."

Now it all became crystal clear why Subrata had been frequenting our home several evenings a week and was entertained with tea, egg samosas, and other specialties from Mother's kitchen. Getting me to embroider these handkerchiefs was nothing more than the final piece of Mother's master plan. She was going to talk with him and write to his parents! What of my opinion about my own marriage?

The fantasy I had occasionally woven at age thirteen about falling in love was no longer central to my existence at age fifteen. Now I was dreaming of bigger things. Rows of leather-bound books were waiting for me in Kolkata to transport me to a fascinating world of knowledge. Even the very idea of going to college gave me goose bumps. Yet Ma was thinking I would give all this up to marry an engineer whose loose overweight body reminded us children of a roasted eggplant which could be peeled easily if one held it by the stem! That she could even think that I would sacrifice my grand future in Kolkata shocked me more than her dream of marrying me to a man of her choice. I knew she had no clue about my dreams. Still, her reluctance to ask me even once about my opinion hit me hard, although I had a vague feeling that in her mind she thought she was doing me a favor by choosing a young man with a good potential career for me to marry. That was the best way she knew how to do her maternal duty!

I had always known that Ma loved my older brother Subhas—whom I call Dadamoni—more, and all her dreams for a glorious future centered on her firstborn son. My academic achievements and obedience to her authority had not succeeded in making me her favorite child, although she was proud of me. I did not know then that marrying off the eldest daughter at a tender age was considered an essential duty for conservative parents. Later, much later, when I became a psychotherapist, I also realized that the love and affection perhaps between all mothers and their daughters are mixed with a dose of envy and competition. Averting my tear-filled eyes I simply said, "As soon as the exam results are out, I plan to go to college in Kolkata. Marriage can wait a few years until I finish my education."

"What's wrong with studying after marriage? Subrata's family lives in Kolkata. They may not mind you continuing your education from their home. Besides, I don't recall asking your opinion about this." Dismissing further conversation, Mother began to gather the sewing things. I got up, dropping the needle and silk threads on the floor.

I was sure that Father would never agree to this plan. He had always supported me in my studies. I could not help noticing how proud he had been each year when I received prizes for standing first in class. I found him in the garden. With a small trowel he was weeding the bottom of a row of okra plants. When I asked him about this conspiracy, he smiled before saying, "Your mother is determined to have a big wedding for you. It's her dream. But the dream can wait another four years. If your scores are good, she won't have any argument against your going to college. Don't worry, I shall talk to her. In the meantime, you should sit down and make a list of the books you wish to take to Kolkata with you." Relieved I went to my room.

I had a pang of sadness as I looked at my bookshelf and my desk with my papers, notebooks, pen, and pencils. What would happen if I really had to leave all this and be married off to a stranger? I knew that marriage was a woman's destiny. But why does a girl have to jump into it so soon? And why was this question not raised about my brother at all? Why were girls and boys treated so differently? As children, when we were visiting our village home for vacation, I never noticed such discrimination. Could it be because we were so many children gathered together for a short time? I did remember that at dinner the delicacies such as fish heads and the sweets like *rasogollas* always went to the boys' plates, but we were all showered with the same love and affection. As a matter of fact, we girls were favored more by the uncles, and to our grandfather his granddaughters were always special.

As I write now, wonderful memories of the part of my childhood spent in the village homes of both sets of grandparents come crowding into my mind, letting me forget the previous memory with my mother and erasing the earlier pain. In a second I am transported to the villages in the eastern part of Bengal, which are now in Bangladesh, an independent nation since 1971 when it separated from Pakistan. Both sides of my family, as a result of the partition of India in 1947, lost all their properties and had to relocate some seven hundred miles from their original homes. Unlike many other Hindu families, they were fortunate in that they did not lose anyone in the riots. My relatives on both sides were well-to-do landlords. Father's family lived in the town of Habigunj and the village of Baniachong of the district of Sylhet, and Mother's family lived in Kayasthapalli, a village in the district of Mymensingh.

Grandfather's Home

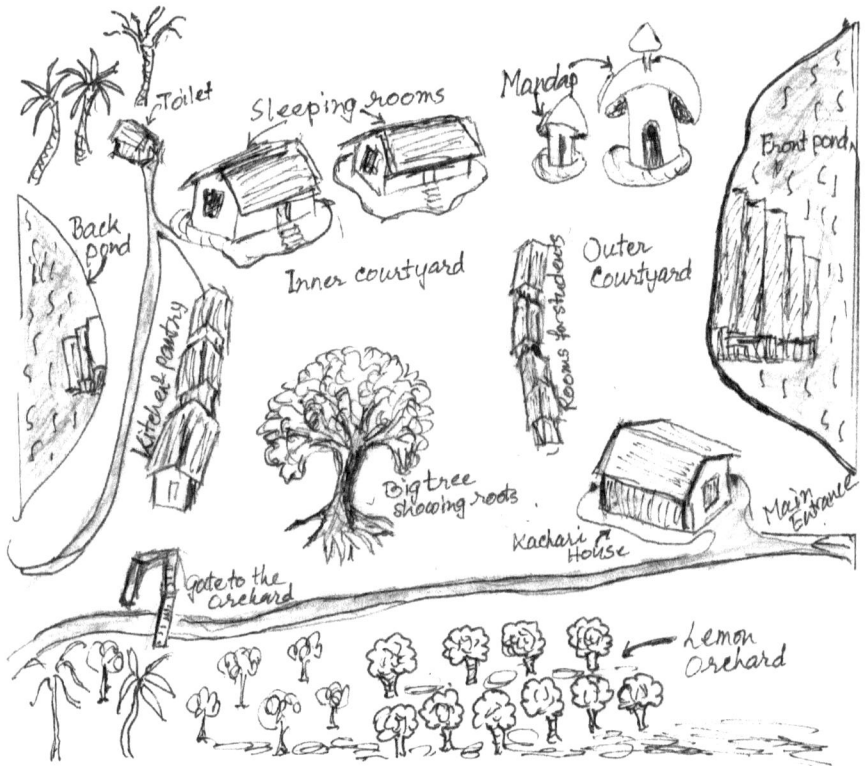

Toilet

Sleeping rooms

Mandap

Front pond

Back pond

Inner courtyard

Outer Courtyard

Kitchen & pantry

Rooms for students

Big tree shooting roots

Kachari House

Main Entrance

Gate to the orchard

Lemon Orchard

THE VILLAGE HOME

It was the autumn month of September, when our ox-drawn carts carrying my parents and four of us children and my oldest uncle's family of six arrived at the front yard of my father's ancestral home in Baniachong. I was seven years old and had been here a few times before. But all I could remember were fleeting images of my grandmother pounding betel nuts in an iron mortar with a pestle, her red mouth chewing the betel quid, a red-bordered sari draping her head. My grandmother died soon afterward from choking on a piece of betel nut caught in her esophagus. It happened on the evening of Lakshmi Puja—worship of the goddess Lakshmi, who protects homes and families and bestows wealth and prosperity—an auspicious occasion for any Hindu household. Since that day no one in our family has ever performed Lakshmi Puja. According to family legend, whenever one of the young men brought his new wife into the family, she was told about this custom, among other instructions. If a member of the younger generations defied this proscription, inauspicious and harmful things would happen. This was just one of many family traditions which were handed down and eventually became family destiny. To this day if a brave new wife sets up a shrine with an image of Lakshmi to worship, a chill runs through her spine and she wonders if she will be punished for this misconduct.

We had arrived in Habiganj a few days earlier from Digboi in the state of Assam, where my father was an engineer in a British oil company. The three-day train trip through the hill country and plains of Assam was captivating for us. We passed through twenty-one tunnels, which Dadamoni and I counted carefully. Every time the train went through a tunnel, I waited eagerly for the darkness to end and at the same time hoped that it would go on longer. Defying mother's admonition, I stuck my neck out of the train window to look down on the thread-wide white rivers way down in the deep gorges that at other times appeared high up on the hill slopes as waterfalls. The slapping wind on my face and hair felt exhilarating. But it also blew grains of coal from the locomotive engine into my eyes. Mother had to use the corner of a clean handkerchief to carefully take the coal particles out, and we were strictly forbidden to stick our heads out again. Passing trees with elephant-ear leaves were dark and moist. Occasionally we would have a glimpse of snake-long white orchids hanging down from the vines encircling those moist trees. We knew that this part of Assam had the highest rainfall in the world. As we approached Bengal, the landscape changed from dark forested hills to wide fields sprinkled with mango, banana, jack-fruit trees, and bamboo clumps. The scene rolling by outside the train window was both old and new to me—familiar trees in a new landscape—and I was excited, wondering about the future adventures.

The house in Habiganj, one of the large towns of Sylhet, a district well known for its natural beauty, orange plantations, and upright population, was occupied by our oldest uncle, whom we called Barojetha. He stayed in town to practice law, which he did rarely. A handsome, authoritarian man with a hot temper, Barojetha ruled the family with strong hands, yet showed great affection for children, which included all of us. In fact my father's brothers and sisters—five that we were close to—were all warm and affectionate people.

On the way from Habiganj to Baniachong, some eleven miles distant, we could barely see through the dust kicked up by the ox hooves. Gradually we got used to the jolts and rough rhythm of the oxcart, an entirely new vehicle for us. The autumn sky in the distance was sapphire blue, with scattered cotton clouds, which seemed to have come down to become the silver cats' tails that swayed like huge brooms on the horizon.

Baniachong—the largest village in the world, we were told—

is now a famous village in Bangladesh. Father's family lived in a spacious home with distinct outer and inner quarters. The outer quarters were ruled by the men of the family and were used to receive guests and outsiders; the inner part was run by the women and was the place where the family lived, played, ate, married, grew old, and died.

It was just after sunset when the carts approached the village home. The western sky was still lit with long strokes of pink and white. On one side of the big yard our three carts stopped and the backs were lowered for us to get off. On the other side there were bamboo mats full of golden paddy drying. A few yards from the house we could see a large pond, which was called the Pond of Steps. Red and white marble steps went down all the way to the water and even a few feet below. After the dusty ride I felt like walking down to the cool, clear pond for a dip.

Mejojetha (the second oldest uncle) and Mejojethima (his wife) lived here with their six children. The youngest, a girl whose nickname was Buli, was slightly older than me, and Hena, Barojetha's oldest daughter by his third marriage, was slightly younger. The three of us became close in no time, although Buli and I were closer. I found Buli more experienced in matters of life I knew nothing about, and Hena was still a bit too naive for me to confide in fully. Besides, she wasn't good at keeping our sworn secrets. Of course, my relationship with Buli wasn't an unadulterated pleasure either. It was fraught with competition, occasional mistrust, and mischief. But it lasted beyond these obstacles and was renewed each time we visited the country home.

THE HOOKAH

The front house had wooden filigree along the eaves. This was the outer house or *kachari bari*, consisting of a large room which served as an auditorium where our grandfather—whom we called Dadu—and Mejojetha met with villagers on business related to the estate.

Grandfather sat on an ornate chair that looked like a throne. Next to it on a low stool stood a hookah, or water pipe, with a long snake-like tube attached to it. Everything about this water pipe fascinated me—the red hot disk of tobacco on its clay top, its *guruk guruk* sound, along with the aromatic odor of tobacco when grandfather put one end of the tube in his mouth. The water pipe was the thing that pulled us toward this formal room.

One afternoon, when the grown-ups were taking a nap after lunch, Buli and I sneaked out to the outer house and peeped inside grandfather's parlor. Nobody was in sight. We went in, and I took the tube of the water pipe and blew into it. A spray of water fell all over the place. My embarrassment increased tenfold when suddenly out of nowhere Budhu—one of the older cousins—materialized. He had been behind the door watching us.

"What a mess! You girls know nothing about these matters, yet you have to interfere with everything. Since when do girls smoke a hookah? Watch me." With a flare of authority, he snatched the tube from me, wiped the tip with his palm just like I saw grown men do when they shared a hookah, and began to smoke, the sound and all. Although there was no fire or tobacco, we were impressed but said nothing. I was determined to learn how to smoke a water pipe the correct way.

One evening a few days later I peeked into grandfather's chamber and saw him smoking his hookah alone with his eyes nearly closed—an expression of satisfaction on his face. That enchanting aroma and fine smoke were circling around him. He took the pipe out of his mouth and asked, "Oh, is that you, my dear? What can I do for you?"

"Dadu, could you teach me how to smoke your hookah?" I felt emboldened by his gentle words.

Dadu frowned a bit before laughing loudly, then said, "All right. Come, come close." He sat me on the wide arm of his chair and passed the tube to me. Gratefully I put it in my mouth and drew a couple of breaths. It made the same *guruk guruk* sound, but my mouth tasted bitter and I began to feel dizzy. I returned the tube to my grandfather as quickly as I could. I never tried to smoke the hookah again, nor did I tell anyone about it. I know Dadu never told anyone either.

FISH AND NEW RICE FESTIVAL

Early one morning Buli's older sister, whom we called Mishtidi, shook Buli and me vigorously, saying, "Hey, wake up. Come and see what happened at the pond." We followed her—sleep still on our eyelids—though it soon disappeared as we approached the front pond. Near the red and white marble steps there was a small crowd of people and a lot of commotion, including shouting and screaming. The boys of the family were already there, all talking at the same time as if they were a big part of the activity. Two narrow boats were being raised from the water, each full of fish. Hundreds of fish were jumping all over the boats—some escaping into the water followed immediately by the boys, who stood waist-deep in the water. Mejojetha, Father, and Sundarkaka (Father's younger brother) all stood there admiring this great catch. I had never seen so many live fish in one place. They seemed to me creatures full of life and eager to escape, and I felt a bit uneasy that they would be killed to make tasty dishes. Already the neighbors had gathered to take their share of the fish. Fish like these had to be eaten fresh. Even our household of nearly thirty people wasn't big enough to make use of this large catch, although some of the fish could be kept alive under water inside the hull of a boat.

Around this time in late September or early October our family celebrated the harvest festival. The rice paddy was being gathered and dried in the sun by the poor women in the village to be husked. A whole series of steps had to take place between harvesting the field and rice ready for cooking. Farmers were hired to cut and collect clumps of ripe paddy, using sickle-shaped knives to cut the paddy reeds and make bundles which were then carried on oxcarts to the house for drying. When the paddy reeds were dry enough for the paddy to separate from the ears, three or four oxen were set to going around and around over the dry paddy. Their hooves helped the paddy to separate from the stalks. Their muzzles were covered with bamboo masks so that they couldn't eat any of the grains. I used to watch this laborious process and felt sorry for the cattle who worked so hard for us and were not allowed to share our food. Once the paddy was separated from the stalks, the farmers' wives carried huge baskets full of paddy to their husking pedals and a few days later brought back the freshly husked rice along with the broken kernels, which they winnowed and separated from those that were whole. This cracked rice was cooked in milk with sugar and raisins to make rice pudding and was served for the harvest festival.

We sat in a circle and ate this tasty dish while another circle of women—the farmers' wives—sang folk songs to mark the occasion. Years later when I worked in the West Bengal villages as an anthropologist and was served breakfast with cracked rice pudding, the tune of the folk songs came back to me along with the taste. I always loved this rustic dish made with cracked rice.

DURGA PUJA

The primary reason that the whole family gathered in the village home during this season was to celebrate the worship of the goddess Durga. Durga, whose name literally means fortress, was born out of anger and frustration of the male gods of Hindu pantheon. The gods were at a loss because Mahishasur, a powerful demon born of a water buffalo, was determined to destroy the universe unless the gods allowed him total power to rule the three realms: heaven, earth, and the underworld. When the gods saw that a beautiful female figure materialized from the energy of their collective anger, they knew that this goddess had come to protect the universe. She had a golden complexion of fire, beautiful and powerful with ten arms. She rode a lion and had a third eye on her forehead. The gods immediately bowed to her and offered ten lethal weapons for her ten arms. She was ready to subdue Mahishasur, and she succeeded in killing him after ten days of ferocious battle. During this battle Durga became Kali—a dark goddess of fury who killed her enemy and adorned herself with a garland of skulls around her neck and another of severed arms around her waist as a skirt. But Durga, the fair version of Kali whom my family worshipped, was powerful but beautiful. She was also a mother of four children, and she visited her father's home with her children during the four days when she is worshipped by the people on earth.

The members of Father's family held this major festival for everyone in the village, including their Hindu subjects, who received gifts of food and new clothes on this occasion. The *puja* itself lasted five days, beginning with the sixth day of the lunar fortnight and ending with the tenth. But the preparations began long before that.

In a tin shed next to the *mandap* where the goddess would be placed for worship, the professional clay-modeler and his two assistants gathered their utensils and materials—straw, wood, bamboo, clay, rope, paints, rags, and various tools. The same artist fashioned the image every year. He came from a family of clay-modelers specializing exclusively in creating images of gods and goddesses. Their family seems to be the most respectable among all artists in clay. Every morning after breakfast and every afternoon when the grown-ups took their naps, my cousins and I would run to this shed and sit in a trance watching them work. I watched them create, from a few handfuls of straw and rope, heads, arms, and legs on bamboo structures. It was hard to believe that these simple structures would take the shape of the beautiful goddess, her four children, and their various animals. Sometimes, when we had missed a morning or afternoon's visit, the progress was astonishing. In one corner of the shed was a portly figure without a head. This had to be Ganesh, Durga's oldest son. Once the assistants had kneaded heaps of clay, the skeletal figures became fleshy, and in a few days the faces, noses, even fingers and toes were in place. On the next day the eyes became focused and the lips smiled. Finally, Ganesh received his elephant head, beautifully decorated with curved designs. That day, sitting mesmerized in front of the tin shed, I discovered the truth that real talent can bring even the gods of heaven down to this earth.

Goddess Durga riding the lion and killing the buffalo demon

When the images were painted and glazed, it was an extraordinary event. Within a few days Durga, her two daughters, Lakshmi and Saraswati, and her two sons, Ganesh and Kartik, came alive. My eyes were dazzled by the shining weapons, which looked like polished silver in Durga's ten arms. The morning sun that spilled through the slats of the makeshift bamboo walls hit the white metal of the weapons—a sword, a spear, a club, and more. Yet her beautiful face wore a smile. The buffalo demon whose chest was bloody with the spear from one of the goddess's hands looked as if he would burst open from fury and the lion would pounce on him in a moment.

Saraswati's swan was poised with its long neck bent, Lakshmi's owl looked straight ahead, and Kartik's peacock showed off its tail ablaze with rainbow colors. Only Ganesh's little mouse was hidden under his foot—barely visible. The day before the *puja*, Durga and her whole family were moved to the *mandap* where auspicious festoons of mango leaves and other decorations made the room festive. The priest held a small ceremony to infuse life into the images, and from that point on we were forbidden to enter the *puja* room. Incense, flowers, oil lamps, and the bell in the priest's hand all marked the boundary between the divine space and the mundane world.

Noticing a veiled figure next to Ganesh, I asked Buli, "Have you seen that figure before? Where did it come from?"

"Oh, that's Banana Bride, Ganesh's wife. She was made from a banana tree."

"What are you talking about? The elephants love to eat banana plants. Suppose Ganesh suddenly feels like eating his bride?" I was really worried.

"Don't be stupid. Does anyone eat his own wife? Besides, it's a god we're talking about," Buli snapped. The priest asked us to leave the premises. He would do the evening *arati* with a seven-flamed copper lamp and put the deities to sleep. Tomorrow, the first day of the *puja*, would be a big day for the goddess's family as well as all of us, her worshippers.

The next morning I awoke to the beat of drums. We bathed in a hurry, put on our new dresses, and ran to the *puja mandap*. The sounds of drum, cymbal, and conch mingled with the fragrances of sandalwood paste, autumn flowers, and incense. Hypnotized, we lingered, made offerings to Durga with petals torn from flowers, repeating Sanskrit mantras after the priest:

Ya Devi Sarvabhuteshu Matri-rupena Samsthita
Namastasyai, namastasyai, namastasyai namo namh.
Ya Devi Sarvabhuteshu Shakti—rupena samsthita
Namastasyai, namastasyai, namastasyai namo namah

and on and on.

Then came the second day of *puja*, which was most significant because on that day the sacrifice of animals took place.

BUFFALO SACRIFICE

This year, in addition to goats, a buffalo was to be sacrificed in front of the goddess to appease her thirst for blood. The rumor was that Barojetha had made a vow that he would offer a buffalo to the goddess if the goddess would grant him a favor, though no one knew what that favor was. I did not understand what a vow was or what a buffalo sacrifice was about. During the last couple weeks, I had noticed a hefty water buffalo tied at the front house. One of the servants would take the beast out for a graze or a bath in the front pond. The man rubbed the buffalo's broad back with a brush of coconut fiber, making its gray hide shine the color of polished steel. That morning, as I was watching the animal munching its breakfast from a huge clay basin, Buli came up.

"Do you think he knows his fate?" I asked her.

"Who, the buffalo? Are you kidding? Of course not. He is lucky to be chosen for such a holy purpose, don't you think?" Buli seemed totally unconcerned. I was upset with her, upset with everything. Decades later I realized that I too did not know my fate, my future, or the purpose of all the unexpected twists and turns of my life, which seemed to have a theme and plan after all. Perhaps that is the way of the universe; otherwise we would be denied the excitement of exploring the mystery of our life's journey.

"I'm not watching this brutal business. No one can drag me to witness this cruelty," I announced.

"Aren't you the least bit curious? Will you ever get a chance again to see anything like this? Imagine Barojetha cutting its head off in one stroke. I'm not missing this for the world." She made it sound as if we were extremely fortunate even to have such an opportunity. I just couldn't agree. On such a happy occasion as the *puja*, why did they have to include something so atrocious!

Buli moved close to me, took my hand in hers, and whispered, "Have you seen the big sword on the wall of Dadu's bedroom?"

"The one that shines like silver when the light hits it? There is an eye etched on the end of the blade. I always thought it must be the goddess Durga's third eye that can see and foresee everything," I said.

"That's the one. When this sword comes down in Barojetha's hands with a *ghachat* sound, separating the head from the body of the animal and blood gushes out like fountain . . ."

Unable to stand her sadistic details any more, I put my palm on her mouth. "Stop, stop. How do you know so much? You just said you'd never seen a buffalo sacrifice." I was quite angry at her attempt to impress me with the gory details, which she knew full well I didn't want to hear. Perhaps she wanted to show off how brave the village girls were.

The morning of the sacrifice I awoke with a premonition—something big was going to happen. We fasted so that we could offer *anjali* (flower offering) to the goddess. I saw Barojetha bathed and dressed in a blood-red, raw silk *dhoti* and scarf, moving around with the priest with a solemn air. I sneaked out alone to the front house to see the buffalo. The servant who had been taking care of the animal was getting it ready for its final ceremonial bath. He rubbed a big jar of *ghee* all over it before pouring on water. As we watched, the priest recited mantras. I wondered if the buffalo also had fasted in order to participate in its sacred demise. I felt dizzy. All the anticipation of fun and joy of the *puja* now mingled with fear and ominous morbidity. I was afraid yet eager for what was to come next.

A crowd gathered in the front yard—all the family members, neighbors, and many villagers. We circled an empty area in the middle around a newly erected wooden structure in the center. The buffalo was cajoled and coaxed to come to the center, but it resisted. The poor animal must have realized its fate by now. Finally, three strong men dragged it there. The priest drew a design in the shape of a trident with vermilion and oil on the buffalo's forehead and uttered loud mantras as the men put its head on the groove of the wooden structure.

The boys in the crowd began shouting and screaming as if they were cheering a winning soccer team. All the noise and hubbub made me dizzier. A group of boys moved right in front of me. I couldn't see anything. I didn't want to see. Still I did look up and see the flash of light from the engraved eye on the sword as it came down. I closed my eyes and covered my ears with my hands. I did not hear a sound. Perhaps the buffalo was already dazed by the power of the priest's mantra. I desperately hoped so. My eyes opened at the warm smell of blood, a smell I still recoil from every time I enter a butcher's shop.

I saw the same three men pulling the huge body of the beheaded beast away from the area. The priest placed the head on a silver platter and gave it to his assistant, who carried it to the *mandap* to be offered ceremonially to the goddess. The priest passed a marble bowl full of warm blood to Barojetha, who touched it briefly to his lips before passing it to Mejojetha. Mejojetha did the same and passed it to my father, and thus the bowl of blood went around from the oldest brother to the youngest and then to the children.

"See, they're all drinking blood. You'll have to also," Buli whispered in my ear.

"What about you? Aren't you going to do the same?" I was suddenly angry, very angry. I didn't want any part in this, this cruel festival. How I wished I could run back home to Digboi, where in my mother's little shrine Lord Krishna, a bamboo flute in his hands, smiled from his picture, and the pleasing fragrance of fresh trumpet flower, incense, and sandalwood paste made life feel more secure. The marble bowl had arrived in our row. I quickly ducked to the ground, the bowl passed. Buli followed me to the floor and exclaimed, "Yaak! I had no idea blood smells so bad!" I said nothing, just got up and went to the *puja mandap* to offer my *anjali*. I wanted to ask the goddess if she really needed a poor buffalo's head. I knew that she had once killed the buffalo demon in a ferocious battle of ten days and ten nights to save the universe. Did she still need to eat the demon's parent? I knew I couldn't ask anyone these questions, least of all my knowledgeable cousin Buli.

In the *puja mandap*, the priest uttered more mantras as he threw flower petals toward the silver platter with the buffalo head in front of the goddess. He gave each of us a handful of petals, and we closed our eyes and repeated the mantras after him and tried to throw the flowers at the goddess's feet. Some fell on the platter. At the end of the third throw we knelt down and bowed our heads down to the floor for the final prayer.

"So, what did you ask from Mother Durga?" Buli asked as we rose from the ground and brushed our knees.

"I'll tell you later. First, you tell me, did Barojetha cut the buffalo head off with one stroke?"

"Of course. If he hadn't, all kinds of calamities would have fallen on our family and even the whole village—epidemics and such like." She was relieved that I was back to my normal questioning self again, and she could play the role of the one who knew everything.

That afternoon when we all sat down to lunch in the huge courtyard between the outer and inner parts of the home, I wondered where the pieces of meat came from. Barojethima told us that we were eating the goat meat from the sacrifice of the day before. Later I heard that the buffalo was given to the poor people of the village who shared everything—hide, meat, and all.

The third day of the *puja* was mostly reserved for evening performances. My mother—the youngest daughter-in-law of the family at the time—took charge of directing us in various performances to entertain the family and neighbors. A temporary stage had already been erected at one end of the big hall of the outer house. Chairs and benches were lined up for the audience. The number that Buli, Hena, and I performed was a simple dance to a song sung by our older cousins from the wings. I still remember the first line, which went like this: "We are three flowers just bloomed on one stalk."

We were dressed in silk saris with sequins on them, and our faces were heavily painted with powder, lipstick, and rouge. Our eyes were painted with kohl to make them appear larger. We kept moving our hands, fingers, and bodies, following Mother's instructions from the wings. At one point, as I was turning around, my sari slipped off my waist, exposing the undershirt I usually wore under my dresses. I was mortified and dropped down on my heels on top of my bunched-up sari. Someone in charge of the stage had the good sense to drop the front screen. Buli and Hena kept dancing and were furious that they were not allowed to finish. My first debut on stage did not foretell a very promising future.

Vijaya Dashami, the last day of the *puja*, was special. Along with the sad tune produced by the *shenai*, a wind instrument, played by a group of musicians on a platform erected above the main entrance, everyone and everything looked heavy with sad anticipation of the goddess's departure. We knew that Durga and her four children would leave her father's home for the next whole year. Her image would be immersed in the river. I stood in front of the *mandap* looking at the goddess whose eyes seemed moist. Rows of married women came to have their vermilion—the sign of good fortune at having one's husband alive—blessed by the goddess. I sneaked in and became part of the moving row of married women. I had heard that they were supposed to look at the reflection of Durga's right foot in a clay pot of water. I was so intrigued by this that I had to find out firsthand what happened. By the time I got to the pot of water and peeped in, I saw the reflection of the goddess slightly quivering from all the pushing and shoving.

The quivering image of the goddess in the water of the pitcher standing at her feet that day gave me goose bumps as if something vital had just happened to me—something beyond my reach and understanding. A reflection in the water bringing similar goose bumps happened another time in my adult life. But that story must wait for later.

By mid-afternoon the boys began to dance in a devotional frenzy in front of the *mandap* as a farewell offering to the divine family. They each held two large clay containers of burning dried coconut husk with incense thrown in to produce a lot of smoke. Some of them had an extra container between their teeth. With heads thrown back and eyes closed they danced to the loud drumbeat. We stood by watching. Buli whispered in a loud voice that the boys had taken a drink mixed with hashish to get in the mood. I didn't quite believe it. But the way they were dancing, she might have been right. Pieces of red burning husk spilled from the incense pots all around, and they stepped on them without noticing. They kept swirling around like a group of mad marionettes pulled by invisible threads. This must be the way Durga's husband, Shiva, danced the cosmic dance when she died, I thought. The dance ended when the boys were totally exhausted. They were dazed and in another world.

The preparation for taking the images out to the river began in earnest right after the frenzied dance. Three or four boats were put together to carry the images across the pond and through the canal that eventually connected to the river. Men held on to the images as the boats made their way slowly, everyone shouting, "Hail Mother Durga! Hail Mother Durga!" Women and children stood at the bank—some blowing on conch shells, some singing, some weeping silently as if a daughter was returning to her husband's home. The goddess was also the mother and protector and was leaving the helpless worshippers for another year. The emotions were high and touched everyone deeply.

Buli and I planned to sneak onto the boats with the crowd, but we were held back by some of the elders. Boys, on the other hand, put on shorts and jumped into the shallow water and climbed into the boats. Being part of such a solemn expedition made them feel important; they looked back at us proudly. Buli and I sat on the steps of the pond long after the boats and the images disappeared. The sun had gone down in the meantime, and the dusk crept in, making the water dark. We could barely see our feet.

"No matter how much we worship Mother Durga, the gods and goddesses are from another world. They come down from heaven, give us their blessings, and leave until our effort to worship invites them back again," Buli said slowly.

"Do you think that if we didn't make images, call the priest, and worship with all this pomp and grandeur, they would still come down?" I wondered.

"Who knows? The poor people don't have the money to do all this. Maybe Mother Durga doesn't come to them. I hope we never stop worshipping. At least we bring her for the whole village," she said with her usual wise flourish. Somehow I felt uneasy, not quite understanding the connection between the goddess's presence and all the festivities and preparations. In Digboi, in my mother's little shrine, we sang devotional songs every evening, and she meditated in front of her gods for a few minutes every morning with fresh flowers and fresh fruit and sweets. I was sure the gods were there.

"So, here you are! Your mothers are looking for you. They thought you girls must have left with the goddess." One of the maids spoke from behind us and began to giggle, showing her blackened teeth in the oil lamp she held up. Annoyed by the interruption in our philo-sophical speculations, we got up and went back to the house. After the men and boys came back from the river, the grown-ups hugged one another, the young touched the dust of their feet in *pronam*—a gesture that shows greetings of respect to the elders by the younger relatives—and the elders touch the lowered heads and utter blessings, which can range from "Live a long life" to "Be a mother of many sons." Mejojethima gave us sweets made from evaporated milk and shredded coconut. We went to bed exhausted and feeling empty. In a few days we forgot the grief of losing the goddess because we knew she would return with her children again the next year.

MOTHER FAINTS

Late one morning before we went for our bath I stopped by the kitchen for something and found the aunts and maids standing in a circle around someone on the floor. One maid was waving a palm-leaf fan. I inched close to find that it was Mother! Mejojethima grabbed my hand and pulled me aside.

"Your mother is not feeling too well; nothing to worry about. Could you be a good girl and run to the *kachari* and call your Mejo-jetha? Ask him to get the vial of smelling salts from Dadu's medicine chest." She spoke gently and moved back to the circle. I ran to the outer house wondering what smelling salts might be. The name had a smell of sickness attached to it. After I had brought it to her, I was not allowed to stay in the kitchen. Later, when Mother was resting in our bedroom, I approached her bed quietly.

"Ma, what happened? Are you sick?" I asked.

"Nothing big, I was just feeling nauseous. It could be the heat in the kitchen. Don't worry. Take your sister with you when you go for your bath. Now get moving, it's getting late." She did not sound that sick. I could not remember ever seeing Ma sick. Maybe she would be better if Father came back from Assam and lived with us.

The next day I lay in Mejojethima's wide bed pretending to nap. Two aunts and several of the older female cousins were all there.

Suddenly my ears perked when I heard Bardi (our oldest cousin) and Mejojethima talking.

"Don't you get it? It's hysteria, what else? It's the oldest trick in the book to attract attention from the men folks," Mejojethima said and ended with a snicker.

"Has this happened before, do you think? It's all very strange. Could it be a symptom of something else?" Bardi responded.

"Maybe. Even if it is, do you think we'll be told? Not a chance." The conversation then shifted to other family politics. I lay stiff, not moving a limb. It was clear they were discussing my mother. I felt quite upset to find out that my cousin and aunt were not as kind to Ma as they were to us children. For the next few days I avoided spending nap time in Mejojethima's bed.

One evening a few days later, I entered our bedroom to find Mother alone wiping her eyes with her sari. She turned her face away immediately so that I would not see the tears. To distract me, she asked in a natural voice, "Have you memorized your multiplication table? Isn't the tutor coming tomorrow?"

I knew that the conversation I had overheard the other afternoon in Mejojethima's bed and Mother's fainting spell had something to do with her tears. Her tears always made me sad. I blurted out, "Ma, the other day in Mejojethima's bed I overheard them talking about you. I did not like the way they said things . . ." I trailed off.

"What was it that they said?" Ma pulled me by the hand, sat me on the bed near her, and asked.

"I don't remember the exact words. They were talking about your fainting in the kitchen and laughing at you." Ma looked at me with a faint smile and touched my head gently before saying, "Don't you worry your little head about adult talks. It's nothing. I'm glad you told me. Even if they may be critical of me, your aunt and cousins love you very much. They may be jealous that I have such a smart daughter like you." As soon as she uttered those words Ma got up from the bed, letting my hand go fast as if she was embarrassed.

This was one occasion that I can recall when I saw a side of my mother which was always carefully hidden. I also knew that she was still not ready to share her sorrow with me. I was not old enough to ask her about these things. But I was old enough to sense the loneliness she must feel living with relatives by marriage while Father was away. I wondered whether, if I were older, Ma would sit me next to her and confide in me. Perhaps not. Years later we had many arguments and differences of opinion, but never again did we sit next to each other and open our hearts. I also wonder how many mothers and daughters really can be open to one another with their private feelings.

A TRIP ON JEWEL-BOATS

A few weeks before the *puja*, when the rains had stopped but the sky was still covered with scattered clouds, Baba, Mejojetha, and Sundarkaka decided to take a boat trip through their estates to collect taxes. Older male cousins were asked to join them. I begged Baba to take me and Buli along.

"We won't be any trouble, I promise," I pleaded. My father would go back to Digboi right after the *puja* to return to his job, and we would be separated for several months. He could not refuse my request. So against their better judgment and considerable protests from the male cousins, we were included. Hena was not allowed to accompany us. She was too young, her mother argued. Dadamoni, Mejda (Mejojetha's son), Father's youngest sister's two sons, Hira and Budhu, and we two female cousins made a group of six children and three adults, along with two servants and four boatmen. Naturally we needed two boats. These were spacious country boats with wide hulls and plenty of sleeping space beneath finely knit bamboo roofs. They were made of dark and glossy wood like old iron and were called jewel-boats, maybe because their bowsprits were decorated with beautifully inlaid brass of ornate designs. My favorite design was a large eye, just like the one engraved on the steel sword that Barojetha used to behead the sacrificial buffalo.

We were in the care of the servants, who helped the four boatmen when necessary. Otherwise they fished, ground spices with a mortar and pestle, washed our clothes, and cooked. They shopped for groceries in the villages where we anchored and where Baba and his brothers did their work. Sometimes people brought live chickens and vegetables as offerings. I loved to stand on the upper deck and take in whiffs of cooking from below deck. I could tell they used too much hot chili, but we were having such a good time, no one complained. Buli and I knew that the boys were annoyed by the disturbing presence of two girls on such a masculine expedition.

One day Budhu could not help himself. He asked, "By the way, do you girls know how to swim? Suppose there is a raging hurricane and our boat capsizes, who will rescue you?"

Buli looked a bit worried, but I spoke before she could show any concern. "Why, whoever rescues you will also rescue us. Knowing how to swim is no good in these waters. Crocodiles will devour all of us as soon as we fall in," I said with certainty. After this bluff, I looked at Budhu's face and knew he would not meddle with us for a while.

Although I had made up the bit about the crocodiles, it could easily be true. There was water everywhere. My father's ancestral home was in an area of mostly low ground and wetlands. After the monsoon season, rivers, lakes, and ponds joined together and the land was transformed into a sea. When the boats came close to the shore we could hear the *ghash, ghash* sound as we went over submerged paddy and other water plants. These plants remained under water for a good three or four months and emerged at their full height during autumn when the sun from clear blue skies ripened them into golden stalks. I craned my neck as much as possible to try and see the submerged paddy, but all I could detect was dark green water. Apparently this type of paddy plant needed to be under water to mature, one of the servants informed me.

One evening I went down to watch the boatmen cook. Buli had gone ashore with the uncles. I liked being on the boat observing the world around and underneath. We were anchored for the night. One boatman was grinding turmeric on a slab of stone with another stone for a pestle, making a *garr, garr* sound, splashing water once in a while on the hard root. His triceps jumped with the motion of his arms. The other boatman had just finished frying some potato chips. He put a handful in an aluminum bowl and said, "Here, have some." He smiled broadly, only two yellow teeth showing on the upper row. I enjoyed tasting their food. It was like a picnic. I would not have minded a taste of the red gravy with pieces of tiny fish. I knew it was fire hot and forbidden and did not dare ask for some. At home we would not be allowed to eat from the servant's kitchen. Besides, I could be sick from such a hot spice. For now I had to be satisfied with the potato chips.

The sun set, leaving streaks of gold on the dark water. It reminded me of the narrow gold border of Mother's wedding sari. But before I could think of Mother and everyone back home, I saw the quick movement of a snake drawing curves on the water moving away from the boat. A chill ran through my spine, and I screamed. The boatmen left their cooking and came running.

When I told them what I had seen, the one with two yellow teeth said, "Oh, ho! It's only a water snake, little sister. Nothing to be afraid of. They are not poisonous. Besides, they won't come into the boat. Of course, in the case of the Gila monster, it's another matter." He went back to his cooking.

"What is a Gila monster?"

"Something like a big gecko. T h i s b i g." He spread his arms wide. "It makes a sound like this—*tak, tak, tak* and *khak, khak, khak*. If it bites you, you are definitely dead—full of poison." I began to laugh from the way he made a face to show the sound. I had never seen a Gila gecko. The only geckos I had ever seen were the little ones everywhere on the walls, chasing insects and making hardly any sound. I disliked them. But I knew that if a gecko ever falls on a girl's head, she is destined to be a queen because they can stick to the ceiling without falling. I did not say any of this to the boatman, who seemed incredulous of my ignorance.

"What kind of country is it where you live that they don't have geckos and Gila monsters?" He asked. Now I was self-conscious. No way was I going to be defeated.

"I live in Assam, the easternmost state of India. We may not have Gila and gecko there, but we have huge pythons—very big—as long as this boat, even longer. They wait quietly in the paddy field or on a tree in the jungle. And we have rhinoceros and elephants." I stopped to watch the effect. The two boatmen stopped their work and looked genuinely impressed.

"Really? Have you seen a python with your own eyes?" the one with yellow teeth asked.

"Yes, but only once." I told them the story of the python.

"One day Dadamoni, my older brother, came running to tell us that two men from the nearby tea garden had brought a dead python to the hospital. The hospital was very close to our house, and its chief medical officer, Dr. Nandi, was Father's friend. We all walked over there. Dr. Nandi told us what he had heard from the men.

"Two workers had gone to the tea garden as they did every morning. It was before dawn, still dark. They sat on a log, sipping tea from bamboo glasses, waiting for the sun to rise. Suddenly the log began to move. They thought it was an earthquake. The sun was up by now, and they noticed the black and white designs and shine on the log. They began to scream and ran all the way to the British manager's bungalow. The manager got his gun and shot the python, which was still in the same spot. The manager suggested they take the dead snake to the hospital, where they could sell it for the poison.

"By the time we went to the hospital to have a look at this giant creature, something so rare, there was already a crowd around it. Several English ladies were among the people asking to buy the skin. Foreign ladies love to own shoes and handbags made out of snakeskin. These shoes and bags are very expensive and fashionable." I stopped after talking so much and looked at the boatman. I couldn't see very well in the dark.

"You went to look at such a big snake! Weren't you afraid?" the younger boatman said.

"Not really. Why should I be afraid of a dead snake? Of course I was nearly sick from seeing the dead goat that came out of the python's tummy. It looked like a rag doll without any bones. Yuck . . ." I could see the scene again in my mind.

The boatmen were utterly absorbed by my story. I was satisfied that I could impress them with an unusual happening from my place of origin. Another servant called me from the upper deck for dinner. The anchored boat was floating on quiet water, glistening with moonlight. I had been so absorbed in telling stories that I hadn't even noticed when the moon came out. The water snake must have returned to its hole. I climbed up, still wondering why a snake sent a shiver up my spine.

During dinner Buli asked, "What do you talk about with the boatmen all the time?"

"This and that. I like to watch them cook." I didn't go into any details. Somehow I didn't feel like sharing the world of the lower deck with anyone, not even Buli.

In the early morning the boatmen and the servants hung their wash on a rope they had tied from one corner of the boat to the other. One of the servants woke us from our sleep with hot tea. The anchor had been lifted, and the boat had already begun to move again. I loved watching as one of the boatmen pushed the boat away from the shore by digging a long bamboo pole down into the water while the other one paddled with the oars. The oars went in and out of the water—*chhalat, chhalat, chhalat.* Even in the cool early morning, the boatmen had beads of sweat on their bare backs. One day, both boatmen jumped out to the shore and began to pull the boat with long ropes tied to their waists. Buli explained to me that since we had to go upstream, this was the only way to maneuver. Watching the gullies of sweat on their backs, I felt ashamed sitting comfortably on board the boat. No one else seemed to mind.

After a week or so, the boat trip grew stale. We were bored and fidgety. The grown-ups were busy doing their work on the shore while we were stuck on the boat. The boys took this time to tease and bully us. The longer we stayed on board the boat, the more we bickered and fought with them. One morning Mejda and Dadamoni used the boatmen's fishing rods and tried fishing. I watched their serious faces from the upper deck. A long time passed. With the increasing heat and humidity, my skin began to itch. I lost patience and went down below under cover. Immediately there was a loud commotion. I came out and saw one of the boatmen trying to stop the rod, which was swirling around in Dadamoni's shivering hand. At the other end was a medium-size, wiggling, snakelike fish. I was shocked when the boatman told us that it was a very tasty fish called *loitya*. I couldn't overcome my fear of anything snakelike, even though I had been brave enough to witness a full-size dead python. I made a mental note to avoid this particular fish when it was served on our plates.

Several decades after this boat trip, in the summer of 1973, I was traveling by car with some friends in the countryside of France. It was unusually hot that year. We stopped near a lake for a dip to cool off. The moment I began to swim, I spotted a snake by my side, etching a silent line on the water. Immediately the scene from the boat trip thirty years earlier came back with a shiver all over me. I left the water as fast as I could. Just like those boatmen, my friend's ten-year-old son laughed and remarked, "It's only a water snake, not poisonous."

⁕

DEADLY FRUIT OF OLEANDER

During monsoon season Baniachong had so much water that the rooms of our home appeared to be floating. We had to use small dinghies to move from one room to the next. The boys learned how to use bamboo poles to negotiate these boats easily. We went to *pathshala*, a kind of preschool, in such a dinghy rowed by an older boy. His mother accompanied him. She was a sort of matron, our school mom. We called her *mashima* (aunt), and she held the youngest of the students in her lap. She also picked us older ones up and held us in her lap if we cried for any reason. The little boat stopped at several homes and picked up students. The teacher was a young man who gave us lessons on alphabets and numbers. We copied Bengali and English alphabets on slates with chalks over and over until we memorized their shapes. I loved going to school in a dinghy so much that hours of practicing writing felt like a small price to pay.

One day on the way to *pathshala* I saw a water vine with bright red fruit. I asked our *mashima* what the vine was called. "Oh, these are ordinary wild things called "crow's food," not edible, possibly poisonous," she said. All day I wondered about this anomaly. Water snakes were not poisonous, but beautiful red water vine fruit might be. I wished I could taste one fruit and find out. I never had the chance. As far as I can recall, we stopped going to *pathshala* after the rainy season. A tutor came to our home to give lessons to five or six of us between six and ten years old.

One day Buli told me that the young daughter-in-law of the Sen family—our neighbors—had committed suicide by eating oleander fruit. Not knowing what suicide really meant I said, "How did you find out?"

"Haven't you noticed all the whispers and talk? Ma and Baroje-thima went out through the back door to the Sens' house. The police commissioner came by boat to our house to ask for directions to theirs. You haven't noticed any of this?" Buli stopped to take a breath. I waited patiently, knowing full well that in time she would tell me more. I needed to understand exactly what suicide was.

That evening, when we were sitting on the steps of the front pond, four men walked past us carrying a long bundle of cloth on their heads and shouting, "*Balo Hari, Hari bol.*" Buli whispered, "Here they go to the burning *ghat* with her dead body." By now I sort of understood what suicide meant. As usual my curiosity was piqued. I wished I could see the dead woman. I had never seen a dead person. In the dark of evening the sound of "*Hari bol*" gave me chills. I wondered if the ghost of the young daughter-in-law of the Sen family would come back to haunt us.

"Is poison the only way to commit suicide?" I asked Buli.

"Of course not. But this is the only death I know of which was caused by poison from the oleander fruit. Apparently she ate several slices of oleander fruit." Her response came with an air of knowing.

For several days after that, I could not shake off this information about the death of a young woman who had killed herself by eating the poisonous fruit of a flowering bush. Curiosity kept pushing me to know more about exactly how it had happened. Did she suffer pain or was her death instant? Did she change her mind after she had eaten the fruit? About seven years later, Mrs. Biswas, our neighbor in Digboi, committed suicide by swallowing phenol. Her death reminded me of the tragedy in the Sen family in my grandfather's village. Two married women taking their own lives within a period of several years. Are some women so sad that death is better than life for them? I wondered if even Buli could give me an answer to that.

A COUNTRY FAIR

"I shall go to the fair . . . I shall go to the fair . . . eh eh eh." Hena appeared from nowhere, jumped all around me as she sang these words and then disappeared as suddenly as she came. I ran after her.

"Hey, listen to me. Where are you going? Please tell me," I begged. I knew from her glee that whatever it was, it was special, but I had no idea what she was talking about. Hena was not one hundred percent happy with Buli and me. She was suspicious of our liaison and knew that she was not included in our loop. After trying her with our deepest secrets, our experience taught us that Hena was not completely dependable. We knew that under duress she was apt to divulge information to the boys, especially Budhu, the cousin who was quick to find our weak spots after the incident of the hookah in *kachari* house. However, we always took her side when she was harassed by one of the boys.

One day she came in tears and complained, "Shyamalda has stolen my doll. I cannot find her anywhere." We girls had to be united on such occasions against the bullies, our male cousins. But when she betrayed us by telling the enemy camp of our plan to steal fruit from the neighbor's garden or other such secrets, that was a different matter. Besides, forgiveness was not one of our strong points. So it was not easy for me to ask Hena for a favor. Yet I tried one more time.

"Please, please, tell me where you are going. I know how nice you are."

"I'm going to the fair, to the fair where I shall buy many things." She said it in a singsong voice, pausing after each word to taunt me. Then she said in normal voice, "Mejokaka has given me money to buy a big doll. I'm not going to share it with anyone." She moved away, singing the same line again and again.

That evening at dinner when Buli and I sat side by side waiting for the fish curry, I asked her, "Where does the fair take place? Aren't you going?" I did not want her to know my ignorance, that I had no idea what a fair really was.

"Of course, all of us will go. This is a major fair—lots of shops, a Ferris wheel, magicians, candy shops, and so much more—all in a huge field. Why? Haven't you ever seen a fair? Isn't there a fair in your Digboi?" Before I knew how to cover my embarrassment, the maid dropped a fat slice of *guchi* fish on my plate. Buli got a smaller piece, most of which was bone. She began to suck on it, occasionally stealing a glance on my plate. I covered my fish under rice, away from her greedy glance.

"We have many things in Digboi. There is no fair, so what?" I was defiant and began to relish my fish. After a while I felt bad enough to break off a small section of my fish and put it on her plate. Buli immediately put it in her mouth. She was satisfied.

"Why don't you ask your mother for some money to spend at the fair? I shall tell you exactly how to spend it. Let me see . . . the bearded lady will cost four paisa, then there is the bear dance, monkey tricks, and the old woman's hair candy . . . all told, it will come to several *anas*. If you can manage a rupee, we may even have extra for the fries and bangles."

I had forgotten to finish my dinner. I had no idea what she was talking about, as if she was speaking a foreign tongue. My uncontrollable curiosity transported me to a mysterious world where one could watch bearded ladies and dancing bears for a few paisa. I could not understand what the old woman's hair was about but decided to keep quiet for now. We finished our dessert—milk mixed with red molasses. We raised the brass plates to our lips, gulping the sweet liquid with a delicious *hoosh hoosh* sound. I was eager to go to our room and ask Ma for money for the fair.

Ma was in good mood. That afternoon I had seen one of the servants give her a thick envelope. It must have been Baba's letter from Digboi. This might be a good time to ask about the money.

"When will Baba come, Ma?" I ask.

"In two weeks." She became busy straightening the bedspread, avoiding my eyes, perhaps to hide her pleasure. I waited a few seconds before saying,

"Buli and Hena are talking about going to the *mela*. May I go with them?"

"Which *mela*? Oh, the one next week? I almost forgot. Of course you'll go. It's the biggest *mela* of the year. You'll never get another chance to see it once we're in Assam. But you'll have to stay with your older cousins, not just with Buli and Hena. There will be a big crowd of people, you could get lost. You may only go if the older kids are going." I was so pleased with the permission that I didn't raise the issue of money. That could be arranged in time.

For the next week every night before falling asleep, I kept wondering about this unknown event called *mela*. Was it something like a wedding? The worship of the goddess? Buli told me that it took place in a huge field with temporary structures of tents and stalls. I couldn't comprehend exactly what it might be like. One night I even had a dream of a gigantic woman whose head was full of long black hair and whose face had a white flowing beard! She kept gesturing at me with her hand. I woke up afraid and did not mention the dream, not even to Buli. In the light of day, I almost forgot the dream.

The day before we were to go to the fair, when I came to our room for a nap after lunch, Ma took out a coin from an old cigarette tin and gave it to me.

"Here are four *anas* for you to spend in the *mela*," she said. "Now, don't spend it on junk and remember to hold Dadamoni's hand tight all the time. Otherwise a baby thief may kidnap you. These things happen in a big crowd." I was so pleased to get a full quarter of a rupee to spend, I did not mind the prospect of holding on to my older brother's hand. Besides, once we were in the *mela*, how would Ma know whose hand I held tight? Most likely it would be Buli's.

The next morning after breakfast, ten of us cousins climbed in the back of two bullock carts. I held my money and a small handkerchief in a tiny handbag. I wanted to wear my printed dress, white shoes, and socks from the last *puja*, but Mother did not allow that. "It will be very dusty in the *mela* and would ruin your beautiful dress and shoes," she said. I had agreed to wear the slightly tight dress from one year back. I could not possibly make her upset after the generous allowance of four *anas*. Besides, I was too excited to worry about clothes. The bullock carts jolted along over dirt roads with potholes and uneven surfaces. We kept falling on one another and giggling all the way. When we reached the fair, it was already afternoon.

When we entered the *mela* grounds I was completely startled. In fact I did not know words to express my feelings of anticipation mixed with an unknown apprehension. The din of a loud band deafened my ears. Waves of people moving in all directions raised a lot of dust from the ground. There were merry-go-rounds, a Ferris wheel, stalls with various activities, and balloons held by young children. The boys in our group immediately moved to a stall where they began to shoot at small targets with toy guns. Buli explained that whoever could hit ten targets would get a velvet rabbit. None of them had succeeded so far. We girls pretended not to notice. Soon the boys lost interest and suggested we all go for a ride on the merry-go-round. I was thrilled. My head was still reeling from the ride when Buli pulled me aside in front of a small booth.

"How much have you brought? These two tickets I will purchase with your money. Next round is on me," she whispered. Nervously I handed over the coin, my total treasure. Things were moving fast, as if some puppeteer was pulling strings from behind the scene, making things happen.

Didimoni, Buli's older sister, said in a voice with authority, "Now wait here, you two. Don't move from here, and don't talk to any strangers. We'll be back shortly." Accompanied by Mishtidi, she entered the stall where a man was selling glass bangles of many colors. I would have loved to join them in trying on bangles. How the man held the bangles between his fingers and slid them gently onto the wrist of his buyer! But Buli had other plans. She bought two tickets and pulled me by my hand into an enclosed dark area. We managed to find some space on a bench close to a makeshift stage. Suddenly, along with ear-piercing music, a round spotlight lit a very short man on stage. He spoke rapidly through a handheld loudspeaker. The only words I understood were "the tenth wonder of the universe" and "the Siamese twins."

"Isn't this man really short?" I whispered in Buli's ear the moment the man and the music stopped.

"Don't be silly. He is a midget, not a short man. He'll remain this size all his life."

"Really?" I had never seen a midget before. But that was just the first of my surprises. Strange deformed people began to come and perform with even stranger music. In the flashing red light they appeared grotesque. A woman's severed head on top of a bamboo stick began to talk and before I even had time to think how that could be possible, someone placed two babies on a baby blanket in the middle of the stage. To my horror, I saw that the babies were joined from the waist down; they had only two legs but four arms and two heads. I was no longer surprised, but scared.

"Let's get out of here, I don't feel well," I whispered again.

"Wait, we haven't seen the most important item yet. Have you ever seen a bearded woman?" As soon as Buli finished, the drop screen parted, and there in the middle of the stage sat a woman inside a glass booth. She had a long flowing white beard and long black hair just as I had seen in my dream. The audience began to cheer, whistle, and scream. I began to feel like I couldn't breathe. I jumped up and pulled Buli along with me, out of this dark world of nightmare into the dazzling afternoon sun and dusty air. Once outside I felt a thousand times safer.

"Didn't I tell you the strange things I would show you? Here, take the rest of your money." Buli looked satisfied. I took the two *anas* from her palm and put them inside my little handbag. We began to walk toward the glass bangle stall to find Didimoni and Mishtidi.

Buli looked around and said, "You think they're still at the bangle stall? I'm sure they're in the gypsy booth getting their fortune told. They want to know when they will be married." She began to walk, and before I could ask all kinds of questions about the gypsy, I found myself in front of a small stall with a young girl in it, who looked to be around my age. In front of her was a row of tiny soaps wrapped in colored tissue. The girl sat quietly without any effort to sell her merchandise. She looked as if she was hungry. I felt sorry for her. I asked, "How much?"

"Two *anas* each." I picked a soap wrapped in glossy violet paper and paid her my last two *anas*. The soap smelled of lavender. I recognized the smell. A few years before, my mother's friend, the lady health officer, had presented Mother with a lavender perfume she had brought from England. When I first smelled that perfume, it had brought to mind a picture of a foreign flower. Memories of my first adventure and that special acquisition mingled with the fragrance of lavender.

Many years later when I went to England on my way to America, I saw lavender bushes and flowers. Their fragrance immediately took me back to that tiny soap I had bought at the fair nearly fifteen years earlier. And when I was returning to India after six years in the United States, our trip through Europe took us to the south of France. The acres of lavender fields near the perfume factories took me back to my first childhood possession, the tiny lavender soap. The foreign fragrance of lavender had accompanied a pleasant memory only to end in a full circle in the lavender fields of French Provence, a painful time of the breakup of my marriage.

Suddenly we saw Budhu standing in front of us. He was munching away on freshly fried *pakoras* from a newspaper cone in his hand.

When we got our share of *pakoras*, I wanted to go back to the soap stall and give a few to the shy little girl. But it was getting late and the gang had gathered to leave the fairground, which was getting quieter. A few kerosene lanterns were lit already. Mejda rushed us on. "Let's move. It's getting late. The grown-ups must be worrying already."

Outside the main gate, the bullock carts were waiting. It had been the most exciting day, and I did not know if I would ever be able to tell anyone about these adventures. I was tired and happy and sad that the day had come to an end. The moving rhythm of the cart wheels made me drowsy. The fleeting pictures of the Siamese twins and the midget man appeared like a dream now. Inside my handbag I held my little soap of foreign fragrance. That night, before falling asleep, I remembered that I had never found out how the candy called "old woman's hair" tasted.

THE LEMON ORCHARD

A courtyard separated the two sections of my paternal home—the outer house or *kachari* and the private living quarters. This yard was swept clean every day by one of the servants, sometimes washed with water mixed with cow dung to prevent insect invasions. In winter it was a place for the quilts and bed linens to sun and air. In summer and autumn various jars of mango and tamarind pickles in oil stood in the sun to cook. To steal pieces of pickle out of these jars in such an open space was a major challenge. The boys seemed more successful in such thefts. Every morning a maid hung saris and other wash across the courtyard on clotheslines, and we girls played hide and seek through the waves of colors that moved in the breeze. The maid kept warning us not to pull any of the wash down to the ground.

The suite opposite the *kachari* across the yard had two bedrooms with a covered verandah—one for my grandfather and the other for Mejojetha's family, who lived in the village home permanently. This was known as the main house. The kitchen, pantry, and storage area were attached to this suite. Three other rooms overlooked the same courtyard on other sides, where transient families stayed, such as us. Near the *kachari* stood a row of small rooms where some of the servants slept. In the past, poor students from the village had lived in these rooms, enjoying free board and lodging. My paternal great-grandfather was a successful attorney and a generous landlord who believed in helping poor villagers by giving them a free education. My father often quoted his grandfather, whose last words to his young grandson on his deathbed had been, "If you wish to 'give' to the poor, give them education, not money." Many of us in generations to come seem to have followed this ancestral advice unconsciously by becoming teachers and professors. Others teach without actually holding teaching jobs.

Between the main house and the kitchen area stood a large ancient tree which bore fruit the size of hand grenades that tasted like custard apple. I have forgotten the name. We girls loved that tree both for its delicious fruit and for its wonderful shade and exposed roots, which created a perfect place for us to play house. Years of rain and sun had polished the roots into a dark wooden labyrinth. In their little groves, Buli, Hena, and I set up our dolls' houses. After lunch, when the grown-ups took naps, we would sneak out of bed and gather under the tree. We would coax the kitchen maids to give us pieces of vegetable and some uncooked lentils or rice. The leafy branches of the tree protected us from the scorching sun. In fact, we never noticed the heat. There was always a breeze that came from beyond the back pond and brought up the musty coolness of water. Sometimes we invited some of the male cousins to join in our games by pretending they were guests who came to our make-believe meals. They were bored by such games and often wanted to play shop, where we sold our meager portions of rice, lentils, and vegetables and the boys bought them with pebble money. They liked to haggle over the price for a long time.

One day our oldest cousin Bardi, who was in her late teens, came and joined us and said, "You girls have pretended to cook long enough. Wouldn't you really like to cook and eat some real food for a change? Let's have a picnic. Just follow me." Didimoni and Mishtidi also joined in, resulting in a group of six girls of various ages. Bardi went to the pantry and got some provisions. As the oldest girl of the family and one who had lost her mother as a child, she was spoiled and indulged by the elders. She had free access to places we couldn't dream of entering.

We followed Bardi across a bamboo gate next to the edge of our house and entered a lemon orchard. I had heard about this garden for years but had not been allowed to go in. We entered it with trepidation, knowing full well that Mejojetha would not like such trespassing at all. This orchard was Mejojetha's creation, and he guarded it as his most precious possession. It was large, with hundreds of lemon trees, many laden with fruits of various sizes in shades of green and yellow. He had collected lemon seedlings from many countries—some as large as grapefruits, some as small as grapes, and many in between. Some were good for juice only, others were for flavor. Some trees had no fruit, only blossoms, making the air heavy with scent. At the bottom of every tree dirt piles made mounds and the aisles between the rows were picked clean. Now I knew where Mejda and Budhu occasionally got the large round lemons like pomelos, asking us to steal salt, pepper, and oil from the kitchen so that they could make a mouth-watering concoction of the pulp. We would wait with eager anticipation until the boys reluctantly handed down small portions to our outstretched palms.

I had heard the rumor from Mother that the land where the lemon orchard stood belonged to another branch of the Roy family. The two sides had had an ongoing feud for two generations, ultimately leading to a legal confrontation which our side of the family won, and the other side fled. Eventually their homestead was demolished, and the lemon orchard was planted on the ruins. All this supposedly happened long before the birth of Father's generation, and the lemon orchard must have been planted before my parents were married. Whenever Mother got upset with her in-laws she would refer to this story with a hidden reprimand to Father's ancestors. Baba would listen quietly and leave the room indicating that the story must have some truth to it. Piqued by my usual curiosity, one day I decided to find out.

"Ma, who were the people that lived on the land where the lemon orchard is now? What happened to them? Where are they now?"

Mother looked around carefully before saying anything. She took her time to finish the legend in several installments. The tale was so enchanting that I kept pestering her to continue. I listened to every word she said and later put it together in my mind.

Many years ago—not even my oldest uncle was born yet—a young man from the other side of the Roy clan brought home a beautiful bride. The whole village raved about her beauty. Some said, "too much beauty is unlucky, let's hope she lasts," etc., etc. The two sides of our family shared the pond behind the house mostly for washing and bathing. Every afternoon, women of the two families went with their brass water pitchers to the pond for leisurely baths. They dipped, swam, and gossiped as they enjoyed this cool break from the many responsibilities of a large household. This was their private time. On the really hot summer days, some of the women would return to the pond a second time, late in the afternoon, for a quick dip . . . it was not customary for the women to use the bigger pond in the front of the house. It was too public.

One summer afternoon, the beautiful new daughter-in-law went to the pond alone to take a quick dip. Perhaps she needed to escape both the heat and the restrictions of the family for a few minutes. There was no one around. The pond was secluded and shaded by rows of mango trees, coconut palms, and other bushes that circled it. A young man from our side of the clan, a college student who was visiting from Calcutta, went to the pond with the intention of fishing. Edging against the branches and bushes with his fishing rod, he approached the still water of the pond. He found a small clearing, put a bait of rice on his hook, and cast the line.

After waiting for a while without a single bite, the city youth grew impatient. He shifted his position and as he leaned against a coconut palm, he noticed a young woman slowly stepping up the moss-covered steps on the other side of the pond. The golden hue of the sliding sun transformed her into a glistening golden image covered by a wet yellow sari wrapping her body. As soon as he saw this apparition, the young man gasped, his heart pounding rapidly. He took a deep breath and closed his eyes to steady himself. When he opened his eyes again, the apparition on the other side of the pond had disappeared. For the next three days, the young man from the city pursued his fishing expedition fervently, and on the fourth day he gathered all his courage and stood right in front of the golden figure as she emerged from the water.

Mother did not go into the details of what happened after that. She only said that a month after this encounter, the news spread in the village that the beautiful new bride of the other side of the Roy family and the young college student from ours had eloped early one morning. Since then, nobody knew what happened to them. After this event, the two sides of the family had stopped talking to one another and became enemies. The relationship deteriorated over time to the point where they could no longer live side by side. Grasping an opportunity, my ancestors drove the others off the property and occupied their homeland.

Now this was the story my mother had heard from a neighbor. It was never corroborated by anybody in our family. I liked to believe the story, because in my eyes this wonderfully romantic tale gave a special stature to my ancestors. I could not help admiring a village bride and a college student showing such courage for romantic love. I had a sneaking suspicion that my mother also approved of their actions.

"I wished I knew who these young lovers were and how we were related," I said to my mother.

"It does not really matter how you're related to them. It's just so interesting and unbelievable that two young people of that era dared to do something so scandalous for the sake of . . ." She suddenly stopped. Without thinking I added, "Love. You mean, for the sake of love."

"That's enough! You don't need to understand all this adult stuff at your age. Now go, leave me alone. Let me concentrate on what I'm doing." But she did not go back to her knitting and looked away from my view. I was sure Mother was still thinking of the two young lovers of the Roy family. I too kept thinking about them. I tried to imagine what might have happened to them. I liked to think they had made a happy life somewhere in a big city away from the judging eyes of their relatives. Later I asked several of my cousins about this fable.

They all said, "Are you crazy? Never heard of anything so bizarre. A newly married woman eloped with a distant relative—this is an old village in India, not Hollywood."

"Fine, then tell me how the lemon orchard came into being?" I was determined to get to the bottom of it.

"Who knows? We heard that a poor relative could not pay the taxes on it and pawned the land to our landlord ancestors, losing everything." This could easily have been the truth, but I continued to believe Mother's story. There seemed to be no harm holding on to a hundred-year-old love story.

We girls arranged to have a cooking place in one corner of this lemon orchard, where every grain of dirt still held the smell of romantic love for me. Bardi made a hole in the earth with a spatula and placed three stones in the form of a triangle around it. One of us gathered some branches and twigs and lit a fire in it. I was asked to take the cut vegetables, rice, and lentils to wash in the pond. I stepped down—not the moss-covered tree trunks but cement steps—and looked up, imagining how I would feel if a pair of eyes were peering at me from behind the large leaves of the taro plants. A chill went down my spine. Really, how fantastic life must have been in those days!

THE JAPANESE SPY

For our meals, we sat on the floor of a room next to the kitchen in an oval ring. At the center sat Barojetha, then Mejojetha, Baba, two younger uncles, then the boys of the next generation, then the older girls, and finally the younger girls. I always sat between Buli and Hena. Our grandfather sat at the head with everyone only for lunch. He ate his dinner in his room on a small table. Dadu's personal servant—a young boy who prepared his water pipe—took Dadu's plate to his room early in the evening.

Toddlers between two and four sat around a large brass plate for their dinner. My mother or one of our older female cousins mixed rice, dal, and boiled eggs in a mash and made round balls. These balls had names such as crow's egg, duck's egg, crane's egg, eagle's egg, and so on, and the little ones stretched out their tiny palms for them. They were reluctant to eat food unless it took the form of make-believe bird's eggs. In addition, the grown-up in charge had to tell stories about the king and his four queens or the tiger and the fox. Otherwise there would be a cacophony of screaming and crying. Sometimes I stood by them and listened to the stories. My favorite was the one about the tiger uncle, who came to the house to carry children on his back to their *mamarbari*—the mother's brother's home, a place full of love and sweets. One has to hang on to the tiger uncle's back tightly, holding his ears, but not too tight. If he is irritated, he can lose his temper and the consequences can be severe. The babies opened their eyes and mouths wide, I suppose trying to imagine the consequences. After they had finished eating, a servant had to carry them one by one and hand them over to their respective mothers. Some of the more stubborn babies needed to be carried, walked back and forth, and sung a lullaby to put them to sleep.

Watching all this, I remember being annoyed by the amount of attention little children demanded. But in a big household there seemed always to be someone willing to oblige. Didimoni was one such person. I knew she would make a wonderful and patient mother someday.

In winter evenings, when the little ones were busy eating their food, we slightly older children had some free time between our evening homework and dinner. We would gather our books, slates and chalks, put them away, run for Mejojethima's bedroom and jump in her bed. Her quilt, which had been in the sun all day, made the bed toasty. This was our time to play war or tell stories. The boys made all kinds of noises, pretending to be fighter planes, and threw pillows at one another until one of the older cousins interrupted the war before the main weapons burst open and scattered fluffy cotton everywhere. In the storytelling department, I was the primary speaker. Only Dadamoni and I were experienced enough to tell war stories, because we came from Assam, where the Japanese planes had flown in several times, although they had never dropped bombs onto the oil fields.

One evening after playing for a while, everyone huddled together in bed. Budhuda said, "Hey, why don't you tell us about the time when the air-raid siren went."

I was just waiting for such a question and began immediately. "One evening when the shrill sound of the siren came on, we quickly left the house and went into the underground shelter. Soon we heard the unmistakable sound of the Japanese planes. We were terrified about Baba's safety, since he had gone out on duty in his helmet and khaki uniform and would not be allowed to return until the all-clear whistle. All of the adult men in the Assam Oil Company were enlisted to perform such emergency duties. We also knew that if we were bombed, their chances of returning home would be slim. It was pitch dark everywhere. All the neighbor women and children sat inside the shelter in silence except the mothers, who kept vigil, praying in low whispers. We held our mothers' hands in tight grips. We were scared yet excited that something unknown and dangerous might happen." I stopped briefly to watch the impact on my listeners.

"Well, what happened then? Was Digboi bombed? Yes or no?" Shyamal blurted out. He was really impatient.

"One can have a war without bombs also," I quickly added. "Why do you have to have people die always? The fear of bombing was scary enough for us. You had to be there to understand what I mean." I looked around knowingly. My younger sister Debi and Hena's sister Meera—both under five—came closer to me under the quilt in the distinct anticipation of hearing something really scary. Encouraged I began again. "These shelters were built in a way so that no one can see them from the outside. We crawled through a small door. The inside was damp. A few wooden benches, one clay water pot on the floor, and a small electric bulb hanging from the ceiling were the only furniture. The bulb was covered with black paper except for one small opening underneath. This was because of the blackout. All the lights in our town had been either painted black or covered with black paper for months." As I paused to think about what to tell next, I heard a voice from the floor.

"What about food inside the shelter?" I hadn't noticed that the servant boy who prepared Dadu's smoking pipe was also part of my audience; it was he who now asked this relevant question. He must have come to call us to dinner and gotten absorbed in the war story. I was pleased to see its universal appeal.

"No, no food. We barely had time to get to the shelter once the siren blew. No one worried about food in such times of emergency. I remember another evening. Baba and some of his friends had found a fresh *Rohu* fish and paid a fortune for it on the black market. They divided this rare find among themselves, and Ma had made a delicious curry for us. We sat down to eat this rare treat, and as I took my first bite of fish, the air-raid siren came on. We had to jump up, leaving the rice and fish behind, and run to the shelter. Luckily, the all-clear whistle came on shortly afterward, and we resumed our fish dinner after Ma heated everything up again. Ma was sure that the cat had helped herself to a couple of pieces of fish while we were away in the shelter."

"I'm hungry," Meera suddenly declared, and several others concurred. The fish story had made everyone hungry.

"Let's go for dinner, and we'll have more stories later," I said. After dinner we went to bed. There were no more war stories until a week later, when as usual we gathered in Mejojethima's bed and Buli asked me to continue with the story of war.

"Suppose the air-raid siren came on in the middle of the night, what would you do then?" Buli asked.

"As far as I remember, that happened only once. We awoke, dressed in whatever clothes we could lay our hands on, and ran out. Baba, of course, had to go for duty immediately. Oh, I almost forgot. We had to wear an iron disc with a number hung by a thread around our neck all the time. It was for the purpose of identification in case we were killed." Everyone was quiet.

"What is iden-fic-tion?" Meera asked in a squeaky voice. I myself did not know exactly what it meant. I just repeated what I had heard from the grown-ups.

"They can tally the number on the disc with a list of names to find out who is dead." Dadamoni got his first chance to show off his knowledge.

"Well, you said earlier that you heard the Japanese planes. Have you ever seen any Japanese soldiers? Aren't they very short like midgets with only two slits for eyes and no nose at all?" offered Shyamal. A boy of few words, Shyamal surprised every one with such a detailed observation. I then remembered something and quickly spoke before Dadamoni grabbed the floor,

"Yes, yes. I saw a Japanese soldier once. He wasn't that small, and he had eyes and a nose just like ours, but he looked a bit like the people from Nepal. One day Baba heard over the radio that some Japanese soldiers were captured in the jungles of Burma. They dropped in parachutes, possibly spies."

"What's a sp-sp . . ." Meera began, when Hena kicked her gently saying, "Don't interrupt all the time, let her continue."

"Oaf! Your foot is so cold, don't touch me." Meera was quite angry now.

"The government announced on the radio that if any Japanese paratroopers were spotted anywhere, they must be reported to the police immediately," I continued. "We overheard Baba telling Ma, and he sounded concerned. Several days later, one evening after dinner, Baba and two neighbors sat under the small opening of a covered lamp and studied maps to find the roads from Burma. They also talked about possible ways of evacuation for us in case things got really bad. Catching only bits and pieces of their conversation, we were not sure exactly what would happen if things got 'really bad,' because we had no idea what 'really bad' meant. If we had to flee, what could we take with us? I was determined to carry my favorite doll under my dress. Would we go through the jungle, full of wild elephants and rhinos? We were quite afraid yet excited by the possibilities of such grand adventures." By now, I had lost the thread of my story.

Budhuda reminded me. "Hey, let's get back to the Japanese spy, shall we? Or maybe you haven't seen any after all?"

I ignored his sarcasm and began again. "One day Dadamoni and I were playing near the train track in front of our house—something we were forbidden to do. But we always managed to sneak out as soon as we heard the sound of an oncoming train and put a copper coin on the rail. After the train passed we got a long tongue of copper, warm, shiny, and flat on the rail."

"We've done that also. No big deal! Get to the real story?" Budhuda sounded impatient. But I stayed on my own track.

"Of course, we did the same thing that day and waited for the train to come. I occasionally put my ear on the rail to hear the sound. Instead of the train, we saw three figures appear on the track—two men in khaki uniforms dragging a third man in faded tattered clothes. When they came closer, we could see that the man in torn clothes had some sort of a baggy net attached to his shoulders. This man was quite short. One of the policemen carried three rifles. Dadamoni whispered, 'Japanese spy!' Not knowing what would happen next I automatically stepped back and stood against our gate in case I had to escape quickly. In addition to hitting the spy with sticks, the two policemen were also giving him occasional kicks. The poor spy was barely able to stand straight. He staggered along and fell now and then, only to be poked and kicked again. I took only one quick look at the spy as they passed by. His swollen face had several cuts, although no blood was visible. He seemed oblivious to our presence." I stopped briefly. In my mind's eye, I could see the poor prisoner again.

"Don't stop now. What happened next? Did the police shoot him? Did he fall right in front of you? Tell us, tell us . . ." Budhuda was impatient again.

"No, the two policemen dragged him away, perhaps to the police station. We had no idea what happened there, nor did I want to know. Actually I felt sorry for the spy. Poor man! Perhaps he meant no harm, just dropped in the jungles of Assam by mistake. He was doing his duty as a soldier. In a war started by faraway nations, innocent people became enemies. Probably the police killed the helpless spy." I ended my story. Everyone was quiet, even the belligerent types such as Budhu and Shyamal were speechless.

"So are the stories finished yet? Let's go, dinner is ready, and it's getting late," said Didimoni, breaking the spell of my last words. We reluctantly got up from underneath the warm quilt. The little ones had fallen asleep.

THE MOTHER OF CHHAOL

Among all the people who dropped by the village home, I was most attracted to Chhaol's mother. Chhaol was his mother's only child—a young man of nineteen or twenty— employed to work in the outer house. We were not sure what his duties consisted of exactly, but he came to work every day and helped with various jobs at hand. Sometimes he cleaned Dadu's smoking pipe, sometimes he lit the tobacco in another smoking pipe and passed it around among the visitors (a gesture of hospitality), and sometimes he sat on the veranda and cleaned the glass domes of the kerosene lamps with rags and wood ash. I also saw him helping the boatmen as they pulled the boats full of fish or merchandise. Like Lord Krishna, he was everywhere. Even though his name meant "child," he was not offended to be called that. His mother's graying hair, which was cropped, told us that she was older than our mothers and aunts and was a widow. Like all Hindu widows, she wore a white sari without borders. She was a plump woman with clear skin and a smile on her face. I liked her from the moment I met her. Everyone called her "Chhaol's mother." No one knew her real name.

Like her son, Chhaol's mother was also around our house a lot. She dropped in at all times of the day and helped with chores in the inner house, even though she was not an employee. Whether it was to pound the parboiled paddy into flattened rice, to mix the green mangoes and oil in the pickle jars, to pick lice from the hair of one of the kitchen maids, or to comb and braid our tangled hair—Chhaol's mother was always busy doing some task. She knew all the customs for weddings such as which gifts should go on the decorative tray as part of the dowry or in the worship of a particular god, which flowers were appropriate for Shiva or which ones were liked by Krishna. Chhaol's mother had free access throughout our home. Everyone accepted her presence and her help.

When my two female cousins—daughters of Mejojetha—were married on the same day at the same time, the preparation began six months before. In the quiet of the afternoon when the women of the house were in bed taking naps, Chhaol's mother came and went inside the pantry. I immediately sneaked out of bed and followed her. She sat on the veranda with a floor knife held by two toes of her right foot. A bowl of water held pieces of white coconut pulp. She would cut fine designs out of paper-thin slices of the hard flesh of coconut. I sat watching her cut tiny pieces of coconut as small as nails and shape designs on them. I was amazed by such fine work created by her chubby fingers with just an ordinary cutting knife.

When she was done for the day, she always would give me the last piece of coconut saying, "Here, have one. You sat so patiently watching me. Don't tell anyone that I gave you a piece, otherwise they will be jealous, and you'll get a tummy ache." I put the piece of coconut immediately into my mouth. She never let me have any of the designed pieces, which I imagined to be like decorated feathers of white birds of paradise. I couldn't have eaten such lovely things anyway.

As if reading my mind she would say, "These will be ready only after having been dried in the sun and then cooked in sugar syrup. Of course, they are quite tasty even without the sugar syrup."

"Tell me, don't you feel badly that these beautiful things you have spent so much time making will disappear so quickly into people's mouths?"

"Yes, a little. But before that happens, these treats will be included in the gifts and displayed for the grooms' households to see and appreciate. They will rave and praise your family. If displayed nicely, these delicate pieces of coconut can be made to look like the lace scarves that English women wear, lace knitted from the whitest silk thread. Hundreds of wedding guests will line up to see the dowry from the Roy family and their eyes and mouths will open wide when they see my cut work with coconut." She began to gasp for air after talking so much in one breath. I had never heard her talk so much before.

Perhaps heavy people should talk slowly, I thought. I began to imagine the whole scene in my cousins' in-laws' homes. I am there in a line of guests admiring the cut coconut pieces. I manage to grab a handful of them from the colorful tray. I couldn't go on with this fantasy. I began to feel guilty. Chhaol's mother gave me a piece of coconut to eat each day, and here I was planning to steal one of her exquisite creations.

I pushed down all sinful thoughts immediately and asked, "Tell me please, how you have learned to cut these so beautifully?"

"Oh, I can't even remember. When I was married, my mother-in-law took me to the Boses' house, where she was a cook. There was a widowed aunt in that family who made wonderful sweets from coconut pulp. I probably learned by watching her. I was young then, I wanted to learn new things." She stopped and sat quietly with her round hands folded in her lap for awhile, her eyes far away. She must have gone back to those days when she was a young wife and wanted to learn new things.

I had never seen any other woman make such beautiful sweets. Even in those days, when women had more time because they had domestic help, they did not spend much time making artistic sweets, which were so fine and which looked more like delicate lace than sweets to be eaten. Only Chhaol's mother seemed to have unlimited time to do beautiful things for us.

I remember once that Mejda was sick with a high fever, possibly malaria. Chhaol's mother came by with a brass bucket of cold water and placed it on the floor under his head. She put a tapering banana leaf under his pillow ending to the bucket and sat near it gently pouring water with a mug over his head. The cool water washed his forehead and hair before sliding over the banana leaf and emptying into the bucket. Mejda groaned in comfort. When, after a long time, Chhaol's mother stopped and dried his hair with a dry towel, he opened his eyes and looked at her. I was convinced that Mejda got well within a few days because of her cold water treatment.

I could not help feeling that Chhaol's mother never received the appreciation she deserved. Everyone was used to her being around whenever needed. We all took her for granted. I asked Buli about this once, and she told me that Chhaol's mother was grateful that her son had a job in our household. But I did not think that that was the reason she did so much for us. She was just a selfless, kind person.

I had not realized that Chhaol's mother had been absent for more than a week. When I noticed this I asked one of the maids about her. The maid did not know anything. That evening I asked Mother if she knew what had happened to her. Ma assured me that she would find out next day. I knew Ma liked her. Chhaol's mother came by our bedroom some evenings and combed mother's long hair and made a braid and coiled it up on her head in a lovely bun. They chatted and laughed together.

The next day one of the servants came back with the news that Chhaol's mother was sick with high fever. Ma arranged for Mejojetha to send for our family physician to examine her. The doctor gave her some medicine. A couple of days passed. I was distracted by other things and forgot about her.

One evening some of us were sitting on the veranda next to Dadu's bedroom with our books in front of us trying to do homework. Buli and I kept reciting the multiplication table loudly as we rocked back and forth. Dadamoni and Mejda were reading the same storybook they kept hidden under a textbook, which they occasionally quoted loudly from, as if they were truly engrossed in their homework. From time to time, our younger uncle came by to check on us. The younger children were drawing nonsense on the slate and fighting over the chalk. Suddenly a loud wailing came from behind the house. We closed our books and looked at one another. None of us had heard anything like this before, but somehow we knew what it meant. A veil of silence fell over us. No one dared to ask any questions.

Somehow I knew then that death was beyond understanding and came to stop life without any warning. That evening all through dinner no one said a word. Later when I went to our bedroom I found Mother sitting on the edge of our bed weeping silently.

"What happened, Ma?" I asked.

"Chhaol's mother will no longer visit us."

I wept in my bed feeling sad that no one would make the beautiful coconut sweets, which looked like lace made of whitest silk thread. This was the first time I felt the pain of losing someone I liked and admired.

BARDI'S WEDDING

The wedding of our oldest cousin, whom we called Bardi, the daughter of my father's oldest brother, Barojetha, was a major event for the Roy clan. Just like the time of the goddess worship, all of the relatives gathered together to celebrate this occasion. The wedding took place in Habiganj town, at the house of Barojetha, the father of the bride, where he lived with his immediate family and occasionally attended court and practiced law. Like Mejojetha, he also enjoyed his share of the substantial income from the village property.

Not only was Bardi the oldest cousin in our generation, but because she had lost her mother as a child, she occupied a special place in all her relatives' hearts. Bardi was in her early twenties at that time. She and her brother Barda, our oldest male cousin, had been brought up by their stepmother, whom we called Barojethima.

Bardi's wedding was an event to remember. World War II had ended two years before. We were back in Digboi and had resumed going to our schools, which had reopened. But now we had an excuse to return to the fun world of grandfather's home again, full of relatives, food, and play. Sundarkaka and Monakaka—Father's two younger brothers who were living in Digboi at the time—joined our family of seven, and we began our trip via Shillong, the beautiful hill station on the Khasi Hills of Assam. In those days Shillong, a resort at an altitude of nearly six thousand feet, was accessible by road only.

No air travel had been introduced yet. We took a bus to Shillong and spent a few days enjoying the cool mountain air scented with pine before descending the other side toward the county of Sylhet, where the town of Habiganj was located. The view on either side of the road was magnificent. One side had high ranges with white ribbons of waterfalls and on the other were occasional orange plantations laden with fruit.

As we were riding down in a taxi enjoying the view, the car suddenly skidded and fell into a ditch. Just before the accident, Monakaka, who was sitting next to the driver, had been singing movie songs. Recognizing the tunes, the driver too sang along. He must have been distracted enough to lose his attention. Driving on this narrow hilly one-lane road with hairpin turns was not an easy feat. Fortunately, the car landed at the edge of an orange orchard, which acted as a buffer and prevented us from dropping thousands of feet below. My baby brother, who was six months old, fell under three of us yet escaped without any injury! The rest of us had small cuts and bruises. We waited for the public bus to arrive with Baba, Sundarkaka, and Dadamoni. After the initial shock, they were relieved to find us in one piece. Monakaka, in his characteristic fashion, kept groaning and complaining about aches and pains everywhere. Because of the accident we were delayed in reaching the river we had to cross.

It was already dusk when we arrived at the ferry station. Suddenly a torrential rain started. The driver cursed, complaining that the hills sent untimely showers whenever they pleased, making traveling a nightmare. Soon we realized what he meant. The force of wind and rain began to dislodge the parked, overloaded bus, which to our horror began to slide toward the river. The river, in the meantime, began to swell rapidly beyond its size. The men got off the bus and tried to stop the slide of the bus by rolling boulders and rocks under the front tires, though without much avail. Inside the bus we children sat stiff with fear, worrying about drowning as the bus crept slowly toward the water. Women began to whisper prayers, holding their young children tight. The children began to cry loudly from hunger and fear. The men were all outside, getting drenched in the storm. As a last effort, several young men stood in front of the gliding bus. At the driver's suggestion, more passengers got out of the bus into the rain.

Then the rain stopped as suddenly as it had come. Everyone

breathed a sigh of relief; the men took their shirts off and wrung them out while the women's lips moved in silent prayers of gratitude. Within a few minutes, the clouds were gone and tiny stars appeared in the dark sky. Soon a ferryboat arrived to carry the bus to the other side of the mountain stream. The boatmen carried kerosene lanterns and told scary stories about floods and landslides. Once on the other side, we felt safe. The rest of the trip was uneventful. After spending the night in Sylhet, a prosperous city of courts and colleges, we reached Habiganj by train the next afternoon. We were greeted by a houseful of people all talking loudly. In no time, the dangerous adventure of our journey was forgotten. We joined others in grand anticipation of the wedding festivity. I was, of course, delighted to reunite with my friends Buli and Hena after two years.

The auspicious day of the wedding drew near. A group of caterers pitched tents behind the kitchen and began to cook our meals, since the regular kitchen was too small to prepare food for so many guests. Altogether we were more than thirty-five members of the extended family. Huge woks—as big as coracles—were full of rice, vegetables, fish and meat curries, chutney, and sweets. Bardi, the bride-to-be, seemed to be in another world. For several days before the actual wedding, she was the center of various rituals conducted by the priest. One such ritual was a ceremonial bath where the older married women sang wedding songs and sprinkled water on the bride-to-be from new brass pots, accompanied by the blowing of a conch shell, an auspicious sound. In addition the women made a strange noise by moving their tongues inside their mouths, which sounded like *woolu, lu, lu*. (Later in my travels I noticed the same kind of sounds being made by African women in a ceremonial setting.) I watched these activities in rapt attention and dreamed of that day when I would be the center of such fuss and attention, although getting wet several times a day in the middle of winter seemed a little less appealing. However when I saw all the beautiful saris and gold jewelry selected for the bride, the dream became even stronger. Unfortunately I was only eleven and needed to wait at least another ten long years for all of this to happen.

Two days before the wedding Barda, brother of the bride, found me alone and said, "Come by this afternoon to the western room where Sundarkaka sleeps. We have important things to tell you." The shock of Barda speaking to me alone was so great that I could not move for several minutes. At the time, Barda was about eighteen or nineteen years old, fair-skinned with a thin moustache and a small beard. In my eyes he looked like the young Rabindranath Tagore, poet laureate of India who had received the Nobel Prize for Literature in 1913. A photograph of this handsome poet hung on our living room wall in Digboi. When Barda invited me, his eleven-year-old cousin, for a special meeting, how could I not feel flattered? It was really hard for me not to broadcast this unexpected news to Buli or Hena. I refrained from telling anyone. Something in his voice told me that I should keep it to myself.

In mid-afternoon, when all the grown-ups were taking naps, I slowly got up from the bed and changed. While I was fixing my hair in front of the mirror on the wall, I heard Mother's voice from the bed.

"May I ask where you are off to in the afternoon heat?" Although drowsy, the voice clearly betrayed sarcasm, which I chose to ignore and lied without hesitation.

"I'm going with Hena to the neighbor's. The girls there are going to teach me how to play marbles. Don't worry, we won't go on the main road. We'll go by the back lane. Go back to sleep, Ma." I was amazed by my ability to tell such quick lies. I closed the door behind me gently, lest Baba woke up also. Dadamoni must have left already for Barda's meeting. After reaching my destination, I found three other cousins in addition to Barda and Dadamoni sitting on Sundarkaka's bed. Sundarkaka was not there.

"Here you are. Come in. Has anyone seen you?" With these words Barda got up to close the door behind me.

"I don't think so. Ma was awake, but I told her that I was going to play with Hena." I found myself a bit nervous but excited. I had no idea what kind of conspiracy I was soon to be part of. It all began to sound like a story in a detective novel, and I was about to be the main character in it. I was the only girl chosen by the boys to participate in something important. I could not wait to find out what it was.

"Now, listen carefully," Barda said. "We chose you for an important job, and we believe you will not disappoint us. You were chosen because you are small and fast and, most importantly, we believe you can keep a secret. Please don't prove us wrong." Barda paused and looked at me for a long time. His words dropped into the room like heavy objects. Mesmerized, I just nodded my head.

"If you open your mouth, the punishment will be severe. Do you understand?" Budhuda joined in.

"After you hear about the job, tell us if you think you can do it." Mejda was always the practical one.

"Of course she can do it. Isn't she always stealing food from Mother's kitchen?" Dadamoni commented. I began to feel uncomfortable. What exactly did they want from me? Stealing? What did they expect me to steal? Now the excitement was mingled with anxiety.

"All quiet, please. First let her hear the whole thing. We don't have time to waste. Sundarkaka may appear any time," Barda's heavy voice intervened.

It was for Barda that I agreed to jump into something dangerous. I would do anything for him, but not for the likes of Budhuda or Dadamoni. They only knew how to tease and taunt. When Barda told me what I was expected to do, I was so terrified that I could not utter a word.

Watching my expression, Barda quickly added, "Don't you worry a bit. We will be close by to rescue you, in case something goes wrong. I personally shall carry you in my arms and run through the bamboo groves. So, are you in?" The promise of escape in his arms took away whatever hesitation I might have had. I conjured up courage just like a soldier in a battlefield. I told myself, *Anything for a great cause, anything for a great general like Barda.*

"Yes, I will do it," I said.

"Good. I shall explain everything, step by step, later this evening. When I go to buy cigarettes for Monakaka after dinner, be prepared to accompany me. I shall call you, so that no one will be suspicious. Now you go first. We must not all leave together." Barda looked at me, tilted his head slightly, and smiled his hypnotic smile. I left the room totally convinced that in the future Barda would definitely become the brigadier general of the army of independent India.

The whole afternoon and evening, I thought of this meeting and mastered all my strength to resist myself from telling Buli about this huge responsibility with which I was being entrusted. I had to sacrifice the pleasure of seeing Buli's face. Reluctantly, I had to learn the first unpleasant lesson of life, that I could not have everything. However, the secret excitement of being part of a forbidden act added to the joy of the impending wedding celebration and turned the situation into a major adventure for me. The inherent danger in this plan began to scare and attract me at the same time. That evening, I walked to the cigarette shop with Barda. He explained the course of action. The plan was airtight if everything went as expected. Barda assured me again of my safety. That night I barely slept.

It was the evening before the wedding. The sun had just gone down. The first shadow of dark was still to come. The servant boy sat on the back veranda cleaning all the glass domes of the kerosene lamps. According to instructions, I wore a black top and a pair of black shorts and put my shoulder-length hair back in a tight knot. I found my way behind the cooking tent. It was already dark next to the tall trees, tightly clustered. Some night birds were making strange sounds. I felt a slight shiver. I wondered if there were snakes in these woods. In no time, the gang of Barda, Budhu, and Mejda arrived. They too wore dark-colored undershirts over dark shorts. No one made a sound. We could hear the cooks inside the tent talking.

"This is the last batch. So far three thousand *gulab jamun* and two thousand five hundred *rajbhog* have been made," a voice said.

"Fine, but who is going to get up early tomorrow to mash cottage cheese so that everything is done before the family is up? I shall make loads of syrup and when the groom's family arrives, we will drop the *gulab jamun* in hot syrup just before we serve them. They will think these were freshly made. Hah, hah!" They seemed not only content but happy with this cheating plan. Then he added, "Hey, would you take this big bowl to the shed? Watch out. Don't slip on anything in the dark. Carry the oil lamp in one hand."

Barda immediately signaled me to follow the carrier of the bowl of sweets. The younger cook began to walk along a narrow path with the bowl of sweets on his head, which he held with one hand and a lamp with the other. He went toward a shed—a bamboo and straw structure temporarily constructed especially to store the sweets for the wedding guests.

That afternoon Barda's gang had cut a hole within my reach on one of the walls of the hut and covered it with straw. My job was to fill a small aluminum bucket with sweets and pass it through the hole to them waiting outside, where they would empty it into a bigger container and pass the bucket back to me through the hole for the next installment. When they decided that they had enough, one of them would rescue me through the door. Stealing the key to the door from one of the cooks was Budhu's job. After depositing the sweets in bigger basins in the shed, the servant boy was sure to lock the door. This was the only part of the plan about which I was not so sure. Despite Budhuda's cunning intelligence, it was the hardest part.

I followed the young cook to the shed. He put the basin down, fumbled with the key and opened the padlock. Barda gently pushed me in after the cook. Once inside it took a while for my eyes to get used to the dark. The oil lamp was casting more shadow than light. I was astounded to find huge clay basins filled with syrup right to the brim and sweets—red *gulab jamun* and white *rasogollas* nearly as large as tennis balls, swimming in the syrup. I hid behind the door, and in a few minutes the cook emptied his bowl into one of the large containers, turned around, and left, pulling the door shut behind him. There was the unmistakable click of the lock. I was alone in the dark. Like ghostly ping-pong balls, white *rasogollas* stared at me. Then I saw the hole in the wall, which was now exposed by my accomplices outside. In order to reach the hole, I had to climb inside one of the basins, crushing many sweets under my feet.

Someone whispered in the hole, "Take the bucket and return it with sweets. Come, quick." I began to fill the bucket and transfer it through the hole. My legs and arms became sticky with syrup, and I began to itch all over. After four transfers, Barda whispered in the hole, "That's enough. Stay near the door, someone will open it for . . ." Before he could even finish I heard a lot of noise outside, including a scared "Oh no, we're doomed. It's Barojetha!"

Then I heard Barojetha's irate voice. "What on earth is going on here? Who dares to steal so many sweets just before the wedding? Who is the mastermind behind all this? Don't think you can get away so easily! I shall personally supervise the flogging of each one of you." I could hear his footsteps stopping outside the door. I was scared out of my wits, but I realized that it would be really stupid to be caught before I had even one *rasogolla*. I began to stuff the sweets in my mouth, as many as I could in the few minutes before Barojetha put his head inside the door, followed by a cook with a lantern. Finding me standing inside one of the basins eating handful of *rasogollas* surprised Barojetha so much that he could not say anything for a full minute. Then he began to laugh and picked me up from the basin with both hands and put me down on the floor as if he were getting rid of an insect. I could not help but burst out crying from fear, shame, and guilt. Only prolonged hiccups interrupted my sobs, and I felt like throwing up all the sweets I had so quickly shoved inside my throat.

I grabbed Barojetha's leg and in between hiccups begged him, "Please don't tell Ma and Baba anything. They will kill me."

"Okay, I won't tell—on one condition. You'll have to tell me everything and everyone's name that are behind this," he said. The cook, in the meantime, went around the shed and retrieved a big bucket full of sweets—the very sweets I had transferred earlier. With great regret, I realized that the gang had to flee without the loot. I knew then that I could never ever betray them.

"I shall tell you later. May I go now? I need to clean up." I told Barojetha. Realizing that I was only an accessory to the crime, Barojetha patted my back saying, "Go, get out of here."

Next day, everyone was busy with the wedding. I avoided any association with my accomplices. They too avoided me. No one talked about the event again. There was a big argument during the wedding over the dowry. I was sure that as a veteran attorney, Barojetha found our unsuccessful petty theft negligible compared to the unreasonable demands of the groom's family. Or, perhaps he had totally forgotten the event.

We did not go to grandfather's home ever again after India became independent and was partitioned in 1947, with bloody riots between Hindus and Muslims. Both Habiganj and Baniachong fell to Pakistan and later to Bangladesh, and both my uncles' families had to move to India, hundreds of miles away from their homes. No one in the family has any idea what happened to the homes or who lives there now. Unforgettable stories of a short period of my childhood must still be in the bricks and dust of those homes, just like the story of the romance between two of my relatives, generations back, must linger in the dust of the lemon orchard next door.

Grandmother's Home

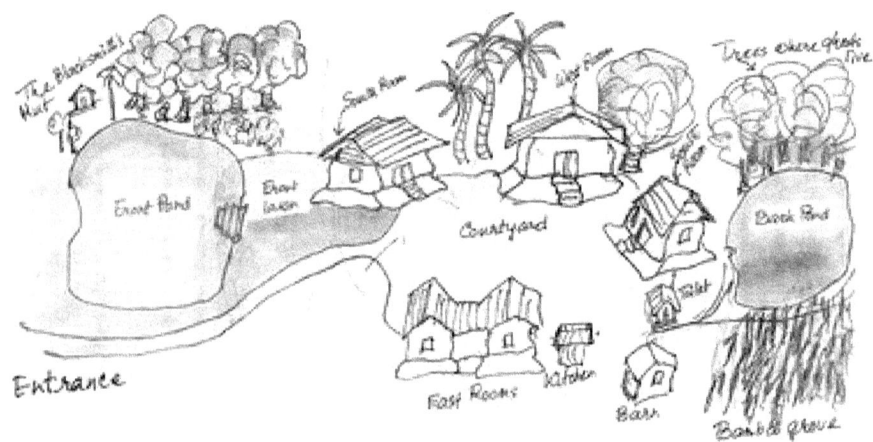

The Blacksmith's Hut

Trees where ghosts live

Sweat Room

West Room

Front Pond

Front Lawn

Back Pond

Courtyard

Toilet

Rest Rooms

Kitchen

Barn

Entrance

Bamboo grove

THE PALANQUIN

When we left Assam to escape the Japanese bombs during the very last part of World War II, we spent one year with my maternal grandparents in Kayasthapalli, a village in the district of Mymensingh, now in Bangladesh. As children, we often heard Mother compare her village to that of Father's. Her list was always long, citing virtues such as a better climate, nicer dialect, better food, and so on. We never heard Father argue with her about this. Perhaps he knew Mother's argument had more substance to it than just a comparison of the two villages. I also always suspected that her problem with Father's village went beyond the weather and the food. She had a hard time adjusting to a house full of relatives by marriage—a couple of sisters-in-law, to be exact, who were not always sisterly.

The biggest difference between my father's ancestral village and that of my mother was the water. Baniachong, Father's village, was in a wet terrain and mother's village was on dry land. In Baniachong, during the monsoons, rains connected the lakes, rivers, and ponds into one large sea. In Kayasthapalli, the rivers and lakes were contained within their boundaries, even during the rainy seasons. The terrain was open, interrupted only by scattered trees and clusters of houses. These were mostly fruit trees—mango, jackfruit, coconut, wood cherry, custard apple, and many others—standing like guards. The meandering roads, covered with fine white sand, stretched alongside the trees and homesteads—some of these with roofs of tin or thatch. We traveled on one such road to reach our maternal grand-parents' home.

We took a narrow-gauge train from Mymensingh, the district capital, to a small station called Gachiahata where the train line ended. We then took a palanquin and a smaller litter, called a *duli*. I had never seen these vehicles before. In both of these we were carried by four strong men. The palanquin was like a very small room that had an opening in the front and a pole on either side for the men to hold. Baba and Dadamoni sat inside the more spacious palanquin, Ma and I and my sister sat in the *duli*. (This was before my two younger siblings had been born.) Four men carried each vehicle on their shoulders and walked in a fast rhythm chanting *hei ho kaya, hei ho kaya*. This sing-song sound matching the carriers' pace put Debi, my younger sister, almost in a stupor. The *duli* was covered with a cloth for privacy. I tried hard to see the roadside through a slit in the middle.

At some point we passed by a cottage where I could see the yellow flowers of a pumpkin vine climbing up to the thatch roof. I was reminded of the fairy tale where the jealous first queen had the newborn babies of the king's favorite second queen killed and buried next to the barn. In time, a pumpkin plant grew on that spot, and the pumpkin flowers cried in the breeze and told their sad story. We passed by so quickly that I could not hear any moans in the air. A little later we passed a cluster of huts, and a group of children ran out and waved at us. The boys wore *lungis* and the girls striped saris. Some of the girls had nose rings. I wondered how these little girls tolerated having their noses pierced. I was eight years old and still did not have my ears pierced, even though I could not wait to wear earrings.

By late afternoon we reached our destination. It was a neat and clean home, not as large as Father's family home in Baniachong. A patch of fine grass separated the main house from the front pond. In the afternoons, Mother's father, whom we called Dadamashay, often worked on the front lawn, weeding and edging the grass where we children sometimes played who stole the handkerchief? and the servant boy collected and folded the dry wash in neat piles. There was another pond behind the house where the maids washed dirty dishes. Next to this pond was a bamboo grove. A little way off a cluster of large trees covered most of the sky, allowing in only a bit of daylight,

making the place spooky. The house consisted of several rooms, sol-
idly built, with tin roofs around a courtyard covered with packed clay
that looked like cement.

Grandfather spent most of his day in the front room, or *kachari
ghar*, which faced south and the front pond shared by the neighbors
who were also distant relatives. Opposite this room across the courtyard was the north room where grandfather's brother and his wife
lived. They were a childless couple and very fond of us children. The
two rooms to the east and west housed sleeping rooms for the rest
of us. The east room was part of a suite with several smaller rooms;
one of them was a shrine for household gods and goddesses, while
another served as a storeroom for old trunks and chests. A third room
was a vegetarian kitchen for Rangamashima (Mother's older sister),
who was widowed at the age of fifteen with one son. Her husband
died in his early twenties of tuberculosis, for which there was no cure
in those days. A kitchen, a pantry, and a shed for firewood stood
between the north room and the east room. At a little distance was a
barn for the cows. The toilet and the bath were quite a distance away
behind the kitchen on the edge of the bamboo grove.

DIDIMA

The east room complex was the world of our grandmother, whom
we called Didima. There were at least fifteen grandchildren, children
of her three daughters and two sons. Her youngest son had not yet
married. We all hailed from different towns and cities around the
country and had gathered here to spend the year because of the fear
of bombs. We children spent most of our evenings in Didima's suite,
crowding around her opulent body to listen to her stories of the epics,
gods, and demons, until we began to doze and were escorted to the
kitchen for dinner. In the summer heat, some of us would sneak up
and put our hot palms under Didima's dangling breasts, the coolest,
and our favorite spot. One or two of the younger ones even suckled
her dry breasts for fun. She would admonish us saying, "Get away,
get away from me. I have no peace left as long as these broods hover

around." But we never failed to notice a glint in her eye and a smile as she pretended to shoo us off.

Our memories of Kayasthapalli's home are forever clothed in the warmth of Didima's indulgent affection. She made our temporary home a haven of love and security. Now I know that much of this security had to do not only with her affection but also her personality. She exuded a unique combination of strength, compassion, discipline, and playfulness. She had a huge heart, which did not, however, soften her conservative ideas and prejudices of her time. For example, even as children, we noticed her partiality for her sons and grandsons over the daughters and granddaughters. The hierarchy was clear and fixed. In her eyes, the highest and most covetous positions belonged to the sons of her sons; then came the sons of her daughters, daughters of her sons, and last the daughters of her daughters.

I remember my mother complaining to her friend, a neighbor close to her age, about my grandmother's partiality toward her sons' wives. She said, "My sisters-in-law cannot do anything wrong. Ma is always critical of me even after all these years when I'm a grown married woman with children." I do not remember if her friend uttered any consoling words. Years later when my grandmother was old and nearly blind, my mother would visit her every weekend, traveling on a crowded commuter train carrying bags full of gifts of food and other necessities. I accompanied Mother on one of these trips and noticed that Grandmother never once thanked her for the trouble she took to be there. Instead she kept talking about her sons. I could see Mother's disappointment in her sad face. I also heard stories from relatives that Grandmother always told the neighbors how lucky my mother was to have a husband who was so handsome even though my mother did not deserve such a husband because she was not as fair.

So the other criterion was skin color. The fairest of the grandchildren were first to receive special treatment. A son's son who was fair, of course, hit the jackpot. This reminds me of another incident. My mother's oldest sister's daughter was quite dark skinned. Although a fairly accomplished and gentle-natured girl, the family was having a hard time finding a suitable groom for her because of her skin color. Each time a family with a prospective marriage proposal came to look at her, my grandmother's advice was to let the fairest member of the family greet the guests at the door, to let them know that this family also had fair-skinned members. The Bengali language has words representing every shade of skin color, something people from another culture may not even see, let alone name.

Along with some of her great skills, such as cooking, Didima also handed down this prejudice to her daughters—my mother and aunts. It was only later that I discovered that this attitude was held not just by our family but nearly the whole subculture of Bengal and the rest of India. Unfortunately, such prejudice was considered normal behavior. Those of us who were not fair-skinned were particularly self-conscious, a trait which I managed to shake off slowly and gradually as I grew older. Now I can look back and laugh at such behavior. However, I now know that prejudice based on shades of skin color is pervasive nearly all over the world. I shall never forget what happened to one of my colleagues, a woman who was a scientist.

Because of her dark complexion, Reba was sure that her parents would never find a good match for her in marriage and that she herself would have to choose her partner. That was not easy, since a fair complexion was a big part of a woman's beauty in the eyes of even the younger generation of men. But eventually a young man fell in love with her, and they married. They went to their village home, where his family gathered for a wedding reception. When Reba sat in her wedding regalia under a veil, the relatives and neighbors came to see her, bringing presents. An old woman raised her veil and remarked, "Oh no, this bride is darker than the bottom of a burnt pot!" Her expression and words were so cruel that Reba felt crushed.

This happened several times and finally the bride put her veil down and left the room. She gathered her belongings together in a suitcase and told her husband that she was going back to Calcutta. It was up to him to do what he thought was appropriate. When I met Reba the next day and heard the tale, I was very proud of my friend. Not many women exhibit the courage she showed, risking the loss of her good name, not only with her in-laws but also with her husband. Fortunately in her case, her husband understood and supported her and left with her for Calcutta.

Being a dark-skinned daughter's daughter I was not a favorite of my grandmother, yet I never felt myself to be an outsider in her wide orbit of affection. For the most part the generosity of her soul superseded her prejudices. Despite her flaws, I loved my mother's mother, especially because I never had a chance to know my paternal grand-mother, who died when I was three. Didima was very patient with all our unreasonable demands. Most important, she had the capacity to be like us in age when she played with us. For example, she joined us when we sneaked out of our beds in the middle of the afternoon to make hot and sour things with the green fruits of the neighbors' gardens while our mothers were busy napping.

Father accompanied us to Kayasthapalli but left after a week. As a son-in-law he was the most coveted guest, and he could not jeopardize that position by overstaying. I noticed how reverentially Didima treated Baba, even though he was a generation younger than she was. She never addressed him directly and talked with him through a child, as if through a medium. For example, one day when Baba sat down to lunch, Didima said to me, "Ask your Baba if he likes the fried fish? Would he like one more?"

"Tell her that it's excellent. I'm quite full. Thanks," Baba said, looking at me. I didn't have to say anything, yet my presence seemed necessary for them to conduct a conversation! It all sounded very strange.

"Didima, why do you talk to Baba like that? He was right there within earshot, why go through another person?" I asked her as soon as I had a chance.

"A son-in-law is an honorable guest. He deserves due respect even from a mother-in-law. You can't understand such values. Things are changing so much, no one knows what respect really means any more," Didima said. I was more confused than before. I decided that the adult world did not always move logically or meaningfully. They just made up rules which suited them.

THE GHOSTS IN THE BAMBOO GROVE

In Kayasthapalli, since no cousin was close to my age, I roamed around freely by myself exploring new sights and smells, especially along the pond and the bamboo groves behind the kitchen. There was a mystery about this area of less sun and greater shadow. This pond was partially covered with a sheet of green algae. The maids pushed this green sheet aside with the bottom of a pot to reach clear water barely reflecting the patch of blue sky through the bushy heads of so many trees. The air was moist, mixed with the musty smell of earth that came from the bamboo grove. For the first time in my life I saw beautiful red bamboo shoots, which are like flowers and quite rare to see.

One morning, Haridashi—one of Ma's distant cousins who lived in the next house over—walked into our courtyard holding the hand of a girl aged nine or ten and asked for Didima. She ordered the girl to touch the dust of Didima's feet in *pronam* and introduced her by saying, "This is Mayna, my niece. She will spend the summer with me. I thought she might like to play with . . ." She signaled toward me on the veranda. I was playing with some pebbles by myself, and the last words rang like music to my ears. The girl was obviously a bit older and taller than myself and wore a sari tightly wrapped around her bare torso. Immediately I was jealous. I wanted to wear a sari, too, and look like Mayna, grown up and self-assured.

"Live many years and have many sons," Didima said, putting her palm on Mayna's head in a typical blessing to a girl. And then to me, "Now you have someone to play with."

It was very easy to be friends with Mayna. We both wanted a friend to do things with, to confide in. Besides, I really missed Buli, who had been my constant partner in every adventure in Baniachong.

One day I told Mayna with pride, "I bet you've never seen a blooming bamboo shoot. I can show you, let's go." Mayna kept quiet for a minute before bringing her mouth close to my ear.

"Since you go to the bamboo grove so often, I bet you know who lives there," she whispered.

"No, who? Why are you whispering?" I was already cautious. Mayna pulled her sari above her knees and climbed up onto the high veranda, pulling me with her.

She began in a muffled tone, "At the top of big trees such as mango, jack fruit, and such, live *petnies*, the estranged wives of ghosts. They keep vigil to find suitable men to marry. They spit on people's heads to attract their attention. They spit more on girls whom they wish to stop from going into their area. If you still don't stop, these *petnies* will jump down on your shoulder and will never leave you again.

You'll be forever with a *petni* and talk like they do, like this." At this point, Mayna pinched her nose with her two fingers and talked in such a nasal tone that I couldn't follow what she said.

"Cut it out! I don't believe a word. Have you ever seen a *petni* or have they spit on you?" I asked, both incredulous and curious.

"Of course, many times. Let's go. You can see for yourself, since you don't believe me. You town people think you know everything, ha!" Annoyed she got up and snatched my hand and started walking behind the kitchen.

Two maids were cleaning pots and pans at the pond using dirt, coconut husk, and ash. One of them was covering the blackened bottom of rice pots with fresh clay. A covey of ducks quacked loudly around the pots, begging for food. Mayna dragged me along a narrow path by the pond. A few minutes later, she let go of my hand, and we began to walk single file. The path got narrower every minute. I loved the soft touch of wet grass on my bare feet. There were bushes and shrubs along the path. Under them bloomed tiny blue flowers with even tinier yellow centers as if blue stars with yellow dots had come down from the sky. Soon I saw the bashful vine—as soon as I touched it, the leaves closed as if a shy new bride was closing her long lashed eyes. I almost forgot about the ghosts and their estranged wives. Mayna walked fast and was a good bit ahead of me. All of a sudden she turned back and said, "Why are you lagging behind? Come quick, here it is."

I ran to catch up with her. Together we reached the other end of the pond. The sun could barely penetrate through the tall trees, which now replaced the dwarf bushes. The air was thick with the smell of forest and anticipation. I was not too scared because Mayna, who knew about these things, was next to me. But I still felt somewhat strange.

Mayna came very close and whispered, "Now is the time to chant the ghost-prevention mantra because we're officially in their area. Repeat after me, word by word,

> *The ghost is my son, petni is my daughter,*
> *No one can harm me,*
> *I'm protected by Ram and his brother.*

We continued chanting the mantra as loud as we could over and over again as we walked slowly. After a few steps, Mayna stopped me with her left hand and with her right pointed to the top of a large mango tree. Although I craned my neck as far as I could and tried to see through the crowded branches, I saw nothing.

"Tell me what you saw," I said.

"*Shushsh.*" Mayna put her right index finger to her lips. I fell silent. She looked positively scared and pointed toward the tree again.

"Don't you see the figure in the white sari dangling her legs from the top branch? She is waiting for us to get closer so she can spit on us." After trying hard for a few seconds, I still could not detect any white figure. It was not so easy to see through the dark green leaves. I did see something smoky up there. Meanwhile, Mayna kept chanting the mantra. The whole atmosphere became creepy, and I became frightened.

"Let's go back," I said. We turned back and walked in silence.

After a few minutes Mayna screamed, "Here it is! Here is *petni*'s spit. Look, she just dropped it. We didn't see this spit before." She pointed to a vine and went back to her loud chanting. Indeed, there was a glob of foam hanging from a leaf. I wanted to get closer to examine it, but Mayna suddenly broke into a run while chanting the mantra at the top of her lungs. She must have seen something horrible. I ran after her and reached the pond in no time. The maids and their pots were gone. Even the ducks had disappeared. We stopped briefly to catch our breaths. Then, hand in hand we walked back together into the courtyard.

We were still chanting the mantra under our breaths. Once in the courtyard, Mayna let go of my hand and walked diagonally across the yard. Her slim figure in its tightly draped sari disappeared before I could ask any further questions. I never got around to asking her about what had happened, because every time I raised the topic Mayna changed it.

"Talking about the ghosts brings them back close," she once said.

To this day when I'm near a dark, woody area, I automatically begin to chant the ghost-preventive mantra,

The ghost is my son, petni is my daughter,
No one can harm me,
I'm protected by Ram and his brother.

THE MANGO STORM

Our days and evenings were filled with playing all kinds of games. In the late afternoon, after sunset, we cousins sat in a big circle on the front lawn, which Dadamashay always kept trimmed, and played handkerchief thief. As we sat in a circle keeping our eyes closed, one of us ran around behind the circle dropping a small handkerchief behind a player. If this person correctly guessed it was behind her, then the original runner lost a point and had to go around a second time. On the other hand, if the person had no idea that the handkerchief was behind her, it became her turn to go around. With about fifteen kids participating we always had a lot of fun arguing and giggling.

In the evening if Didima was too busy to tell us stories, we would play snakes and ladders or tic-tac-toe on our slates. Sometimes we would watch Mother and the other grown-ups play *ludo* on a board using two dice. Uncle Lalit, one of Ma's male cousins, joined them in this game, and they played through the night, laughing, joking, and betting with one another. They seemed quite addicted to this game. I enjoyed watching Mother so relaxed and happy. The change in her was remarkable compared to her behavior in Father's village. She laughed a lot and hardly ever put her sari around her head as a veil. She played and ran with her siblings and older nieces in the courtyard. In this regard Didima, who was strict with her daughters-in-law, was lenient with her own married daughters. I thought a lot about it and was curious to know if my uncles' wives behaved in the same relaxed way when they went to their parents' homes.

One early afternoon in May when the grown-ups were in bed taking naps, some of us were playing hopscotch in the courtyard. This was the same courtyard where, on winter mornings, the pillows and quilts were put to sun on a mat and many kinds of pickles stood in big jars of oil, slow-cooking in the sun. Now it was the hottest time of summer and only flat baskets full of beans and other legumes were drying in one corner. We were forbidden to go out in the midday sun. But we often defied such orders and sneaked out. It was better to be out in the open because sometimes a sudden breeze would come from the front pond bringing an unexpected coolness.

It was so hot that day that not even the birds were out except for one solitary crow, who kept crying *ka ka*. For our game of hopscotch, we drew squares in the sandy dirt with a stick and used a broken piece of clay pot for a marker. It was my turn. As I hopped out and turned, suddenly the daylight disappeared. In a few seconds, someone had emptied a huge bottle of black ink over the whole sky, as if the night had fallen several hours before its time. Grandfather came out of the south room and hollered for the servants.

"Get the wash, baskets, everything from outside immediately. The mango storm is on its way. Hey, you kids, get inside, right now." I noticed that his voice quavered a bit.

We ran to the east room where Didima, Ma, her sisters, and two aunts by marriage were all resting with my newborn baby sister. Mejomamima, the wife of our second uncle, ran out and carried the dry laundry in and dropped it in a heap on the bed and then ran out again to gather the baskets of beans. Along with two servants, Dadamashay ran to the barn to check on the animals. The wind picked up; the wooden shutters of the windows opened and closed continuously, *dasht dasht*. Occasional thunder cracked, deafening our ears. Ma and one aunt tried to close and latch all the windows and doors. It was pitch dark inside and out. Baromamima kept looking for matches to light a lantern. From the north room Grandfather's younger brother and his wife also joined us. We were all in Didima's room except Dadamashay, who stood on the south room veranda and looked up to the sky, praying loudly, "Save us, God, save us." The sound of his prayer was almost lost in the howling wind before it reached us. The mango tree between the west and south rooms began to drop hundreds of baby mangoes on the tin roofs.

Cousin Naru blurted out, "What a shame! All the mangoes are dropping, leaving none to ripen. Maybe I should go and see." His mother looked at him with admonishing eyes.

"Don't you move! You go out, and the lightning will fry you into ashes. There will be plenty of time to collect the mangoes tomorrow morning. Just sit tight and be quiet. It may not be a bad idea to pray for the storm to stop." Baromamima sounded pretty scared herself. After this, nobody dared to say anything.

It was only four o'clock in the afternoon by the wall clock above Didima's bed. We huddled together listening to the wind outside, sounding as if thousands of pythons were inhaling and exhaling. Branches of trees were breaking and hitting the roofs. Somewhere a tree fell.

"Oh, my coconut palm just gave up. It was not even six months old," Dadamoshay's brother said in shock. We could hear the cows in the barn mooing loudly. Unable to hold my tongue any longer, I moved close to Mejomamima, whom I liked most among my aunts. She was young and pretty and was closer to my older cousins' age. I saw her in between the two generations, maybe because she was nice to me always.

"What will happen if the roofs of this house are blown away? Are we going to die?" I whispered.

She put her hand around my shoulder and said, "This house is very strong, don't you worry a bit. The storm will stop very soon, you'll see." I was reassured by her stable voice.

But the storm showed no sign of stopping. By now it was five o'clock. All of us children began to grumble about being hungry. But there was nothing to eat in this room. Who would dare to go outside to the kitchen! All this time Didima was moving her prayer beads rapidly with her eyes closed. Except for the new baby, no one made a sound. Even the two cats sitting at the foot of the bed stared vacantly. I had never seen my mother and aunts so quiet for so long. Fear covered us all under the same silence. It seemed like a long time before someone noticed that the sound of the wind had subsided. Soon a new sound of torrential showers followed. But the rains lasted only a short time.

Ma peeked though the crack of a window and a sliver of sun sneaked in. Surprisingly, all the dark clouds had disappeared, exposing the last light of the setting sun. Everyone began to move off of the bed, including the two cats, which pulled their backs up and shook their heads and jumped down. Didima touched the prayer beads to her head, set them aside, and got up. We opened the door to a world of destruction.

The whole courtyard, where we had played just a few hours before, was now covered with fallen trees, branches, hundreds of green mangoes, and a few green coconuts. Not knowing what to expect,

Dadamashay tiptoed toward the barn. He came back to report that the cows and calves were safe but that half of the thatch roof had been blown away.

We stepped down to the courtyard to collect dropped mangoes. The fallen leaves and rain made the yard very slippery, and we began to skid and fall. Soon that became a game, causing a lot of laughter. Dusk fell, and we had to get back inside. Fortunately by then we had already picked up most of the fallen mangoes in our courtyard.

We had a simple meal of hot *khichuri* (a mixed dish of rice and lentils or mung beans) and fried potato and went to bed. The storm had reduced the sultry heat considerably, and we all huddled under a light blanket. Inside the warm security of Didima's cotton blanket, the fear of the dangerous storm was soon forgotten. This scary and eventful day ended with the exciting anticipation of gathering fallen mangoes the next morning, to be followed by a most desirable event: Didima's special recipe of instant green mango chutney mixed with chili, salt, sugar, and oil. Even the thought of it made my mouth tingle. I wished it were morning already.

When we awoke, everything was flooded with sunlight. We finished our breakfast quickly and ran to the mango orchard outside the house. There were mangoes everywhere—half-ripe, unripe, and even very small green ones. A lot of children from the neighborhood were there already, gathering mangoes in baskets and in the folds of their saris. Along with the excitement, I also felt a little sad thinking about the poor mangoes, which did not get a chance to mature. But if the mango storm dropped them each year, then perhaps this was the law of nature. We took our loot to Didima. She was very pleased.

"Wow! You got a lot. Let's sort them first and then you will have Didima's special." She smiled with satisfaction and sat on the floor next to the heap of mangoes. She made separate piles by size and ripeness and ordered us to take them to various places. "Naru, take this pile to the vegetarian kitchen. Maya, you take these to the kitchen and tell the maid to slice them with the skin on for pickles. This pile, I shall cut later to be dried in the sun. But first our instant chutney, right?" She looked at us.

"Yes!" we said in unison.

We brought salt, sugar, green chilies, and oil from the kitchen. Didima dropped several green mangoes in a bowl of water and then peeled and cut them in fine slices. Then she mixed everything together for what seemed like a very long time. Watching her prepare this delicious concoction, a sour sensation along my tongue made my mouth water. I could barely wait. Didima took a bit of the chutney in her two fingers and dropped it in her mouth to taste. Then she added a bit more sugar and finally called us. We crowded around her with our outstretched hands. We got our share, and the rest was put aside for the grown-ups. The taste of that instant mango chutney was amazing and only Didima could make it so.

WHO STOLE THE QUEEN'S HEAD?

Our grandmother could make many kinds of delicious food, but her specialty was various types of sweets made from milk products. In Kayasthapalli, milk was available in abundance and at a low price. Every morning Dadamashay came back from the market followed by a servant who carried two brass buckets full of milk. The milk from our own cows was just about enough to feed the younger children. The boiled milk from the market was used for making yogurt, cheese, and evaporated milk, the last two being the primary ingredients of Bengali sweets.

My favorite was the fried crust of the milk. A thick crust was allowed to form on top of boiled milk that was left to stand over a burned-out fire for hours. Didima then carefully lifted the crust and put it out on a clean plate in the sun. After the crust was dried, it was browned on a pan over the fire, exuding butter and then covered with caramelized sugar. The taste of this sweet was rich and wonderful. Because of the long labor involved in the process, it was made only on rare and special occasions. Some of us could not wait, and we sneaked into the kitchen in the afternoons to steal the crust directly from the wok of milk on top of the dying wood fire. It was not easy to steal milk crust without leaving traces of milk drippings. But it was always worth the effort.

Some of the sweets were made with a thick paste of sweetened evaporated milk that was prepared over high heat for many hours.

This milk paste was then pressed into stone molds made by Didima herself. With the help of only a small knife, she painstakingly carved mirror images of flowers, fruits, birds, and other animals and figures inside stone bowls of different sizes. Even we children could not help marveling at her beautiful creations when we ate the lovely milk flowers or birds.

One such mold was of Queen Victoria's head. Using a red marble bowl, Didima had cut out the head of the queen wearing a crown. Filling this life-size mold required several pounds of thickened milk. A touch of food color on the lips and two cardamom seeds in the eyes made the creamy white head lifelike. My father, who was once offered this masterpiece, could not bring himself to break and eat it. We often talked about this legendary sweet and waited for her to make it. Finally this happened. Didima made the queen's head for a special guest, a political dignitary of the congress party who was visiting the village.

Didima made the head several days before the arrival of the dignitary and put it in an aluminum container, hidden away from her grandchildren. The news circulated in no time, and several of us looked everywhere for it without any success. Even if we had found it, perhaps no one would have had the courage to eat the head of Queen Victoria! No one that is, except one.

Dadamoni was an expert sweet thief who had an uncanny nose for sweets hidden anywhere. Sometimes he used one or two of us to keep watch at the door, but usually he preferred to work alone. This way, he would not have to share his precious loot. On this occasion even Dadamoni was not sure. As the time for the guest to arrive drew near, he became desperate. Secretly we were happy that even he seemed to have failed this time. When the illustrious guest finally arrived, Didima arranged pieces of cut fruit and pastry on a polished brass plate before opening the container of the sweet. Her scream was so loud that Baromama (our oldest uncle) came running to the pantry. The aluminum container was empty!

Headmaster of a high school by profession, Baromama began an immediate investigation. We were all afraid of this uncle who was strict and authoritarian. He tried to coax us all into a confession, promising that there would not be any punishment. Not one of us could provide useful information. We knew that not even Dadamoni could be involved this time. Unable to solve the mystery, Baromama gave up and eventually the event became another family tale. Years later, when several of us came back to Calcutta to attend a wedding, as we sat together one rainy evening reminiscing about the war years in our grandparents' home Dadamoni confessed for the first time how he had found the queen's head.

"When all of Didima's usual hiding places yielded no result, I decided to let it go. Then one afternoon I was sitting in Dadamashay's room chatting with him. He asked me about my school. As we talked, I looked around and saw the large photo of Rangamashima's dead husband that hung on the wall. I wondered what happened to him that he had died so young. Then I saw a black line on the wall between the large photo and the floor. After a while I noticed that the dark line was moving. Meanwhile Dadamashay began to doze. I went close to the dark line and discovered that it was a line of ants coming down from behind the photograph all the way to a tiny hole on the floor. I could not recall seeing any ants on this wall before." Dadamoni paused and looked at us. We waited anxiously trying to figure out where the story was going. Finally he decided to end our suspense.

"Who knows the significance of a row of ants?" He asked. Before any of us could speak, he quickly added, "Now I knew where Didima had hidden the queen's head. It had to be in the space behind the photograph." He stopped, presumably for our exclamations. Although impressed by his detective acumen, we could not forgive him for devouring this precious and beautifully crafted queen's head all by himself.

"We get the story of your clever discovery. But how on earth did you get to the space behind the photograph so high on the wall?" I asked.

"With great difficulty. It took me a long time to push the container down from behind the photo with a broomstick. Besides, climbing up a cane stool placed on top of a chair and poking at the back of the picture required quite a balancing act. Thank God Dadamoshay slept soundly! Fortunately for me the container didn't open, not even from the fall, although the queen's head was a bit damaged. Her crown broke off." He finally ended his tale of brave theft.

"You ate the whole thing by yourself! Didn't you get a tummy ache?" I couldn't help myself and blurted out.

"From long experience I have learned one lesson. It's safer to work alone than take a chance with weaklings divulging information. One hard question from Baromama, you people would have broken down and confessed," he said.

For sometime after that I kept wondering if Didima would have really punished one of her favorite grandsons if she had known who really stole her precious sweet, the head of Queen Victoria.

THE MUSLIM GIRL

Didima, along with her many-faceted talents, was also an amateur family doctor. She not only knew natural remedies for broken limbs, cuts, bruises, colds, fever, and gynecological problems but also how to deliver babies. Even though Dadamashay, her husband, practiced homeopathy, all his patients preferred to come to Didima, who was not only effective, but her services were free of charge. The villagers trusted her because she used familiar things such as herbs from the garden and spices from the kitchen. Once a man fell from a coconut tree while trimming the dead fronds and broke his leg. He limped to Didima's kitchen and got a bandage of turmeric and lime. A week later he came back walking normally and took the dust of Didima's feet and touched his head to show his respectful gratitude. Whenever we grandchildren had any medical symptoms—stomach ache, tooth- ache, headache, cold or fever—Didima's medicine worked like magic. But there was another side of her that I came to know that I neither understood nor admired.

From time to time, a pretty girl about my age came to the house with her mother. The mother took a big basket full of paddy from Di- dima and came back a week later to deliver popped rice, flattened rice, and so on. Sometimes other things, such as shelled peas or cleaned mung beans, would be in her baskets. The girl's hair was light brown with blond streaks and tangled. She wore a tiny brass nose ring. She helped her mother clean our courtyard by pouring buckets of water as the mother thrashed around with a broom made of coconut leaves. I never heard the girl speak. A mystery surrounded her. I so much wanted to talk to her, ask her to play with me. I had a feeling she was different but did not know how.

One day I asked my grandmother, "Didima, who is this girl? She is so pretty. May I play with her? Why doesn't she ever come up to our porch and talk to me? Does she have an infectious disease?"

"Here you go again, a small head full of big questions! I'm afraid this habit of yours is going to land you in big trouble. Don't ask so many questions, okay? This girl is Muslim. We don't mix with them. Be careful never to touch her. Now off you go. I have no time to waste chatting with you." Didima dismissed me and left for some important errand. I did not dare broach the subject again, but her comments kept stirring inside me. Something told me that it was not a safe topic to ask the adults. I wondered if Mayna could answer my questions.

This was the first time I became aware of the problem between the Hindus and the Muslims. Yet, I had no idea what the problem really was. A few Muslim families in the village were well off, but the ones who came to our house were poor. They worked for us and got paid in paddy or old clothes.

A few days later when the mother and daughter came carrying a big basket of shelled beans, I ran out to the porch. I saw Didima pouring a small basket full of rice in the sari fold of the woman. Both of them were careful not to touch each other. After Didima went inside, I whispered to the girl, "What's your name?" She appeared shocked, stared at me, and averted her eyes without saying a word. Her mother gathered the rice in her sari in a bundle, tied it, and put the baskets on her head. She grabbed her daughter's hand and began to walk out of the courtyard.

I have never forgotten this Muslim girl in my grandmother's home, whose hair was tangled and light and whose name I never learned. As I grew older, my grandmother's prediction about the danger of asking too many questions became clearer, although I never could change this habit, partly because I did not see any benefit in being quiet when I wanted to know the answer to some question I had. To this day, thousands of questions drive me; one of them is whether a solution exists to end the problem between the Hindus and the Muslims and between the Israelis and the Palestinians.

I recall another occasion when my question to Didima, despite her annoyance, gave me a very profound response which I have not forgotten to this day. Once when I was in college, a few of my cousins and I were visiting Didima in her new village home, which was built after the partition of India, when many Hindu families sought asylum in the western part of Bengal. She was telling us about a village scandal of a young man eloping with his aunt by marriage, leaving the whole village in shock. "But Didima, you told us the story of god Krishna whose dearest lover was his uncle's wife Radha. No one seemed to mind the god's falling in love with his aunt. Why are you so upset with similar behavior when a man did it?" I asked boldly.

"I see your bad habit of asking tough questions hasn't changed. What gods do, mortals must not; we have gods to do things we humans are not meant to do. Don't ever forget that," Didima said without any hesitation. These words shut me up. I knew she had said something extremely significant. Years later I quoted my grandmother many times whenever I gave lectures on Hindu mythology, implying the wisdom of her words.

THE BLACK STONE NEAR THE POND

Every afternoon in the summer months I accompanied Mejomamima to the front pond. My job was to sit on the top step and keep watch. According to the village customs the young daughters-in-law of established families were expected not to go out of the house alone. I was delighted to be picked to be her chaperone, even though I never quite understood why the daughters-in-law had to be watched whereas the married daughters were free to go anywhere by themselves. My mother and her sisters even played *ha-du-du*, running all over the inner courtyard, and snakes and ladders or cards with their male cousins deep into the night. Of course, they were not allowed to do any of this in their in-laws' homes. I had noticed this distinction when my mother was at her in-laws, that is, grandfather's home.

I really enjoyed this opportunity to daydream while watching Mejomamima bathe. She was always quiet. Sitting on the last step with her feet in the water she rubbed a cake of Hamam soap in a small red towel and gently scrubbed her face, the back of her ears, armpits, and legs. Then she stepped down into chest-deep water to wash off the soap. She came out of the water and squeezed the bottom of her sari and covered her wet sari with a dry one. As she climbed up the wet moss-covered steps, her skin glistened like gold in the afternoon sun. She looked like a water nymph from one of the fairy tales Didima told us. When I saw her firm breasts and thighs under the wet sari I was impatient to grow up as quickly as possible. At age nine I knew that was not possible. So I sat there imagining myself grown and beautiful with round breasts and firm thighs.

One afternoon sitting there I began to wonder what might be on the other side of the pond. The next day Mejomamima did not go for her afternoon dip. She looked distracted, her hair uncombed and unwashed.

"Are you sick, Mamima?" I asked.

"No, not really. You'll know when you grow up. I shall not go to the pond next few days," she said slowly.

Determined to ask Mayna about this mysterious condition, I decided to use the free time to my advantage. Now I could venture to the other side of the pond and find out what might be there. If the ghosts and *petnies* made the bamboo grove their home, perhaps other kinds of scary creatures lived at the far end of the pond in front of the house. All my life, I have been prone to excessive curiosity that gets me into trouble. This time was no exception. I couldn't resist the tempting invitation of possible danger and adventure.

The next morning when I saw Mayna, I forgot to ask the question about Mejomamima. Instead I asked, "Have you ever been to the other side of the front pond? Do you know if the ghosts live there too?" Surprised by the question, Mayna looked at me for a few seconds.

"Why are you suddenly so curious about the other side of the pond? Sometimes I don't understand you!" she snapped. "I heard that a blacksmith lives there, and someone saw wild cats with huge red eyes like burning coals in that area. I think it's actually a big cat, a tiger. Frankly, I have no desire to get that close to a man-eater. Drop these crazy ideas. Let's go fishing instead. I have stolen some stale rice from my aunt's kitchen. It would be perfect for bait."

"Maybe," I merely replied. Despite my interest in fishing, this time I was more inclined to explore the unknown even if I had to go alone. The more I considered the possibility, the more I was pulled by the dark path through the shade and undergrowth of the tall trees which cut off the sunlight. Just the thought gave me goose bumps. How dangerous could a wild cat be?

The next day, armed with a stick, I slipped out. Once I had turned past the front edge of the pond, I saw my granduncle, Dadamashay's younger brother, fishing, standing very close to the water. He was turning a small wheel on his fishing rod, making a *krrr, krrr* sound. He had taught us all how to fish. He was our friend. He had some kind of illness which made him faint without any warning. But that did not seem to interfere with his ability to fish. He concentrated so hard on what he was doing that he did not see me pass by.

I began to walk along the long side of the pond away from the houses and deeper into the woods crowded with tall trees and under-cover of bushes and shrubs. The narrow path I was following became narrower and suddenly disappeared. I had to use the stick to make my way, thrashing through the undergrowth. A bird flapped its wings as it flew from one tree to the next, the only sound I had heard since I stepped into this dark forest. I was scared, even though I didn't like to admit it, even to myself. Without realizing, I began to repeat the ghost-prevention mantra that Mayna had taught me.

> The ghost is my son, petni is my daughter,
> No one can harm me,
> I'm protected by Ram and his brother.

I lost track of time. Eventually, I found myself on the other side of the pond. The trees began to look smaller, and I could see the water of the pond clearly on one side.

There, not far from the pond, stood a small bamboo hut. Mayna was right. This must be where the blacksmith lived. I went toward the hut and saw smoke coming out of a pipe on top of the roof. I tried to look through a chink in the bamboo wall. It was hard to see anything because of the smoke and scanty light inside. Slowly my eyes became accustomed to the shadows, and I saw a hearth with a fire on the other side of the room. A short dark-skinned man was pulling a rope on top of the fire. From time to time, a flame leaped up, blown by a baglike contraption pulled by the man. After a while the man let go of the rope and began to hammer a red-hot piece of iron. The sound was deafening. I put my fingers in my ears and turned away. I was so hypnotized by this primitive image of a blacksmith hammering a red-hot piece of iron near a fire that I almost forgot that if the man saw me, he might chase me with his hot iron rod. A man who beats hot iron in a secluded hut at the edge of the dark forest could not be friendly to an intruder.

As I turned away from the mysterious hut I noticed that the sun was not as strong as before. It was getting late. I needed to go back through that dark forest again. But something pulled me to explore behind the hut. I had to go that way. There was a clear patch under a bush with tiny green berries on it. I recognized the berries, called *lukluki*, which I first saw in this village. They were a mixed color of magenta and blue when they ripened, and one had to roll them gently between the palms of the hands to make them soft before popping them into the mouth. They were deliciously sweet and sour. I would tell Mayna about this hidden treasure. We could sneak away and pick our own berries when they ripened.

Then my eyes fell on a shiny object right near the root of the *lukluki* bush. I sat on the dirt and had a good look. It was a black stone, polished and shiny, sitting half-buried in the ground. For some reason, I felt it was sacred and that I was not supposed to touch it. As I looked at it I was transported to an unknown world where hunters, who are as black as a shiny black stone, make weapons by the fire and worship the black stone before going for a hunt. Somehow I felt a primordial connection to this ancient world; I knew it well. I touched the ground around the stone with my bowed head and came out of my reverie slowly. I now understood why so many villagers all over India worship ancient trees or polished stones.

The sun was about to disappear behind the woods. I stood up after putting a few grass flowers around the stone, promising to return. I knew I had to come back and that I could not tell anyone about this, not even Mayna. As I hurried back, I had no idea how I had come through the dark forest. Yet, I had no fear at all. The black stone showed me the way back safely.

It was a few days before I could return to the stone. I went back to it as often as I could for as long as we were in the village. This was my secret world, which enveloped me with a security that I loved then and searched to find all the rest of my life. I never forgot the shiny black stone on the far bank of the front pond at my maternal grandparents' home.

MURDER IN THE PADDY FIELD

In the late hours of morning, when the sun almost touched the top of the roof of the east room, Didima got into the front pond with some of us to teach us how to swim. We clung to her body like a brood of baby whales. Moving slowly down until the water reached her chest, Didima put her hands under our bellies and helped us float. We splashed around like freshly hooked fish, scared to death that we would slip away from her wet body. Once, after closing my eyes and putting my fingers in my ears, I dove in and found no bottom. I zoomed up instantly and, holding onto her arm, tried to kick my legs, spraying water in all directions. Once we felt secure being close to her body, she gently pushed us away, and we had no choice but to learn how to float. After swallowing several pints of water and being scared to death, I finally learned how to swim, not in the most scientific and elegant way, but enough to manage laps in a pool as an adult. Every time I get into a swimming pool, I think of those days in the pond with Didima in front of their home.

We always waited with anticipation for Didima to surprise us by saying, "I'm thinking of going to Dinu Ray's lake today. Whoever wants to join me should be ready in five minutes with towels and a change of clothes." We would rush into our bedrooms, find some clothes and towels, and run to catch up with her. A folded wet towel on top of her head—to avoid the hot sun—and a rolled clean sari under her arm, Didima was already walking away, cutting diagonally through the neighbor's courtyard where Mayna's aunt lived. We walked single file like a row of chicks behind a hen, on narrow dykes separating tiny plots of paddy fields. The sight of the cool water, after what seemed like a long walk, drove us on. Once we reached the lake, Didima set us free. This lake was shallow with a hard floor of packed sandy soil without snails or tangled moss. We could easily walk in the water by ourselves and play, while Didima dove in a few times, hair and all, and swam a few yards.

On the way back, we covered our heads with wet towels as protection against the hot sun and followed Didima home. The water play under the noon sun had tired us and made us famished. As if knowing how we felt, Didima would take a slight detour and visit the home of a teacher named Makhan. Near the entrance of the home was a vine of bright blue flowers with yellow spots in the center. These flowers looked like tiny sea shells, and I knew they were called *aparajita*. The teacher's mother, a widow, chatted with Didima briefly and called us in. We were given round sugar candies and cold water. We drank the water fast and put the candy on our tongues and walked back. Although tired, we could not wait for the next trip to Dinu Ray's lake, one of the largest ponds in the village.

But we did not make it back to the lake for some time to come. A few months passed. The crop in the paddy field ripened to gold and was cut, the stubs sticking out like the unruly hair of a punk teenager. Neatly tied bundles of straw stood here and there, like straw footstools all over the fields. The color of the sun, too, turned gold as the monsoon cloud receded, exposing more and more of the blue sky. We knew that autumn would be here soon.

One morning, I saw Mayna's aunt walking quickly toward Didima's bedroom. Sensing something urgent, I followed her and found them whispering. They looked very serious. I had to wait until after breakfast—freshly cooked soft rice and fried tiny potatoes—before I could run next door. I found Mayna with her book open, pretending to read. As soon as she saw me, she closed the book.

"I'm glad you're here," she whispered. "I was about to go looking for you. Something horrible happened." She grabbed my wrist and began to walk out of the room and across the yard behind the house. When we were alone she said, "We have to go to Dinu Ray's house. Early this morning someone murdered the two Ray brothers, Torini and Tarini, and left their bodies in the paddy field."

"What nonsense! How do you know all this?" Then I remembered her aunt and Didima's meeting this morning. Mayna looked straight at me.

"Let's go and have a look. It's still early, and I'm sure the bodies are still there. This is our only chance to see a real murder. What do you say?" She spoke fast.

"Suppose the killer is still around." As soon as I said it, I knew it was a stupid thing to say.

"Yeah sure. The killer is sitting there with the bodies on his lap! Sometimes you say such dumb things." Without much ado she began to walk, with my wrist still in her hand. I was still worried about being discovered. Mayna seemed undaunted. I had little choice but to follow her.

We walked as fast as we could on the familiar road toward Dinu Ray's lake. We encountered nobody, as all the people of the village had already gone to the paddy field. As we approached the field, we saw a small crowd. We glided through toward the center and saw three policemen talking to people. One of them was writing in a small notebook.

Mayna pressed my palm slightly and whispered, "Look, there is the bloodstained shirt!" I looked hard through many legs and detected two pale feet draped in the thin border of a *dhoti* stained with blood. It was impossible to see anything else. Suddenly I saw Mejomama on the other side of the three policemen.

I whispered, "Mejomama is here. We better get back." Despite her curiosity, Mayna had to turn back. Even she knew that if we were caught, it would be a disaster. No one expects two nine-year-olds to be at a murder scene. We walked back without a word. Once near the house, Mayna went directly to the front pond and stepped down to the water. We washed our hands, feet, and faces and sat on the cool mossy step in silence.

I could not shake off the sight of the two pale feet draped in bloodstained cloth. In my mind's eye, I began to see the bodies of the two brothers, their heads severed from their shoulders, blood gushing out, wetting the dry ground and turning the golden stubs of paddy purple. I did not know if Mayna was seeing such bloody scenes in her mind as well.

Many years after this event, I went to India and visited Mejomama and Mejomamima at their home in Kanpur. Our conversations turned to reminiscing about their home in Kayasthapalli during the war years, where all of us spent such a memorable time together. Now I had my chance to ask him the question I had wanted to ask for the last twenty years: How were the Ray brothers murdered?

"It was a horrible thing," Mejomama began. "Apparently one of their subjects had an argument over taxes or something with the older brother. The angry man came back with a hatchet early next morning when Torini Ray was taking his morning walk and cut off his head. The younger brother, Tarini, went to look for him and when he arrived at the scene, the murderer killed him too before running away. No villager confessed or pointed out who might have done it, and the case was never solved." Mejomama stopped for a few seconds and then looked at me. "But how do you remember all this? You were very little at the time."

"Maybe I remember it because I was so young," I said.

Again, after so many years, I clearly saw in my mind a pair of pale feet and a bloodstained *dhoti*.

THE WINTER CIRCLE

Several times a year, along with a group of women, Didima observed *bratas* to placate various deities. *Bratas* are seasonal household rituals mostly observed by the women in a rural family to placate one god or another for the protection of the family and the children. The word literally means "vow." If the prayers are answered, the participants vow not to forget to pray and worship a particular god. In Didima's household, *bratas* were observed in addition to the daily *puja* in the little shrine set aside exclusively for her favorite gods and goddesses.

This room had a hand-carved miniature wooden throne, where pictures and brass figurines of Lakshmi, Krishna, Shiva, and Ganesh were arranged. There was a bronze figurine of a crawling Gopal or baby Krishna eating a glob of butter. Having been brought up by dairy farming parents in one of his incarnations, Krishna was fond of butter and often stole it from his mother's kitchen. Beside these deities stood a framed photo of a thin scantily clothed monk with a long white beard. We used to tease Didima about this half-naked old man, and she would tell us how learned and wise her family guru was. Our job was to pick fresh flowers every morning for her *puja* and bring them to her. In return, she gave us small pieces of fruit and sweets after the *puja* was over. We had to touch them first to our heads and then pop them into our mouths, hoping the gods would be kind to us. *Prasad*, food that was offered to the gods and blessed by them, had to be eaten whether we liked it or not.

Unlike Father's family, Mother's family never observed the worshipping of the goddess Durga on a grand scale but had small everyday *pujas* and *bratas*. Didima was the prime organizer of these *bratas*. She knew the rules and customs as well as every legend behind each ritual. We were still too young to participate in the *brata* of Shiva Ratri (Shiva's night), which was designed for the teenaged girls asking to be blessed with husbands as desirable as the god Shiva. Shiva was considered the most loving and faithful husband to Durga, and every Hindu girl was brought up to believe that a husband like him was most covetable.

One afternoon as Didima was distributing *prasad,* I asked, "How old do I have to be to do *brata* with you, Didima?"

"Why, would you like to? The *brata* of winter circle is only a month away. You may join us. There is no age limit for this one. I'm glad you're eager to observe these traditions already." I was more curious than religious, attracted by the novelty of it all—the clay dolls and various natural objects, along with storytelling sessions, and ending with the *prasad* of homemade sweets. It promised to be a day of new experience. I had a vague idea that the clay dolls used in a *brata* were somehow connected to the black stone I had discovered on the far side of the pond. I didn't know why, but I expected to find similar feelings of being close to something big and sacred, which made me feel secure.

The next evening when Mayna and I were walking hand in hand in her family's courtyard chatting about things, I asked, "Have you ever done a *brata*? Would you like to join me in observing winter circle *brata* with Didima and others?"

"Yes, yes. I have done all that several times with my grandmother. No big deal." Mayna was not interested. She added, "Remember, you'll have to fast all day and dip in the cold water early in the morning. And then, you'll have to sit quietly listening to the same story you've heard many times, no matter how much your tummy growls from hunger. Finally, the good sweets will go before you lay your eyes on them! You may get a tiny piece of one if you're lucky." She stopped to take a breath.

Although I was a great admirer of Mayna's qualities, I never liked her matter-of-fact attitude. Sometimes she sounded like such a know-it-all. That's why I did not tell her about the black stone. I decided to go ahead without her. Besides, my two older female cousins would be with me.

The day before the *brata*, Didima made sweets from milk and tiny balls of roasted sesame seeds and molasses. On the day of the ritual, we girls were awakened before sunrise and made to take a dip in the front pond. We shivered as we put on our new saris. Didima picked some fine grass and gave a bunch to each participant. We went back into the water knee-deep and, facing east, repeated after her a mantra—a prayer to the sun to keep the family safe and healthy and send us the young girls good husbands—then dipped the bunch of grass in the pond and sprinkled water in the air. We sprinkled water twenty-one times before throwing the grass in the water. As we came out of the pond, the first ray of the winter sun touched our bare arms to our welcoming relief. Didima led us to the southwest corner of the courtyard.

She dug a tiny hole with a small hoe and poured water in it from a brass pitcher. She drew a white circle around the hole with a tiny piece of rag soaked in liquid rice paste, and said, "This is the sphere of water, which is life in miniature. Now we have to draw things of life around it." We all began to draw whatever she asked us to. With a piece of rag dipped in rice paste, I drew the sun on the right and moon on the left of the tiny water hole. Mayadi, one of my older female cousins, drew ears of paddy at the bottom, and Didima drew a tree at the top. In between were drawn other things that girls need when they get married, such as jewelry, clothes, a mirror, and a comb. I had no idea that Didima could draw so well with nothing but a piece of wet rag for a brush.

As the floor painting dried, Didima poured a little water on the dirt that had been dug out from the hole and made a thick putty. She then shaped tiny figurines of gods and goddesses and put them in the sun to dry. When the dolls were a bit dry, we each got one to hold and to repeat a mantra after her. I could barely follow the words. Some of them had to do with the cycle of seasons and life and a girl's future. After the mantra, we touched the dolls to our heads and dropped them into the tiny water hole. I was a bit disappointed to see them drown. I was hoping to add them to my doll menagerie after the ritual. But I also knew that the figurines of deities couldn't be used for playing. They were sacred.

The outdoor ritual was over. The sun was high in the sky, showering heat. We followed Didima to the household shrine where she gave us *prasad* of fruit and sweets. We sat in a circle and began to listen to the story behind this *brata*. Didima told the story as if she knew every word by heart.

> *Once upon a time, a wealthy merchant had a beautiful daughter for whom he couldn't find a suitable husband. The merchant and his wife were very worried about the daughter's future. One day a holy man came for alms, and the girl stepped out to give him a bowl of rice. He told the mother, "Observe the Winter Circle brata, bathing early in the morning on an empty stomach. Your daughter will be married in no time. But you must follow every step carefully." The wife and the daughter performed the brata following the rules to the letter. Within a month, a barber brought a marriage proposal from another good family in the next village.*

Didima ended the story and looked at us and added, "If one cannot do the winter circle *brata*, there are several others for the same purpose. Well now, you girls have done well, and you all will have no problem getting good husbands." She sounded content.

Even at age eight, I had already learned that marriage was not only a big event in a woman's life, it was inevitable. We finished eating *prasad*, washed our hands, and left the shrine. The whole day I was wrapped in a pleasant emotion that came from being touched by something sacred, by something bigger than life. I felt sorry that Mayna had missed it.

Forty years later I spent a night with a Jewish friend in her New York apartment. At dinner, we talked about our respective childhoods. Since she came from a reformed Jewish family, where they hardly ever observed any religious rites, she was curious about my experience. I told her about Durga *puja* as well as various *bratas* in which I had taken part as a girl. We talked until late and went to bed. Early the next morning, I dreamed:

I am on one side of a small pond, and my mother, aunts, and grandmother are on the other side. They put some handmade clay dolls on a paper boat in the water and push the boat toward me.

I was awakened by the siren of a police car and realized that even though my life is so far away in time and space from childhood, that special experience connected to eternity is never lost.

FROG WEDDING

Our stay with my mother's family was nearly over when the war ended. We were to meet Father in the city where Mother's oldest sister and her family lived. I was excited by this prospect since I was very fond of this aunt and her husband and my cousins. Even though we had spent almost a year together in the village, being in the city had its attractions. We could ride the horse-drawn carriages to the cinema or to the beach of the big Brahmaputra River that originated in Assam, my birth state. The grown-ups, however, had other plans.

One morning, we were told that we would spend a few weeks in Baailkha, a nearby village where my aunt's in-laws lived. Although disappointed, once we reached this village, I forgot about the city immediately. I began to explore the huge orchard on their property, which had trees so big and so strange that I felt I was on another planet. This was the first time I saw clove and cinnamon trees and bushes of cardamom. Their spicy fragrance permeated the whole garden. I wondered if the spice islands of the Pacific were always fragrant. There were other fruit trees which I had never seen. Amazingly big jackfruits hung from short and stocky trees, making them look like short women with many heavy breasts. I discovered a fruit by the name of *rose jaam* for the first time. When I bit into a ripe fruit, it really smelled of rose! I wandered through this paradise and tasted every new fruit and forgot my sadness at leaving Mayna and my grandmother's village.

However, disturbance appeared in paradise unannounced. This

year the monsoon had not come to Baailkha in June as expected. It was already August and still there was no sign of the rain. The grown-ups talked about nothing but the drought, and their voices became increasingly apprehensive. When I went to the orchard again, I noticed more dry leaves on the ground. Even the bark of the cinnamon tree was twisted and cracked. Its pungent fragrance made the dry air oppressive. Many flower bushes were already dead.

One afternoon my cousin Maya and I were playing. She showed me how to drape a sari on a doll. Naturally we talked about the topic on everyone's mind: "If the rains don't come in a day or two, they may have to arrange a frog wedding. I overheard Baba and the neighbors talking about it yesterday," Mayadi said pensively.

"What is that? Do the frogs get married?"

"When the drought reaches a dangerous point, extreme measures must be taken. The frog wedding is the last resort, and it never fails," she said knowingly. I couldn't quite visualize what she meant but looked forward to something unusual. Not only had I never heard of frogs getting married, I could not remember even seeing a frog closely. I always thought frogs were playthings for naughty boys and never considered them serving such an important purpose.

A few days passed when there was not a cloud in the sky, and the preparation for the frog wedding began in earnest. My aunt's husband would give away the bride, and the groom would come from one of the neighbors. A priest was to officiate at every step of the ritual of a Hindu wedding. The wedding date was set. Many people were invited. Caterers pitched their tents. We children were excited by the promise of festivity and delicious food. We forgot about the drought.

The priest consulted the almanac to decide on an auspicious hour. It was to be right after sunset. On the day of the wedding, the women in my aunt's house prepared small decorative baskets to carry dowry— sari, jewelry, sweets, and much more—to the groom's family. By late afternoon, my uncle and the priest led a procession of our family and all invited guests toward the venue of the wedding, a narrow creek on the edge of the village. The priest carried the frog bride in a small bamboo cage. I kept wondering: Where did he find a willing frog? How did he know it was a female? Unfortunately I did not have Buli or Mayna by my side to supply me with answers.

The older women began to sing wedding songs, while the older girls kept blowing the conch shell—an auspicious sound. A group of musicians followed the procession, playing bagpipes and other wind instruments. We finally arrived at the creek, which was dry. A large group with the groom in a cage was already there. We made a semicircle near the creek.

The priest sprinkled some holy water from the river Ganges on the frogs. They jumped inside the cages. The priest built a small fire on a piece of aluminum and set the two cages on either side. The frogs were quiet—perhaps stunned by the turn of events and such careful attention. All they had been used to from humans was abuse in the hands of boys. Their bulging eyes kept moving in all directions as they listened to the priest reciting wedding mantras in Sanskrit. I would have given anything to enter their little heads to find out what they were thinking. The priest moved the frog bride seven times around the frog groom and urged the god of fire, who is the witness to all Hindu weddings, to bless this union. He then announced the end of the ceremony.

He took the newlyweds to the dry river and looked up to the sky and prayed loudly. "Oh, god of rains, please bless us with your grace as soon as possible, otherwise animals, birds, fish, insects, and humans, all will die." The priest then opened the cages and set the frogs free. The frogs jumped out and disappeared with a croak. We had a delicious meal at the groom's family and returned home.

Along with everyone in the village, I too began to believe that the drought would end very soon. Any unlikely mysterious connection between the frog wedding and the rains did not bother me. I felt very fortunate that I was there in Baailkha to witness such a unique event. In a few days, dark clouds appeared, and rain began to fall continuously for days.

Parents Home

My family in 1945

THE HOUSE BY THE BAKERY

In the town of Digboi, where I was born, we moved three times. Every time Father was promoted, we moved to a better house offered by the oil company where he worked as an engineer. The only thing I remember about the first house was a black wooden gate and a dark-skinned tutor who came every week, pushing open that gate. I sat on his lap and Dadamoni sat on the mat, as the tutor tried to teach us the alphabet. This arrangement pleased me a great deal although it didn't last long: for some reason the tutor had to leave the area.

I must have been five or six years old when we moved to the second house, which held three main attractions. Behind the kitchen, outside the back door, there was a flowering tree. Its tiny flowers, called *Bakul*, covered the ground under the tree, and the sweet fragrance entered the house through the backyard. I helped Ma collect them and string them to make garlands for the picture of Krishna in Ma's little shrine at one corner of our bedroom. Our pet hens, which laid eggs for our breakfast, flew up to the top branches of this tree. I never saw any other hens or chickens fly so high.

The second attraction was the train track that ran just outside the house about fifty yards from our front gate. I loved the slight tremor each time the freight trains passed. Although we were forbidden to go near the track, both Dadamoni and I sneaked out and put our ears on the rails to hear the distant vibration of the oncoming train. Sometimes we put a copper coin on the rail and loved the long shiny tongue it became after the train ran over it. The warmth of the metal made us feel as if it was alive.

Best of all was the bakery that stood behind a high hibiscus hedge surrounding the house. One of my duties was to keep an eye on my two younger sisters—Debi and Anu—who were one year apart. Debi was four years younger than me. I needed to watch them when Ma was busy in the kitchen or with other household chores. I soon found out that they did not like to obey any of my orders. Naturally I preferred the company of my older brother, who was closer to my age, despite our problems of other kinds. I often had to comply with his wishes, but I was willing to do that because Dadamoni came up with many ideas for adventures.

One such adventure involved a sneak visit to the bakery. Every morning we woke to the enticing smell of baking bread, which lingered all morning. Dadamoni made a hole in the hibiscus hedge for us to peek through. A young man in a dark *lungi* once discovered us and handed over a freshly baked sweet bun through the hole. My brother broke off a tiny piece and reluctantly gave it to me, but only because I threatened that I would tell Ma if he did not. Within a short time, the man in the *lungi* and Dadamoni had become friends, and he supplied us with sweet buns, cupcakes, and even a small loaf of bread that he had prepared and baked only for us. Eventually the tiny hole in the hedge became a tunnel through which we could slide in and out. I was fascinated by all the activity in the bakery, although I tried to forget that a group of sweaty men kneaded the dough with their feet, jumping up and down. I never dared to ask the young men if they washed their feet beforehand.

When my parents found out that we were regular visitors to the bakery, they did not seem to mind. Even though the men in the bakery were Muslims, my parents never told us not to mix with them. They did not believe in such discrimination. Even after Baba rose high in his profession, both my parents always kept in touch with their original colleagues and neighbors. Perhaps this was the reason why, a year earlier during our stay in the village, I was surprised and unable to understand the reasons when my grandmother forbade me to play with a Muslim girl.

There was a small hospital beyond the railroad tracks. Dr. Nandi, the chief medical officer, was a good friend of my father's. The Nandis had a beautiful home with a garden that I loved. In winter, varieties of exotic foreign flowers, such as chrysanthemum, dahlia, phlox, and peony, bloomed in their garden. A rubber tree in one corner of the garden had a paved pedestal around it. The bark of that tree was as smooth as the skin of a baby. Not too far from the rubber tree was a small pond filled with water lilies and lotuses. The lotus stalks stood up proudly, whereas the lilies floated humbly on the surface of the water. Since then, water lilies have been my favorite flowers. Sometimes I would go with Baba, when he visited his friend, and sit on the pedestal of the rubber tree and enjoy the beautiful garden. I dreamed of having such a garden someday, and I did build a water garden with hardy lilies and lotuses nearly fifty years later when we lived near Buzzards Bay in New England.

Dr. Nandi and his wife had a daughter close to my age, but we never became friends. She was distant. The whole family was like that. But their beautiful garden was always inviting.

Our third house, where we moved when I was ten, was a spacious bungalow in an upscale neighborhood. More on this house will follow.

THE KIDNAPPERS

Our little oil town was surrounded by waves of bluish-green mountains—the foothills of the Eastern Himalayas. During the winter mornings and evenings, a layer of fog spread over the hills, making them seem even more remote and mysterious. I tried to imagine the kind of people who might live there. Was this the place where the Naga tribe lived? When we refused to take our daily dose of cod-liver oil, Ma always threatened that the Nagas would come down from the mountains to kidnap us and carry us away in their shoulder bags. What they did with the children when they reached their mountain home was not mentioned. They apparently made a habit of kidnapping disobedient children.

We children had long discussions about the Nagas. We found out that they were naked headhunters. We considered both these behaviors to be horrible, although we were not sure if they ate children.

Our imagination refused to go that far. Therefore, we decided it was safer to swallow the awful cod-liver oil. We always closed our noses with two fingers when we swallowed the stuff, but we felt secure that the Nagas would spare us this time.

Then one day I encountered a Naga in flesh and blood! I was looking out the window of our living room, wondering if the next train was going to be a passenger or a freight train. Suddenly I saw a man entering through our front gate. He was wearing only a strip of material around his hip, had matted hair, several strings of shells and bone pieces around his neck, and a spear-like stick in one hand. A couple of long bags hung from one shoulder. He did not come to the front porch but stood near the gate and said something loudly, which I couldn't understand. I remained glued to the window, and my heart began to pound rapidly, but my head was clear. No one would shout to attract attention if they wanted to kidnap a child, I thought.

Ma came out of the house with a container of sugar and poured the contents in the man's shoulder bag. He took out a small box from another bag and gave it to her. I watched the whole transaction carefully, paying special attention to the bags to see if those contained anything else. I was curious about the little box and wondered if the box held some magical secret to subdue us. I thought of a tale in the book of stories called *The Grandmother's Bag*, which Baba read to us on some Sundays. In that story, the secret of Prince Dalimkumar's life was hidden in a gold chain, and that was hidden in a small wooden box, which was swallowed by a big carp. Did the box Ma got in exchange of sugar hold some such secret?

A few years later I found out that the Nagas exchanged small boxes of wild musk for tea, sugar, or cigarettes. Sometimes they also bartered colorful feathers of birds and honey-colored resin, gathered from the trees of the forest. I also learned that the Nagas never lived in those mountains that we saw from our windows. They lived quite a distance away in the southwestern part of Assam. The more I learned about them, the more curious I became.

Many years later when I studied anthropology, I wanted to do my first field research among the Naga tribe. I was unable to get permission from the government to do so for political reasons. By that time, the Nagas had been transformed from half-naked "kidnappers" to a militant group in khaki uniforms carrying guns, not shoulder bags.

However, I learned one lesson early in life: the grown-ups would tell scary tales to get children to do what they wanted us to do.

A NEW ARRIVAL

One night we awoke to the sound of screaming, as if someone were in great pain. I looked at Dadamoni, who was also up and sitting on his bed. My two sisters were asleep.

"It's Ma," he said. "She must be very sick." We sat stiff in fear not knowing what to do. I prayed to the goddess, asking her to save Ma from whatever it was. Then I got out of the bed and walked toward our parents' bedroom and tried to peek in. I saw Doctor Uncle inside, Baba on his side. Before they could see me, I left and came back to our room. Then everything was quiet for a while. We dozed off. It was dawn when Baba woke us with a bundle of blanket in his arms.

"Wake up, look, you have a little brother," he said smiling. The announcement shocked us so much that it took us several minutes to grasp its meaning. I looked at the bundle and saw a reddish glob of flesh with closed eyes and tiny fists sticking out of the woolen blanket. It was the middle of January and very cold this early in the morning. All four of us looked at one another saying nothing. Baba turned to go back.

"Is Ma alright?" I asked.

"Yes. She is resting now, so be quiet," he said.

Even though I was almost ten, I had no clear knowledge of how babies were born. But I knew that Mother's screaming and the appearance of this bundle called "our little brother" were connected. I didn't ask Dadamoni for any clarification either. The instinct of a ten-year-old told me that certain things were better left alone.

A nurse was appointed to take care of the baby and Ma for a few days, until Ma was on her feet again. In no time the household returned to its normal course. However, we still didn't know how to handle this newcomer among us. My two sisters were more curious and often sat near the baby's crib and watched his every move and giggled. Within a few days Ma asked me to watch the baby when she went for her bath or lunch. I was proud to be entrusted with such a big responsibility, although I was still not sure that this tiny thing belonged to our family.

One day Dadamoni and I were watching the baby and scrutinizing it closely. Noticing his head covered with a thin layer of fine hair, Dadamoni made a remark. We then decided to try something out. A few days later we gathered a few ants in an empty matchbox and let them loose on the baby's head, just to see what would happen. Perhaps this was the only lethal plan we could come up with to get rid of this intruder. Or could it be just a prank we wanted to play?

We watched with excitement as the moving ants meandered through the baby's flimsy hair. Fortunately for the baby, Ma appeared and rescued him from our hands and from the ants. She scolded us severely. When she said that the baby could have died from ant bite, we were really scared. At that moment the little stranger became our little brother, to whom we all became extremely attached. I was his main caretaker, and a deep bond developed between us, which still exists.

Years later my baby brother's daughter, age eight, came up to me and said in genuine anguish, "How could you? How could you do that to my Baba? If he had died from ant bite, I couldn't have been born!" She must have heard the story from her father. I admitted our guilt and stupid jealousy. It felt good to confess after nearly thirty years!

PICNIC

As children we always looked forward to Sundays, some of which were reserved for picnics. We teamed up with other families. The family of Dr. Paul, Father's closest friend and our family physician, was always part of the group. Mrs. Paul was Mother's best friend, and their two daughters were close to my sisters' ages. Dr. Paul held a special aura for me because I had been told that he delivered me when I was born. We called him Doctor Uncle, and he was summoned any time of the day and night whenever we had any medical problems.

One winter Sunday morning, we climbed into four cars and set off for the forests outside our little town for a day of picnicking. Kanukaka, Baba's cousin twice removed, invited all of us children to ride in his pick-up, which had room for only two people in the front. We all sat in the open back. With every jolt, we fell on each other like chickens in a cage and burst out laughing for no particular reason.

"Hey, you in the back, stop laughing and keep your eyes and ears open for wild animals. If we're lucky, you may see some wild elephants!" Kanukaka yelled from the driver's seat. We girls began to laugh again as if he had just said the funniest thing. A little later, we suddenly heard a horrible sound coming from the woods we were passing. "That's the call of a wild elephant," Kanukaka shouted back. We stopped laughing and tried to visualize the size of the animal that could produce such a racket. I closed my eyes, hoping I wouldn't have to see the monster. Fortunately, no wild elephant appeared! I had to admit to myself that I was not interested in an adventure with real beasts.

We reached a spot in the woods, which might have been cleared by the forest ranger. The cars with provisions were unloaded. Kanukaka dug two holes and, setting six stones in triangular fashion, constructed two cooking hearths and lit fires. Ma and the other ladies got busy with the preparation of food. We broke some branches of a dead tree and followed Kanukaka on an expedition to explore the woods.

"Come back within an hour. The food will be ready by then," Doctor Uncle called after us.

As we proceeded, hitting bushes with our sticks, we noticed that the trees began to be taller and dense with undergrowth. Vines with big dark leaves—the size of elephant ears—snaked up the tall trees, which we had never seen before. Hundreds of wild banana plants had onion-colored flowers. I wondered who ate all the bananas when they ripened. Was it the wild elephants? The sun struggled to enter the thick foliage. A wet smell rose from the damp earth and leafy undergrowth. A chill ran though my limbs. Everybody was quiet as if we had suddenly landed on a new planet. Only the sound of the branches we used as sticks cut into the silence. We were humbled by the majestic power of the forest.

All of a sudden a rumbling sound of marching boots broke the silence. We looked at our leader and knew that it was not a marching band of soldiers. Kanukaka pointed his stick toward the direction we had come from. We turned back without a word. I kept wondering if the noise came from a herd of rhinos or elephants. Our speed increased as we retraced our footsteps. The thundering sound followed us for a few seconds and then shifted direction. After a few minutes, by following a pleasant sound, we reached a waterfall. Its spray cooled our hot faces. Hundreds of orchids hung from big rubber trees. Some of them had long stalks of tiny flowers emitting a wild fragrance. We picked them and put them in our hair. The boys wrinkled their noses, saying, "Yak, how can you wear such smelly things!"

The fresh aroma of cooked food guided us back to the picnic spot. The glossy leaves of banana plants were used for plates. *Khichuri* and fried eggs with potato curry tasted great. A group of older children took the pots and pans to the waterfall to be washed, and Baba and the uncles loaded the cars. We were on our way back before the last streak of sun disappeared from the forest floor. We dozed in the back of the pick-up and this time did not worry a bit about the wild animals. That evening in bed I kept wondering when we would go for another picnic. I also wondered how the animals lived in the scary dark forests. I was happy to be a human being, living at a home with my family and sleeping in a bed with warm quilts tucked around me.

MR. STEIN

Even though India was not directly involved in World War II, as a British colony it had to participate in the war in various ways. Our little town on the northeast frontier of the country had a strategic location, over and above being the major producer of petroleum at the time. The Assam Oil Company—where Baba worked and which owned the town—was sure that Digboi was a primary target. Underground trenches were constructed in each neighborhood, and we ran to hide in them every time air-raid sirens went off. The whole town had to observe a blackout during nearly the whole year of 1943. Even though I was too young to understand the full implications of the war, my parents' expressions made clear the severity of the situation.

I remember the morning when I saw an airplane for the first time. We heard a mild groan coming from the sky. When Baba said that it could be Japanese Air Force planes flying in high altitude, we ran outside and looked up. After a few minutes we spotted a group of tiny aircraft way up in the sky looking like silver sparrows. I had heard stories from Didima about the gods riding flying chariots across the heavens. Now even people could accomplish such a feat! Every time the air-raid siren blew, we heard that special interrupted groan but never saw those planes at a closer distance.

Underneath the edge of our front lawn there was an air-raid shelter, which was completely hidden under a small mound. The small door leading into it was covered by a gardenia bush. The only furniture inside was a few wooden benches and a lightbulb hanging from the ceiling covered with black paper. A clay water jug stood in one corner. The grown-ups had to stoop down to get through the low entrance. Sometimes, I would stretch out on the bench and look at the ceiling. I saw shapes of animals and scary creatures drawn by the moisture on the ceiling. This way I distracted myself from the fear of bombs killing us. The grown-ups never talked inside the shelter, though some prayed silently with their eyes closed. Watching them, we could tell that they were nervous. When the all-clear whistle blew, they stood up and sighed with relief. Our lives went back to the same routines until the next air-raid siren.

One morning as we were walking toward school single file, we heard the roaring sound of an oncoming truck. We moved to the narrow shoulder of the pitch road and stopped. Not one, not two, but more than fifty huge trucks rolled by—each seeming as high as a two-story house. We saw big black-skinned men in khaki uniforms driving these thunderous vehicles. Some of these drivers threw bars of chocolate at us, and they talked in deep voices and laughed like thunder. We were too scared to pick up the chocolate bars. When we got to school our teacher told us that the Americans had arrived and were camping outside our town, building roads and bridges near the Burmese border.

That afternoon Sundarkaka, Baba's younger brother, told Baba that, along with his two friends, he was going to start a construction business to supply material to the Americans. Sundarkaka was staying with us after his college graduation, looking for a job. Now he had found one. He also explained to us that those big black drivers were Africans who lived in America, called "Negroes."

The American soldiers built a helicopter pad and set out to build roads. Sundarkaka's construction company supplied them with the necessary material and labor, thereby making a lot of money in a short time. Sometimes he would come back to visit us on the weekends, and on Monday mornings he would take me with him in his jeep to visit the construction sites. Because of the war, our school was closed for an indefinite period of time. I was very fond of this uncle. I would stay with him and his two friends in small bamboo huts away from the noise of the construction. The only problem was the makeshift bamboo bathroom. I saw worms crawling on the dirt floor each time I went there. But the cook, a gray-haired local man, liked me and made me spicy omelets from large duck eggs.

In the evening, my uncle and his friends would sit on a mat and play cards as they smoked lots of cigarettes. My job was to cut the deck of cards and deal. Everyone wanted me to sit with him to bring luck. They bet small coins for fun. Whoever won gave me the coins. When I returned to Digboi, I had a bag full of coins to show off. They all seemed sad when I left, so I had to promise to come back the next week. I loved all this attention showered on me alone, without my brother or sisters to compete. When I visited the construction sites with my uncle and saw huge trucks, cranes, and machines run by big strong Americans, I felt I too was part of this big event called the war.

One day, Sundarkaka took me to the helicopter strip, which was almost finished. We went over a rough road with many bumps.

"I hope the Americans will finish building this road soon. Your bones will be all crushed if you travel on this road everyday. Oh, I'm aching all over," I told my uncle. Sundarkaka gave me a peck on my head before disappearing among the workers. He came back after a few minutes with a white American man and introduced him to me.

"This is my niece, Manisha, and this is Mr. Stein. He has a daughter your age in America." Mr. Stein stretched his hand and shook mine. This is the first time a foreigner had shaken my hand. I felt grown up and important. A few of Baba's British colleagues had come to our house for tea once or twice, but no one had ever taken us children seriously enough to greet us with a handshake. Mr. Stein was not as big as the black drivers in the trucks; he was even shorter than my uncle. He wore a pair of shorts and a short-sleeve shirt, and his arms and legs seemed almost as dark as Indian workmen, possibly from the sun. But his hair was light, almost the color of straw after the paddy was harvested.

Mr. Stein smiled at me and asked my uncle something I couldn't follow. My English was not good enough to catch an American's nasal words. He said goodbye to me when we were ready to leave. On our way back to Digboi, Sundarkaka told me all about Mr. Stein.

"Gerald Stein was born in a small town in the midwestern part of America. He left his wife and a seven-year-old daughter Annie there to come thousands of miles to fight with the Allied force. Right now he's stationed here to help with the building of roads because he's an engineer. He has shown me his wife and daughter's picture. He talks about his daughter a lot." I realized now why Sundarkaka had introduced me to Mr. Stein. Even though my uncle was not yet married, he felt sorry for this man, so far away from his family.

"Do you think you could speak with him a little in English next time you come to the site?" he added as he looked at me. I nodded but was nervous about the prospect of using my English with a foreigner who spoke with a nasal accent. I felt sorry for Mr. Stein, who was so far away from his little girl. I remembered how I worried about Baba whenever he was a bit late coming home after work. Baba was in charge of the welding workshop, and I was always afraid that he would be in an accident. I asked my uncle many questions about Mr. Stein. I wanted to know how long a letter from his daughter might take to reach him.

Two weeks later when Sundarkaka asked me to accompany him again, Ma was reluctant. "What could you do there all by yourself? There are no children of your age," she said.

I quickly responded, "The cook is very nice to me; he makes eggs especially for me. I like it there. There are so many wildflowers and orchids in the woods! I help the uncles in the evenings by dealing cards. Sometimes I do homework." The last bit was not quite true. I carefully suppressed the information about the worms in the bathroom.

To tell the truth, I was always ready to leave the house. Who wouldn't want to avoid Mother's discipline and my sisters' complaints? I also knew these escapes I enjoyed were for only a few days at a time. I knew I'd miss everyone in my family if I stayed away longer.

On the way to the construction site, I kept rehearsing lines in English that I might use with Mr. Stein. "How old is your daughter?" "Show me her photo, please." When we reached our destination, my uncle went out and returned after a few minutes and said, "I have to go further inland. A workman had an accident. Could you wait in the office until I return? I've asked Stein to come and keep you company. Don't be shy. Now is your chance to practice your English." He picked me up from the car seat and stood me near a small shed and jumped into the jeep again. Before I knew it, the jeep and my uncle had disappeared. I felt lonely standing there among trenches and holes and all kinds of machinery. I entered the small shed and saw a couple of steel chairs and a long wooden desk with papers strewn all over it. I sat on one of the chairs holding my canvas bag of clothes in my lap. I sat for what seemed like a long time. I was very thirsty and looked around for a sink or water tap, but there was none. Then as I looked out the window, I saw Mr. Stein approaching.

He stopped near the open door and knocked on it gently before entering. With a big smile on his face, Mr. Stein shook my hand. I tried to stand up from the chair but slid off the smooth surface and almost fell. He quickly picked me up and put me on the chair again. All of my English lines got mixed up in my head. I forgot to thank him and slowly gathered enough courage to say, "May I have a glass of water, please?"

"Certainly. I'll be back soon," he said. A few minutes later he came back with a boy carrying a big aluminum kettle and a couple of cups. "It's safer to drink tea than water here," Mr. Stein said as the boy poured two cups of tea. With his cup in hand, Mr. Stein sat on the other chair and began to talk, most of which I couldn't follow. My one desperate line must have given him the wrong impression about the depth of my knowledge in English! He tried his best to speak slowly. What I gathered was that his daughter's name was Ann, but everyone called her Annie. Annie went to a school where her mother taught. She also had a dog whose name was Bob. Bob followed Annie everywhere and slept in her bed at night.

Mr. Stein asked me if I had a dog. I shook my head and said, "No." I wanted to say that I was not that keen on having a dog as a pet, but I decided not to say anything, mostly because I was sure I would make mistakes. He continued to talk more about their town, about his wife, and about many things. I think he had to tell someone, no matter how young. I was so impressed that a man of my uncle's age could talk to me as if I were his age. I lost track of time. I knew that I had made a new friend.

At some point Mr. Stein got up from his chair and asked, "Would you like to go to America someday?" This question took me by surprise. I wanted to say yes.

"Maybe," I said, trying to sound grown up. I kept thinking, why not? I could easily be Annie's friend and stay with them. I would have to wait a few years, of course. If I studied hard, maybe someday I would go to that faraway country. He read my mind.

"Now you've a friend there. You come and stay with us," he said smiling.

"Thank you very much." I smiled back.

We both looked out as we heard the sound of a jeep. Sundarkaka was back. Mr. Stein waved and said, "Bye now."

When Sundarkaka heard the gist of our conversation, he was pleased.

"Now you've a foreign uncle, Uncle Stein." I didn't quite like this title. Mr. Stein had called himself my friend, not my uncle.

Soon afterward, Mr. Stein came to our house in Digboi and became a family friend. But with me he had a special connection. The year ended, and we heard rumors that before long the war might be over. But the construction on the northeast frontier continued.

"How about going to the camp one last time? Everybody keeps asking about you. Oh, and Stein is being transferred to Burma; he'll leave in a week," Sundarkaka told me one day. So I went back to the camp one last time. The cook made chicken curry. Several of their colleagues and friends were invited in honor of Stein and me. When we met, he picked me up and held me in his arms. Embarrassed, I tried to slide down. He took me to the dining table and put me in a chair and sat on another one next to me.

"I have a gift for you," he said and took out a yellow box from a bag. "Butterfinger" was written on the box. I didn't have any idea what the box might hold. Mr. Stein smiled at me and said, "Open it when you go home. I hope you'll like them. These are my Annie's favorite."

After dinner Mr. Stein took many pictures of us. He took a few of me alone. The next day I left the camp with a heavy heart. Leaving my favorite uncle behind in the jungle was not easy. Now an additional friend was added to my list of dear people.

That was the last time I saw Mr. Stein. A year later Sundarkaka received an airmail envelope from America with a note and copies of pictures. Mr. Stein sent his warm wishes to all of us and a special hug for me. We could never send him a reply because the return address on the envelope was smudged by rain when the letter came.

FORBIDDEN GARDEN

We moved to a spacious bungalow surrounded by gardens and a lawn in a nicer neighborhood when Baba became the executive engineer in charge of the whole workshop of the Assam Oil Company. I was ten years old and spent the next five years here. In January the year before, my youngest brother was born in our house near the railroad tracks. Moving to this bigger house, I hoped to have my own room where all my books and papers would be arranged neatly. But I had to accept a desk in one corner of the big living room, and Dadamoni had his in another corner.

We made new friends, both girls and boys, although the boys didn't always include me and my girlfriends in their games. Every day we walked nearly two miles each way to and from school. The Boys' and Girls' High Schools were not far from each other. On the way back, we girls walked and talked in a group, and I was always the one who told stories to assuage our hunger as we dragged our tired legs. Once at home, we had our glasses of milk and snacks before going out again to play. Since Dadamoni and his friends were not always eager to play with us, I organized a girls' soccer team. The purpose was to show the boys that girls were as good, if not better, at soccer as they were. The only problem was none of our parents were willing to buy us a ball. I started raiding trees with large fruits such as pomelos, which look like large grapefruits. We would go through half a dozen fruits every evening playing soccer. The boys laughed at our efforts, which had the effect of inspiring us even more. We got muddy and dirty, playing in tall wet grass, ruining our dresses and shorts, and getting a heavy scolding from our mothers.

My tomboy phase lasted a couple of years. During this time I played every forbidden game, climbed every tree, and learned how to ride a bike. One Sunday a month, a barber came on his bike to cut Baba's hair. He would stand his bike along the front gate and walk to the backyard for a smoke with our cook. I would snatch the bike and side-pedal it as long as I could until Dadamoni snatched it from me.

One tree that gave me a challenge was a guava tree on the west side of the house. Its smooth bark was hard to grip, but I didn't stop until I had succeeded in climbing its high branches. I ignored the scratches and bruises I got from this endeavor. I would climb up and taste the green guavas, which were too hard for even the animals to bite.

I had to climb down from such high trees when Ma discovered that I was behaving more like a boy than a girl. She threatened that I would have to wear a sari if I did not behave. Restrictions were imposed, and I was forbidden from going out as I pleased and had to return home every evening before six. One evening I was half an hour late, and Ma worked up such a commotion that Baba got really mad and took hold of my left ear and squeezed it hard. This was the first and the last time Baba punished me physically, and the insult in front of my younger siblings was a lot harder to take than the hurt. I was very angry and didn't know how to react. Before I knew it, I had fainted, and my hands and feet had become cold. When I came to, I saw both my parents rubbing my hands and feet and looking very worried.

I was shocked that Father would punish me in this way. I had always known him as a gentle and kind man, and I knew how much he loved me. I knew also that he was provoked by Mother's long list of complaints against me, a pattern that continued throughout my adolescence. I could not wait to finish high school and leave home and my mother's domination. In hindsight it appears now as if the next ten or twelve years of my life were geared toward escaping my mother's control through whatever means I could come up with. Doing well in school, choosing a husband on my own, and leaving the country for higher studies—all were likely parts of this goal. In late afternoons, when Father came back from work, Mother would offer him tea and snacks along with a long list of my mischievous deeds. Baba pretended to listen and made monosyllabic comments to keep her appeased. I was sure he didn't want to risk a repeat of the fainting incident by punishing me.

Since I was not allowed to play boys' games anymore, I began to go for long walks with my girlfriend Khuku, a neighbor's daughter. She and I would walk through the serpentine paved roads along the hills and valleys. We marveled at the beauty of our little town. It was Khuku who made me aware of the facts of life, though I later found out she was not always accurate. She told me that babies are born after a man and a woman became close by intertwining their arms. It was not until my fifteenth year that I found out the truth from a male cousin, who laughed for a full minute when I told him my version of the facts of life.

In our walks Khuku talked, but I didn't always listen, keeping my eyes open for some exciting action. Sometimes we walked quite a distance to a neighborhood of European homes—two-storied wooden bungalows with large flower gardens protected by walls and watchdogs. On occasions, a whiff of grilled meat hit our nose, which smelled very quaint to us. I was always curious about these homes and their gardens. Entering the compounds, however, was nearly impossible, because we thought that all English people had ferocious dogs guarding their property. In spite of all these obstacles, I was determined to give it a try.

"Let's go inside one of these homes and steal some flowers. Wouldn't that be fun?" I said.

"We could. But we have to be careful not to be caught. I've heard that the English people like to take Indian girls and sell them to be maids in distant countries," Khuku warned me.

One late afternoon, we stopped near a walled bungalow. I pushed Khuku up to the top of the wall for her to check out the situation. If everything looked favorable, she would jump down into the garden and open the gate for me to enter. She went up without any problem. While she was up on the wall, I kept my eyes and ears open for any cars or pedestrians who might spot us scaling a private wall. The good news was that we heard no barking.

"What do you see? Tell me the names of the flowering bushes, quick!" I was getting nervous.

"What a beautiful home and verandah! I'm not sure about the trees. No fruit trees, but many flowers. I don't know the names, perhaps a foreign variety." I was furious by her report. It seemed a mistake to send her up.

"You've done enough! Now come back down. I'll go up. Do you see any dogs? I hope you know how to recognize that animal, even if it's a foreign pedigree." Before I could figure out if Khuku had heard me, I heard a car approaching. I immediately sat down among the weeds, although I realized it would have been more natural if I had begun to walk. Meanwhile the car pulled up near me and stopped. My heart began to pound hard. A British woman in short hair and painted lips rolled down the car window and looked at me.

"May I help you?" she asked.

I began to stutter. Seeing the situation, Khuku jumped into the garden. I managed to say, "My friend's inside. Please help." The lady looked at her husband in the driver's seat for a second and opened the back door of the car, signaling me to get in. I got in and saw a huge bulldog on a towel covering most of the backseat. The lady said something to the dog, and to my surprise, he moved a little, making room for me. The dog's name was Jimmy. I avoided Jimmy's eyes and sat quietly in my corner. Since Jimmy understood English, he must be trained to be polite and would not attack me.

The car stopped in front of the house. A man in a khaki uniform appeared from nowhere and opened the gate. The car drove along a circular driveway and stopped in front of the verandah. The husband went inside. I looked around to spot Khuku. As soon as the lady opened the back door, Jimmy jumped over me and ran toward a bush. He must have smelled Khuku. I ran after him, and the doorman ran after me. Fortunately, the man caught up with Jimmy before Jimmy got to the bush, and he put a leash around the dog's neck. The lady of the house stepped down to the garden, and Khuku emerged from behind the thick leaves of a gardenia bush.

"Is this your friend?"

"Yes." The kind lady put her hand on Khuku's shoulder and asked if she was hurt. She then invited both of us to the verandah and asked us to sit on two chairs. A servant in a white uniform brought a tray with three glasses of cold drink.

We were stunned by the turn of events. Khuku drank the cold liquid in one swallow, put the glass down, and wiped her mouth with the back of her palm. The lady looked at the paper napkins and smiled.

"Where do you live?" she asked me. We both responded by pointing in opposite directions. She continued to smile and added, "Would you like to see the garden?"

"Yes, yes," we both said.

It was a big garden full of many trees we'd never seen. One bush was drooping from the weight of clusters of brick-red flowers. She picked a few and gave them to us. We thanked her for the cold drinks and the flowers and walked toward the front gate. Jimmy kept looking at us from the verandah where he was spread out in a half-reclining position. We shook the lady's hand before going out the gate.

"Now that Jimmy knows you, don't try to go over the wall. Come right in, if you wish to look at the garden," she said before closing the gate.

Once outside, we walked fast to the end of the road and stopped. We looked at each other.

"What do you think?" Khuku asked.

"I'm not sure. The foreigners aren't so bad. Or, maybe she misses her kids, who were left behind in the boarding schools in England. Who knows?" I couldn't help thinking of Mr. Stein at that moment.

"Nah. I think she has a plan to impress us with hospitality and then pack us off to an agency of slaves. Did you notice she didn't even bother to ask our names? She assumes that we are poor homeless kids. You don't know the English people; they're shrewd and cunning. How else do you think they conquered half of the world?"

Somehow I couldn't agree with her analysis. I wanted to tell her that sometimes people are good without any ulterior motives. At least I liked to think so.

"Did you notice that they smell of burnt straw? Perhaps the hot sun burns their pink skin," I said, changing the topic immediately.

"Yeah, I saw how white the hair on her arm is. It looks like hay, you're right." We both began to laugh.

"You know, I'd have loved to take a peek inside the house. But it would have been impolite to ask that this first time," I said.

"Don't tell me you're planning to go back! In that case, leave me out. I'm not sure I would like to be part of it. You know, you're too curious for your own good. Don't forget, *curiosity killed the cat*," Khuku ended with a flare.

"*Curiosity is also the mother of invention*." I felt proud of my quick retort.

I didn't tell anyone about our adventure and never got around to going back to the European neighborhood.

A MAGIC SHOW

Both Dadamoni and I began to read detective novels written especially for young adults. We had a good-sized library in the house. Both our parents were avid readers. Ma read her novels every night after everybody had gone to bed. Dadamoni and I often read the same book and had fights over it. Since he was a faster reader, I would lag behind and bend my head to read the pages he'd already finished. Mr. Blake's series in translation, which were detective novels for teenagers, were our favorite. Dadamoni was so taken by the character of the detective that he would pretend to be Mr. Blake and recite his lines with a theatrical accent.

One day I found him pacing on the front verandah—a black stick in one hand—murmuring words from the book. He had tied a bunch of corn silk to his chin and fixed an old black drape to the back of his shirt with safety pins, as if wearing a cape. When I asked what was going on, he looked at me with disdain.

"I am dressed as the inspector of Scotland Yard. You may have noticed the blond color of my beard. I'm busy solving a major murder case. Don't disturb me." He turned to pace again.

"If Ma finds out that you tore the hair from the corn plants, she'll be furious. Now the corn will not mature properly." I tried to look serious as well. He looked at me as if I were concerned with total trivia while he was preoccupied with important responsibilities.

"Go right ahead. Tell Ma, and see what happens. You're too dumb to know that this 'corn hair' is not the essential part of the corn." With great confidence, he returned to his soliloquy.

I kept thinking of the vegetable garden in our backyard. Both our parents loved gardening. Apart from the rows of corn, there were okra, chilies, cabbage, cauliflower, sweet peas, lettuce, and eggplants. A chicken coop stood behind the vegetable patch. The chicks moved around and ate from the garden, their little necks bouncing back and forth. On winter mornings, my duty was to get the newly laid eggs out from under the golden leghorns. I wrote the date with a pencil on the eggs and gave them to the cook to put in the refrigerator. The garden in the front was full of flowers and was under Ma's care. With a long stick in hand, she would keep watch very early in the morning. The neighborhood children were always eager to steal her beautiful flowers. One day she overslept, and someone not only stole her dahlias and marigolds but also uprooted several plants. Ma sobbed like a child. We all knew how protective she was of her garden. Even so, I didn't dare complain against her favorite son tearing off the corn hair.

One afternoon, after tea and snacks, Mother called all five of us and said, "How would you like to give Baba a nice surprise? Let's stage a drama without telling him." We were immediately ready. Ma had written the play herself. I forget the plot now, but it was about Christ's crucifixion, and I do remember that our youngest brother, three-year-old Bubu, played the role of Jesus Christ. He wore one of Ma's old slips, which came down to his ankles like a robe, and a wreath of leaves on his head. My two sisters, one seven and the other six, became Mary Magdalene and the Virgin Mary. I was a Jewish rabbi, and Dadamoni was Judas.

Baba came home from work and the cook met him at the door, asking him to buy a ticket for the performance. Although surprised, he complied and paid his five rupees. He was ushered into the living room where a few chairs stood in front of a wooden stage—a converted old bed. Ma had sewn several saris together to make the drop screen. Baba sat in the front row—the only row of the house—with the gardener and the cook. The performance began. Ma prompted the lines from behind the doors. When the play was over, the audience clapped profusely. The next item was a duet by my two sisters, whose song sounded more like the recitation of a poem to me. Ma and my two sisters joined the audience for the final act—a magic show organized entirely by Dadamoni.

During the war when we had spent a year in our grandmother's home, we were lucky enough to have attended a magic show by a famous magician, P.C. Sorcar. Dadamoni was so impressed by this man's tricks that he had studied books on how to become a magician. It was nice of him to include me as his assistant, but he didn't tell me exactly what my duties would be. Ma helped me put on a tight dress belonging to my younger sister, hoping it would look like a swimsuit. My hair was pulled back in a ponytail on top of my head. The only other player was our youngest brother. He was given a generous supply of candy to induce him to lie quietly on a table that was placed in the middle of the stage, a white sheet covering him.

First, Dadamoni showed us a few card tricks, which genuinely surprised the audience. Then came the final act. The servant boy was instructed to focus light on the stage by moving a standing lamp that was covered with a red tissue paper. I was told to hit an empty shortening can with a steel spatula, raising a rhythmic racket. Dadamoni ran to the stage, stood in the spot of red light in his black cape, corn silk beard, black top hat, and magic wand. He bowed low in greeting.

"Ladies and gentlemen, as our final act, you're about to witness the most spectacular magical trick. My assistant"—pointing at me—"will help me in this act." I bowed as he had done earlier, without any idea of what I was supposed to be doing. The servant boy took over the job of making noise and focusing the light at the same time. Dadamoni turned toward the table and picked up an old saw—collected from the gardener earlier—and took the bed sheet off the table. He asked me to stand on the other side of the table and to hold the other end of the saw. I saw our baby brother sucking on his last candy, a bit puzzled by his sudden exposure to the red light.

"Ladies and gentlemen, with this saw my assistant and I will now cut this live child in two pieces and, after a few seconds, put him back together again." He signaled me to begin. At that moment a loud cry came from the audience followed quickly by another from the table. Ma jumped up from her chair and ran to the stage and picked up her baby son, who by now was wailing loudly. Perhaps he had finally caught on to the fateful role he was to play. I looked at Dadamoni. His beard was gone, the top hat tilted over his face. Although I felt happy by his downfall, I couldn't help feeling a bit sorry for him too. He looked more like a broken person than a failed magician.

That was the end of Dadamoni's efforts to be a magician. However, he continued to read books on palmistry and later began to practice telling the future, especially to the women in the neighborhood, who were more than willing to show their palms to a handsome young man to find out their fortune.

THE KAMAKHYA TEMPLE

Another memorable time was when Didima came to visit us in Digboi for a month. Our memories of the year in their village were so happy that all of us looked forward to her visit with great excitement. It was always wonderful to have her around—to listen to her stories.

Didima wanted to go on a pilgrimage to Kamakhya, the temple located not too far from us. She told Ma that this was one reason for her to come this far. Everybody was agreeable. Baba turned her wish into a family vacation.

"Let's write to Chhaya and her husband in Nowgong to see if they wish to join us. They're only ten or fifteen miles from Kamakhya. We can visit them first and rest for a week," Ma said, already planning the details. Chhaya was Mother's oldest sister's daughter. They wrote back inviting all of us. Everything was arranged, and one morning we boarded the train to Nowgong. On the way, Didima told us many stories, mostly from her travels to many pilgrim centers. Even in those days, groups of middle-aged housewives would get together and travel to the distant pilgrim centers of India. The tradition continues to this day. There are even special trains bound to sacred places, carrying pilgrims back and forth. Many of these places are located at the confluence of two or three rivers or in the mountains. Hindus believe that their gods live on top of the Himalayas.

The train ran fast, and we sat close to Didima to take in every word. The story I liked most was about Didima's trip to Hardwar, the mountain site where the holy river Ganges comes down to the plains.

Four of my friends and I stayed at an inn in Hardwar, where as pilgrims we could stay for free. We got up at dawn and bathed, put on new saris, and prepared to go to the temple of Shiva with offering plates full of flowers. There were always monkeys roaming free in the temple yard. The worshippers gave these rascals food, because they are considered to be children of the god Hanuman. As I entered the temple yard, I noticed a few monkeys on the big pipal tree.

After I finished my puja, I came out and sat in front of a stone Shiva lingam to pray. I bowed to the god and prayed for a long time in that position. When I had finished, I untied the little knot at the end of my sari where I usually keep some change and my keys. I was surprised to see that I had only a few paisas left. I was sure that I had put more money there that morning. I approached the peanut man and asked him if he would consider selling me some anyway if I promised to bring him more money later. The man agreed and, laughing, told me how I had lost my coins.

Apparently one of the monkeys had been watching me from the beginning. When I was praying with my head down on the ground, he came down from the tree and very carefully opened the first knot of my sari, put aside the ring of keys, and then opened the second knot and took out the coin of more value, leaving the paisas behind. He tied the knots back again with both coins and keys. All the time I was totally unaware what was going on. The monkey went to the peanut man and gave him the coin. The peanut man knew these monkeys well; he measured a handful of peanuts, and the monkey didn't like the amount. He slapped the man's hand for more. Finally he took his peanuts and jumped up the tree, sat there eating them and throwing the shells down. As I looked up, he gave me a grimace as if to tell me how he fooled me.

Didima finished her story and looked at us. As usual I had questions I was dying to ask.

"But how did the monkey know the exact quantity of peanuts the man should have given him in exchange for that coin?" I asked Didima.

Before Didima could say anything Dadamoni jumped in.

"That's easy. The monkey must have observed for a long time how humans buy peanuts. After all, they're our ancestors. They can be more intelligent than some humans, in fact." He looked at me as if I was one of those lesser humans and he belonged to the direct line of intelligent monkeys.

Baba changed the topic and mentioned that we were not too far from our destination.

After a few days of rest we got ready for the pilgrimage. I was excited, because this would be my first time taking such a journey with Didima, who was a veteran in these matters. Besides, I couldn't wait to hear the story about this particular place. It turned out to be far better than I had anticipated.

Our cousin and Ma prepared baskets of food, fruit, and a thermos of tea. A taxi took us to the bottom of the hill and dropped us off. We began our climb. The temple of the goddess Kamakhya, another name for Durga, is on top of Nilachal Hill, which is less than one thousand feet high and located west of Guwahati, the largest city of the state of Assam. Nilachal is part of a mountain range located in the western part of Assam. An asphalt road went all the way up, encircling the hill. Rows of frangipani (plumeria) trees on both sides of the road tried to stand straight on the sloping terrain. Their occasional shade, and the dry fragrance of the dropped blossoms, helped us to walk uphill, which was quite steep in places. There were also stone benches for the pilgrims to rest on, next to thatch huts occupied by *sadhus* who served cold drinking water from clay pots with ladles made of bamboo and coconut shell. We sat on the benches, which were cool to the touch.

While we walked, we took turns carrying the food baskets. After two hours on the road, Baba made a welcome suggestion about a way to lessen the weight of the baskets. We stopped at a shady spot to picnic. Didima had only a cup of tea, nothing else. She needed to fast, she said, so that she could worship the goddess pure in body and soul. One of the water-supplying *sadhus* gave us the name of a priest—his friend—who would help us enter the temple. He said it would be impossible to gain access in the crowd without the help of a priest. After lunch, we resumed our upward journey. Now we children could easily carry the empty baskets. It was late afternoon when we finally reached the summit. After five hours of gentle climbing we were all exhausted. But the view from the top took away the fatigue. There were waves of mountains covered with dark green forests all around us. A cool breeze soothed our tired bodies. We felt we were closer to heaven.

Our cousin's husband went looking for the priest, while we stretched out on the stone verandah of the temple complex.

"Didima, is Kamakhya one of the goddess Durga's many names?" I asked.

"That's right. I'm glad you already know about these things. And do you know how this place became a pilgrim center?" Didima sounded ready to tell the story.

"No story now. We have to go and buy things for the *puja*. Who wants to come with me?" Ma suddenly said before Didima could continue. I had a suspicion that the story had some information meant for adults only. Didima, on the other hand, never worried about such matters when she talked about gods and goddesses.

We followed the priest to the main entrance of the temple. Crowds of people, mostly women wanting to be blessed with motherhood, gathered to worship the goddess. There was a lot of pushing and shoving. The priest took Didima by the hand first, then Ma and my cousin, and disappeared inside the temple. It was clear that only women and the priests could enter the inner sanctum. Finally my turn came. The priest held my right wrist tightly and got us through a crowd of women. It was totally dark inside. After the bright sunlight outside, I felt disoriented. A dampness rose from the floor, and I tried to put one foot in front of the other, like a blind person. After a few minutes I felt cold water near my feet, and the priest guided me down a set of narrow steps, which were slippery. We seemed to descend for a long time until we reached a nook with several oil lamps, which cast more shadow than light.

I repeated the mantras the priest uttered and threw flower petals on a shell-shaped stone, which was anointed with vermilion, oil, and milk. I remembered the worship of the goddess Durga in grandfather's village and the black stone on the far end of the pond in Didima's village. Like the spring underfoot, a pleasant bliss enveloped me. I didn't know the connection between this shell-shaped stone and the black stone of my childhood, but the sensation and feeling were unmistakably the same. The priest drew a line of blood-red sandalwood paste on my forehead. I slowly came out of the damp, dark sanctum of the temple holding the priest's hand.

Years later I found out the story that Didima had been prevented from telling us when we were on the pilgrimage to Kamakhya Temple.

Durga's father, a powerful king, never approved of her choice of a husband, the god Shiva, because of his unconventional ways. Once the king threw a big party and did not invite his daughter and son-in-law. When Durga went anyway, uninvited, and was insulted by her father when she arrived, she could not tolerate his behavior. Out of anger and hurt, she fainted and died. Grief-stricken Shiva came running, picked up the dead body of his beloved wife and began a cosmic dance. The gods in heaven became nervous that his dance would destroy the universe and asked Vishnu to do something. Vishnu threw his chakra—the round knife—through Durga's body, and each part of her body fell at a different place in India, giving rise to different pilgrim centers. Kamakhya in Assam was the spot where the goddess's vulva fell. That's why women came there to worship Durga's vulva—the symbol of creation and procreation—to be blessed by motherhood.

MY "WRITING"

My tomboy activities stopped before I reached puberty. The change from dresses and shorts to saris was a profound one. The first day Ma showed me how to wear a sari, I managed to put it on. I was asked to take a tray of tea things to the living room for Baba and a few visitors. After I put the tray down and straightened up to leave the room, my sari suddenly slipped off my waist and dropped in a bundle at my feet. Although I had a slip on underneath, I was so embarrassed that I thought I would die.

In a short time, I learned to wear a sari securely as I learned to adjust to my coming of age. This traumatic rite of passage was made slightly more tolerable with the "help" of my precocious friends, who constantly whispered relevant information into my ears. For instance, they told me that this was the onset of adulthood, which meant marriage and having babies. I did not think they knew the biological connections. The only difference I felt was a change of moods. I wanted to be more introverted and craved more time to myself. But my girlfriends had a hard time leaving me alone. Whenever we got together, they talked about boys. We seemed to have become more cooperative than competitive about them. We imagined falling in love. The desire to fall in love came long before the real experience. All this happened behind Mother's back, where her vigilance couldn't reach.

The more I was prevented from free access to different places and things, the more I entered a world of imagination, which, fortunately, was beyond Mother's domination. I began to realize that the only way I could avoid her control and rules would be to escape from home, the same home where I had had such a fun-filled childhood. By this time I had already read several novels from Mother's library, which I kept hidden under my schoolbooks. When I began reading Tagore, I was spellbound. His poetry and short stories took me to a world that resonated with my deepest feelings. His words were like music to me, and they described exactly what I felt but didn't know how to express. Baba also introduced us to English books quite early. Most Sundays in winter, he would read to us after lunch while we cuddled under a warm quilt in his bed. The first book that I liked was *The Legends of Greece and Rome*. The stories of the Greek gods, goddesses, and heroes sounded so similar to and yet different from the stories I knew about our gods and goddesses.

The children of our neighborhood decided to form an association, where we would get together once a week and engage in some extracurricular activities, such as playing games, singing, or discussing books. Somebody's uncle took charge and organized the club. Our parents were happy that we would be under an adult's observation and away from mischief. We established a library in our home to which all the families contributed books that we could check out. We were to write our names and the borrowing dates in a notebook that I had provided.

At every meeting, we looked for something new to do. Once I suggested that we publish a handwritten magazine. Only a few agreed to contribute, and they only agreed to do so provided I took full responsibility for producing the magazine—gathering and selecting contributions, editing, and copying them out into bound volumes. I agreed. As far as I remember only three issues came out. I was proud to do the hard work. Only a few of us wrote short poems, limericks, travel accounts, short stories, and letters to the editor. I wrote the editorial page and a story for every issue. The hardest part was to write legibly with pen and Chinese ink on heavy paper. It took me a long time to write out several copies of the magazine, which ran between thirty and forty pages. But I loved doing it: writing longhand was like creating calligraphy. Because it was summer vacation, I had a lot of time to devote to this literary activity.

That summer of my fourteenth year, the most significant event of my life happened. I fell in love—not with a boy but with an author. At the time, I was reading everything I could lay my hands on. One day I found a book on forests and the life in them by Bibhutibhushan Bandyopadhyay, a well-known Bengali author a few of whose books were later used for screenplays by the renowned Bengali film director Satyajit Ray. The words and their rhythm in this book I read were so captivating that I was totally mesmerized. I couldn't stay away from that book all day. I devoured it and wanted to read everything he had ever written. My love for his work was so intense that I wanted to possess the same ability. I wished I could write the same way. This desire burned inside me so strongly that I sewed together a bunch of papers into a thick notebook for myself. I wrote on the first page "MY WRITING" in big letters and hid it in my drawer.

I did not mention this notebook to anyone. Every afternoon that summer, after a brief nap, I would wash my face with cold water and sit at my desk to write whatever came to my mind. I couldn't stay away from my writing book. It pulled me with a force that could only be compared to the strongest narcotic. The attractions I experienced later in love and as infatuation never matched that first love I felt. This was followed by another desire—the desire to have my own room. I had already discovered the enticing solitude that enveloped me when I wrote. I was desperate to have a place of my own where I could be alone with my notebook.

MY ROOM WITHOUT A VIEW

On one side of our living room and at the end of the inner verandah there was an extra bathroom that was never used as a bath. It became a storeroom for old trunks, chests, and furniture. Ma used to talk about getting the cook to clean it up. Somehow the cook never had time for this nonessential job. This room had two doors and one high window. One door connected to the living room, the other opened to the covered verandah, which we used as a dining space. The window faced west, and I could see a few branches of the guava tree through it. One day, after inspecting it, I decided this room would be perfect for me if the trunks and chests could be removed.

Over a Sunday lunch, I asked Ma about it.

"Since this room is never used, do you think I could put my desk there and make it my study?" Everyone at the table looked at me as if I had gone mad. But to my surprise Ma did not reject the idea outright and looked at Baba.

"Not a bad idea. This way I can throw away stuff we don't use, and we would have a reason to clean it up. It has been packed with junk for years," she said. The fact that for a couple of years now I had been first in my class might have been a major factor in her decision. Also, our home, although quite spacious, was crowded at the moment. Several members of Baba's family, including my grandfather and four of my cousins, had come to stay with us after the Independence of India in 1947. Riots between Hindus and Muslims compelled them to flee their village home, which was now in Pakistan. Naturally, Ma was happy to retrieve this extra space for me.

The next day everyone chipped in to clean up the room. My cousin Mejda could not help joking.

"How will you be able to study in a bathroom? Yuck!"

"This bathroom has never been used. Even the toilet bowl is permanently covered with a board. I may use it to build my book shelf," I said without hesitation.

Within a week, the room began to look livable. Ma sewed colorful cotton drapes for my doors and window. Apart from my desk, there was an iron cot in one corner. The cook took it out and gave it a thorough cleaning with soap and hot water. After it stood in the sun for a whole day, he put it back inside. An old mattress, a handwoven spread, and a few pillows made it look like a fashionable divan. Even the old toilet, which was already sealed shut with a board, disappeared under the divan. Everyone was amazed by the transformation of the old bath and storage room. Within a few days, they began to use the room whenever they pleased. Some even began to take naps on my divan. Seeing that my whole purpose was being subverted, I wrote "No Trespassing" on two big signs and posted them on my two doors. That did not deter most of my cousins, but slowly they stopped coming into the room. It was established that the newly converted study belonged to me, and no one else.

In that room, which was eight by six feet, I began to live among my books and dreams. Besides the textbooks on English, Bengali, Sanskrit, math, and so on, I also had my favorite authors, whom I read as often as I could. When I read English writers, I felt a connection to the rest of the world. Every evening I went for a walk either alone or with a friend on the serpentine roads that climbed the hills of our beautiful town. I wrote in my notebook whatever welled up inside me. I kept the notebook hidden and never showed it to anyone.

That year, during the summer vacation, we had a great time. Because of the presence of our cousins, both Dadamoni and I became a bit raucous. Ma kept up her complaints when she was alone with Baba, this time about the children of her in-laws more than about me. She must have been tired of dealing with five extra people day and night. Baba came up with an idea to keep us under control. One day he called the four of us attending the high school—Mejda, Mishtidi, Dadamoni, and me—to a meeting in the living room.

"It's nearly a year before you'll appear for your matriculation exam. I want to test your knowledge of English. I shall give you three tests in three weeks. All you'll have to do is write an essay on the same topic for two hours. Whoever performs the best will receive five books of his or her choice; the next prize will be two books, and the third prize is one book.

When the three tests were over, Baba called us to another meeting and said, "The youngest of you has done the best." I was the youngest. I chose five novels by Thomas Hardy as my prize. This experience taught me a few things about myself. I found myself inspired to work hard, imagining the end result of doing well. I was also determined to do better than my cousins, and especially my older brother. I had a vague idea that if I continued to excel in my studies and do better than Dadamoni, Mother would have to take notice. Perhaps she would love me as much as she loved her oldest son. We all knew how much Mother valued education and that she dreamed of her children doing well in school. I liked competition, and I could be highly motivated to work hard to complete a project that challenged me intellectually. This trait helped me succeed throughout my academic life. Years later I realized that the academic success came with a price and that I had needed to sacrifice something valuable to become so single-minded. But let me not get ahead of myself.

The year after Baba's test was my tenth grade, the last year in high school, and I devoted myself completely to preparing for the final exam. I made a plan about how to proceed with preparation and stuck to it religiously. I stayed in my room for hours studying. Ma was extremely cooperative and instructed the cook to bring meals to my room if I so desired. It was vital that I do well on this exam, so that I could go to college and manage on my own. Freedom from Mother's control was something I looked forward to all my adolescent years.

FIRST LOVE

All the novels that I read from Mother's library behind her back taught me something about romantic love. I had a sense of what it might feel like. Some evenings when I walked alone on the meandering roads of our town and admired the colors of the sunset from bright red to lavender, I felt something that lifted my spirit. It was a kind of joy that came unannounced and without effort. I knew that love between the characters in those novels happened with a similar joyful lift, though full of unforeseen obstacles. I dreamed of falling in love, although there was no particular person attached to that dream.

An unexpected mingling of joy and sorrow filled my heart. The quiet beauty of nature was a perfect setting for letting loose my imagination, which soared high. The distant hills with their bluish-green forests, the quiet breeze, and the sky with ever-changing colors were the only witnesses to these feelings.

In tenth grade, once a week, I had to go to the boys' high school for a couple of hours to take a special class in additional math. The girls' school did not offer this class. The headmaster, who happened to be my uncle on my mother's side, was a strict man. He sat me in his office and gave me the lessons. Once in a blue moon, I was allowed to sit with the boys. I watched the top boy, Amalendu, in their class and felt an affinity with him, since I was the first girl in my class. He and I were competitors and at the same time fellow travelers. Soon I began to weave romantic fantasies about him. My desire to be in love with him began to grow like a squash vine in the rains of summer. I imagined that the two of us lived in a land where we two were the only inhabitants. I kept this to myself and did not even tell my girlfriends.

Then came the day in February when the festival of the goddess Saraswati took place. She is the divinity of learning, science, and music. Naturally, Saraswati is worshipped by students all over the country. On this day, students are forbidden to study; rather they spend all day having fun. That year it was decided that the Saraswati festival of our school would be performed together with the boys' school. I was ecstatic. The all-knowing goddess wanted to help me in my secret mission of coming close to my beloved. This was my only opportunity, I decided, to unload my heart and soul to him. In the atmosphere of festivity, it would be more appropriate to talk about love.

There were rehearsals for plays as well as music and dance performances. Since I was not talented in any of these arts, I signed up for a debating competition between the two schools. I was sure that the best student of the highest class would represent the boys' school. If I couldn't impress him with beauty and other talents, at least I could attract his attention, I thought, with my brilliance in debate.

On the day of the festival, I kept my eyes and ears open all morning to locate him. But I had no success. Then in the afternoon I was asked to carry a big bowl of rice to be served to the students sitting in rows in the big hall. In the corridor, I nearly collided with him. With a faint smile in his eyes, he let me pass. With that smile he let me know that he knew who I was. He was carrying a plate of fried vegetables going in the opposite direction. Inside the hall, I was convinced that from the other end of the room he was stealing glances at me. That evening throughout the music and dance performances I searched for that smiling face in the crowd. But he had disappeared from sight, leaving my evening barren. My friends kept asking me what was wrong. I wished I could disappear too.

The debate was scheduled for the next morning. The topic was personal freedom, a subject close to my heart. We were called to the stage, but he was not among the participants. I scanned the big auditorium, which was full of students, parents, and teachers. Finally my eyes rested on the first row, where he was, again smiling with his eyes as if to tell me, "If you win the debate, only then will you have a chance to be my girlfriend. Otherwise not."

During the debate, I had no idea where all my razor-sharp arguments were coming from. The words came pouring out of a place inside me with which even I was not familiar. When the jury announced my victory, I looked for him the second time. He was not in his chair! In a moment, all the sunlight was extinguished for me. Bitter disappointment sliced my victory into a thousand pieces. Amid the roaring applause I came down from the podium. My classmates and family members all gathered around to congratulate me. As I was leaving the auditorium, I saw him behind a pillar. I left everyone else and approached him without any hesitation.

"Congratulations! You were fantastic," he said. I was ecstatic.

"Thank you. You should have participated. No one would have a chance then," I said. Watching him turn to go, my pleasure was about to evaporate. "Would you be going to the play tonight?" I said quickly. I needed to have another chance to tell him my feelings.

"Yes, I'll see you then," he said and left.

The whole evening I looked for him everywhere. I couldn't be sure whether he had not attended the evening function or whether I couldn't place him in such a big crowd. In the brief light between acts, I searched for his face, desperately but in vain. The glow of happiness from the morning, which had sustained me throughout the day, disappeared rapidly. That night I couldn't sleep for the bittersweet pain my love had brought me in the span of one brief day. I got the first taste of what falling in love might promise.

A few months after this heartbreak, one of my cousins—the only son of my mother's widowed sister—came to Digboi on a holiday. He was in his twenties with a handsome face, and he walked with a limp because of a serious bone disease he had had when he was twelve. As a result, his growth had been stunted. Although short, he seemed not to notice this handicap at all. Perhaps his tragic life, more than his personality, made him lovable to everyone, including my parents. We had heard so much about this cousin that his arrival was a momentous event. I had heard that after graduation from college, he had joined a daily newspaper and had already become known for his journalistic talents.

I became his greatest admirer, and he too paid special attention to me. Being an only child, he missed not having an admiring younger sister, which he now exploited to the hilt by demanding to be my mentor and guide. I confided in him about my love and disappointment. He listened carefully and told me that this was just the beginning of the unpredictability of life ahead. I found in him an understanding friend, someone with whom I could talk about the most intimate things, including even my notebook, though I refrained from showing it to him.

In the few days that he spent with us, without saying a word, he managed to confirm and support my desire to become a writer and to fulfill my dreams. He left a permanent impression on me, which would deepen when I arrived in Calcutta a year later to go to college. Besides my father, this cousin was the principal guide who took me by the hand and allowed me to travel to the exciting land of learning, knowledge, and creativity for the next ten years of my life.

ON THE WAY TO CALCUTTA

Everyone, including myself, was surprised by my performance in the matriculation exam. I had obtained marks above 80 percent in three subjects and was among the twenty most successful students in the whole state of Assam, out of several thousand students. My brother also got into the first division with letters and was granted admission to one of the best colleges in Calcutta. Awarded two scholarships for the next six years of my education, up until a master's degree, I was sure that going to college and university was a certainty. My parents were pleased and proud. Ma had no excuse to prevent me from going on with my education, although her dream was to see me married and settled after high school.

Now was the time to prepare for a journey to Calcutta, the largest city in India and a completely new world some nine hundred miles to the west. The dream to go away, which I had nurtured tenderly for all of my adolescence, was now a definite possibility. Yet to leave my beautiful birthplace—its hilly roads where I had walked on many evenings, the town that had taught me how to dream and write, and Mother's discipline and unexpressed love—was not easy. Most of all, I felt a stab of pain in leaving my little room, my world away from everyone and everything. However, I have always managed to find some kind of personal space—a little room—where I could keep my books and a desk to write on.

Eventually writing became second nature. Now I carry a notebook always and can write almost anywhere if I am so inspired. But back then, the pull to get away, to go to a bigger world where I would learn about big ideas, was irresistible. I knew that I would never be happy without the world of books and ideas. This mixture of excitement for the unknown future and sadness for leaving the secure life I had been used to and had loved for fifteen years kept me spinning for days, as I packed my suitcase with a few of my favorite books and placed my writing notebook under my clothes.

The year was 1951, and at that time it took four days and three nights to reach Calcutta by train. When Father, Dadamoni, and I boarded the train, Ma, my two sisters, and my baby brother all stood in the station with teary eyes waving at us. It took only a few minutes for the train to leave the town boundary behind, and I turned toward the rapidly moving landscape outside. In no time, the train was passing through high hills with tiny ribbons of waterfalls in the distance and narrow snaking rivers under high culverts. Lush jungles covered the hillside slopes.

This train ride was the beginning of a very important life's journey. Two desires—freedom and learning—had been driving me since I was a teenager. Now the speeding train seemed to reflect that passion, making the landscape outside disappear rapidly in the opposite direction, like the life I had just left behind. The restless excitement inside my heart matched the noise of the moving train. As if echoing my feelings, the sound of friction between the wheels and the rail kept repeating "catch me if you can," "catch me if you can," and "catch me if you can."

At night the same sound became "where do I go?" "where do I go?" and "where do I go?" The anxiety that I kept covered with my enthusiasm by day surfaced at night. I had to admit that I was also scared to face the huge city with all its unknown perils, which we read about in the newspapers. Would I be able to adapt to this unknown world? I had been safe in our little town under the sharp and protective care of Mother. I was more confident of my academic ability than of my social skills in coming to face a complex urban life. But the night train had changed its tune already. It kept repeating, "what fun!" "What fun!" Soon it rocked me to sleep.

By the second day on the train, we had already finished all the food Ma had sent in the various containers of an aluminum carrier. Baba always got hungry when he traveled. He looked forward to reaching Nowgong, where our cousin and her husband would meet the train and greet us, hopefully with food. When the train stopped at Nowgong, we stuck our heads out of the windows so they could find us. They came into our compartment with containers full of delicious homemade food, and we were well provisioned for the rest of our trip.

By now the landscape had begun to change, from forested hills to tame tea gardens on gentle slopes. Acres of land spread before our eyes, covered with a knee-high carpet of tea bushes with occasional tall shade trees to interrupt the monotony. Tribal women with conical baskets on their backs were busy picking tea leaves. I had already read the award-winning novel called *Two Leaves and a Bud*, in which Mulk Raj Anand described the atrocious behavior of foreign tea garden managers toward their laborers. Looking at this peaceful scenery, it was hard to imagine those atrocities. As we crossed the state line, leaving Assam behind, the dark green of the tea bushes slowly changed to the lighter green of paddy on flat fields.

"Have you thought of what courses you would like to take?" Baba moved back from the train window and asked us. "I would like to see both of you take science courses, so that you will have an option to study medicine," he added.

"Let's see which college I get into. That'll determine the choice of subjects to some extent, won't it?" I said quickly. In fact, I was not at all interested in science. I knew Baba had this secret wish that someday one of his children would be a doctor. I was so repulsed by my first experience with dissection—a frog in my high school biology class—that I decided never to go near any cutting activity, be it frogs or whatever. But I decided to keep quiet for now. I knew how much Baba dreamed about our future, especially mine. He wanted great things for me. At that moment I remembered that one of my first birthday gifts from him at age five was a biography of Moitrayee, a famous woman philosopher of antiquity. And he had always counteracted Ma's notions about cutting short my education, and I was eternally grateful to him for that. Without Baba's support, I would not be sitting on this train bound for an exciting future. I had to let him weave his own dream for now.

We reached Calcutta on the fourth morning. The first thing I noticed was the crowds of people—all kinds of people. I also saw all kinds of vehicles—bicycles, rickshaws, horse-drawn carriages, cars, trucks, streetcars, buses—all moving along the roads like waves of an overflowing river of humans and conveyances. I wondered how people could live in such commotion, confusion, and noise. It took us over an hour by taxi to reach my aunt's house in the southern part of the city. Already I began to miss the quiet roads of Digboi. Could I really belong to this noisy and crowded city?

GHOSTS IN THE COLLEGE DORM

Dadamoni was admitted to Presidency College and I to Lady Brabourne College, which was a renowned school for girls with a well-run dormitory for out-of-state students. I also could have gone to Presidency College, one of the best in the country, but they had no lodging for girls. After resting a few days, Baba and I went to meet the superintendent of the dorm. She welcomed me as a new resident, and after a brief lecture on the history of the college she got to the more relevant points.

"In this dorm no student is allowed to go anywhere without my permission, except to the college on the other side of the road. The doorman keeps an eye on everyone when they cross the street and reports to me if anyone takes a detour. For such violations, the punishment is severe." She paused for a few seconds and continued, "Every Saturday your preapproved visitors can visit you, but only in the visiting rooms and for no longer than one hour at a time. One weekend a month, your local guardian may take you out after signing in the book, and he or she must bring you back by six in the evening on Sunday. Do you understand?" She stopped and looked at me. I was wondering if the prisons in the country were not more lenient. I just nodded. Baba looked at me briefly, a touch of alarm on his face. The superintendent was not done.

"All personal letters will come and go through me, and if necessary, I shall open them. This college dorm has a reputation to uphold. I hope you understand my responsibility." This time she looked at Baba and tried a forced smile. Baba nodded as I had done. He had not anticipated that I would be under the rule of such a dictator. Sitting next to him, I told myself, "Alas, here I'm falling *from the frying pan into fire.*"

Asking Baba to wait in her office, she then took me inside the building to introduce me to the warden. We entered a three-story U-shaped building. Everything was spotlessly clean. The warden or dorm mother, a middle-aged widow, came toward us and after proper introductions, put her right hand around my shoulder affectionately. The superintendent left.

"Everyone calls me 'Aunt.' You do the same. Don't hesitate to come to me if you need anything or if you have any complaints," she said before steering me to one of the large bedrooms. Rows of single beds with iron frames stood side by side, with a small wardrobe at the head and a small desk on the side of each. I was a bit disappointed to see that I had to share a room with twenty other girls. The dorm mother mentioned that only in the third year was one entitled to a single room.

"This will be your bed, desk, and wardrobe." She pointed to a bed. Then she took me to the kitchen and introduced me to the head cook and told her that from now on there would be another seat at the table for the new first-year students. I went out of the kitchen and looked around. A paved courtyard separated the kitchen and dining hall from the main building. A patch of lawn, bordered by flowering shrubs, ended in a high wall that circled the whole compound. The only difference between a prison and this place was the absence of electric barbed wire covering the top of the wall. The superintendent's house, a small two-story building, stood at the end of the lawn.

On the way back to my aunt's house, I described the layout of the dorm to Baba without mentioning my disappointment. Baba must have guessed my feelings.

"Everything will be second nature in a few weeks, you'll see," he said.

That night in bed, I couldn't avoid feeling apprehensive about my life in the dorm. But I also knew that the die was cast—there was no turning back now.

Two days later we returned to the college dorm with my suitcase, this time to stay. Baba would leave for Digboi the next day. He wanted to see me settled before leaving. Dadamoni had already moved into his dorm, which was not restricted because only boys stayed there.

After exchanging a few words of thanks with the superintendent, Baba got up and said good-bye to "Mrs. Dictator." I followed him to the entrance where we were alone. He looked at me and said, "Don't be disheartened. The rules are for your protection and strict rules may prevent distractions. Besides, every weekend you'll see your cousins and your uncle." Then he changed the topic. "Try to make a few friends—you've always been good at that—and you won't even notice these restrictions. And join the college sports teams. You like to play badminton and tennis, right? Remember *all work and no play . . .*" He stopped. I knew that he was giving all this advice to delay the moment of our parting. I stooped down to touch his feet in the gesture of *pronam*.

He picked me up with his two hands and hugged me. "Please don't forget to write every week. I'll write also." His moist tone touched my core. Tears filled my eyes as we separated. Baba turned to leave. The doorman kept staring at us. Ignoring him, I watched Baba walk toward the bus stop. He took out a handkerchief from his pocket and wiped his eyes. I ran back inside the building and went directly to the big bedroom and to my bed. My roommates were milling around. I tried hard to swallow my tears unsuccessfully.

"You're missing your family, are you? But there is no need to weep. This is a prison all right, but no one will beat you up." A girl with dark brown curly hair and large brown eyes came and sat next to me. "In no time you'll learn the sneaking tricks we know to get around the doorman's prying eyes. We're here to teach you all that. Don't you worry." I wiped my tears and looked at her. She smiled and added, "My name is Neela. Which corner of the world do you come from?"

I didn't like her know-it-all tone even though she sounded helpful. I decided not to show my weakness openly again. Every night when the warden came and turned off the lights, I couldn't control my tears and shed them silently in my narrow bed. I had had no idea I would miss Digboi and my family so desperately. I missed Baba, my brothers and sisters, and even Ma. I had been dreaming of escaping her domination for years, yet now I wished I could go back to our home, where she was such a strong center.

My secret tears every night lasted for about three months. But during the day, I forgot the life I had left behind. The high ceilings of the classrooms in our beautiful college, the new subjects taught by brilliant professors, and my new classmates all brought a thrill that sustained me even in the strict dorm life.

One morning at breakfast a slim, tall girl with thick glasses came and sat next to me. "I saw you in economics class yesterday. What else are you taking? My name is Hashi." When I told her the courses I was taking, she said, "Exactly my combination. Good, we can study together before the exams." I liked her immediately. It was Hashi who told me about the gang of four led by Neela. They harassed the new students so badly that the superintendent suspended all four of them for a semester. But they were undaunted and soon got back to their old tricks again.

"What exactly do they do? Are you talking about hazing? I thought only boys did that sort of thing. Have you been their victim?" I asked in disbelief.

"Yes, I'll tell you about it some other time. Don't be scared. They may decide to leave you alone. It's hard to predict what they may or may not do," Hashi said and left.

About a week later, one Friday evening, I went to bed early and read until the lights were out. I thought about the next day when Sundark-aka, who was one of my local guardians, would come and take me out to spend the weekend with him and his wife. He had moved to Calcutta a few years back and got married. I was eager to meet my new aunt. I looked forward to seeing my favorite uncle after six long years. With such pleasant anticipations I drifted off to sleep.

Around midnight I awoke. My bed seemed to be moving. I immediately recalled the earthquake that had taken place in Assam the previous year. It had been a major quake, lasted seven minutes during early evening. Hundreds of people and animals were killed and property was destroyed. The rivers changed course and tons of dead fish came floating along them. We had had to live in tents for months. It was one of the scariest times of our lives.

As I tried to get off the bed, I realized that it was not only shaking but was also moving forward! I nearly lost my balance and held on to the bed as hard as I could. I was so afraid that I couldn't make any sound; my throat was dry. The bed kept moving. I was convinced that the ghosts from my grandmother's village had come back to take me. Inadvertently I closed my eyes and began to recite the ghost-proof mantra that Mayna had taught me.

> The ghost is my son, petni is my daughter,
> No one can harm me,
> I'm protected by Ram and his brother.

A few minutes later, the bed was dropped to the ground with a loud thud. A cold breeze blew over me. I remembered what Mayna had told me: ghosts always depart, leaving a chilly wind behind! I kept completely still for a few minutes before opening my eyes again.

I could see the main dorm on one side. My bed was now placed in the courtyard between the main building and the kitchen. As I attempted to get off the bed to run back to the dorm, it began to move again, this time in the direction of the dorm. Suddenly someone sneezed. By now my eyes were getting used to the dark. I moved the mosquito curtain a few inches and looked. Neela's gang was carrying my bed and walking as fast as they could. I had an idea. I kept completely still and did not let them know that I saw them. After they put my bed back in its place, I spoke for the first time.

"Thank you all for giving me such a swinging ride in the middle of the night." They had not expected such a reaction. I told no one about this event except Hashi. In between munching spicy popped rice, she had a big laugh.

"They won't bother you again. Now you're initiated," she said.

The four years I stayed in the dorm, I made friends with two members of the gang. I couldn't help admiring their courage to stand up to the authorities, although I never approved of their harassing new students.

I took honors courses in geography, where I met Krishna, who later became a close friend. Krishna was the best student in the class, and we studied together for our exams. Four years later, in 1955, we finished our bachelor's degrees and moved on to the university, where we were classmates again. Two years later, when we took our master's exams, she stood first and I came in second in the university. My other close friend, Moitrayee, who was named after the great philosopher of ancient India, was also a student of philosophy. Like me, she also came from outside Calcutta and stayed in the dorm. She was more sophisticated than many of us. She and I talked through the nights about our dreams and loves—love of books, love of writing, and also love for men—ideal men who were waiting for us somewhere, we were convinced! I read to her the short stories from my notebook, and she read her poetry to me. We also wrote poetic letters to each other. Both Krishna and Moitrayee are still my friends, even though our paths have moved far away from one another.

It was Moitrayee who explained to me what had happened when two of our classmates were called to the superintendent's office for serious questioning. One of them had to leave the dorm. Apparently the warden had found them in bed together and they were accused of being in love.

"What's wrong with that?" I asked dumbfounded. "You and I love each other. We spend so much time together and write letters which are like love letters," I said.

"This is different. They're behaving as if one of them is a boy," Moitrayee tried to explain. She also told me why this was a common occurrence in strict dorms where teenaged girls have no connection to boys of their age.

"The only man we see around here is the doorman with gray hair and a scraggly beard and a horrible personality," I said, laughing, and added, "Do you think we may become like those two girls?" Moi-trayee laughed at my naïveté.

"No way. Do you think I'm going to fulfill my desires with a poor substitute? *If one wants milk, whey would not do*," she ended with a proverb. I was relieved but couldn't help feeling a bit insulted as well.

TOR RASMUSSEN

After I received my bachelor's degree with honors in geography in 1955, I left the college dorm and moved into a postgraduate dormitory not far from the university. Calcutta University, one of the oldest in the country, was a cluster of impressive sandstone buildings with high columns and ornate façades. The university stood on a crowded and busy street named College Street, filled with many bookstores. Its nearly two hundred years of tradition, rooted in the British liberal education system, seemed to be stored in its architecture, which was more European than Indian. Every morning I was thrilled to walk into the Senate Hall to attend my classes, despite the noise of the broods of pigeons nesting under the eaves where the columns met the roof.

The postgraduate dorm for the girls turned out to be far worse than I had expected. The conditions soon made me yearn for my previous dorm! I shared a bedroom that overlooked one of the busiest streets of the city, with five other girls. The disturbing clang of the streetcars was our companion every night till midnight. Every morning I had to stand in line for at least an hour to go to the only bathroom in the whole building. The lunch and dinner menus were composed of various permutations of cold overcooked rice with thin lentil soup and a curry that smelled of raw fish. I spent as much time as I could at the university even after the classes were over.

Although geography was the subject I had majored in, it had not been my favorite field. However, the deeper I got into it, the more significance I began to discover. It grew on me. A well-known anthropologist and geographer taught a class on human geography.

We knew that Professor Nirmal Kumar Bose had been a close disciple of Mahatma Gandhi and had written a controversial book on his association with the great man. In no time, his charisma and knowledge made the subject attractive to me. I was able to see a connection between various landscapes and climatic zones and the social and economic behaviors of their inhabitants. Looking back, I see that my abiding interest in human culture and nature began at this time.

In a small class of twelve students, I was already acquainted with some of them from our college. Soon I became part of a group of three—Krishna, Protima, and myself. We studied together, sat in class and lab together, and giggled over a visualization game I had invented. I came up with the names of vegetables that resembled individual professors. One looked just like a scallion, a bald-headed one was a peeled potato, and still another looked just like a turnip. We spared the professors we liked or had crushes on. They were, of course, perfect. Krishna was reluctant when I suggested skipping a few boring classes. But she was not so reluctant when we hopped onto the tram to go see matinee shows at the cinema downtown. We loved Gregory Peck and never missed any of his films.

Late one afternoon, after classes were over, I went to the departmental library. Most of the students had already left for the day. The librarian was sitting on his chair paging through a journal. As I looked for a book on the open shelves, I noticed a tall, blond foreigner looking at the same shelf. He smiled.

"May I help you?" I asked to be polite. Instead of responding, the man extended his right hand toward me.

"I am Tor Rasmussen," he said as we shook hands, the smile still on his face. His accent and last name told me that perhaps he was from a Scandinavian country. When I mentioned my name, he pronounced it carefully a few times.

"Your name is not that hard," he said. He told me that he was a junior professor at the University of Oslo and was in India for a few months to do research. He was looking for a few issues of the Calcutta *Gazette* from the last century. I helped him find those and then offered to sign them out for him. Quite surprised, Tor wanted to know how I could trust him after meeting him for only a few minutes.

"I just do," I said casually and handed the three dusty volumes over to him. "I know you'll honor my trust by returning them on time," I added with a smile. Tor bowed his tall body in gratitude.

Watching me getting ready to leave, Tor quickly said, "It's awfully nice of you to help me. Could we have a cup of coffee or tea somewhere? I have a few questions to ask."

"Of course. Calcutta's famous coffeehouse is right around the corner. Everyone goes there to talk, but it may not be the best place for conversation," I said. Tor put the Calcutta *Gazettes* into his shoulder bag and stood by to follow me. As we were about to leave, I saw Krishna coming in. She glanced at us quickly and questioned me with her eyes. I simply passed by with a smile.

As usual, the coffeehouse was full of people, cigarette smoke, and noise. Tor glanced over everyone's head and gestured us out of there. Outside, I noticed the evening dropping around us. Some of the bookstores had their lights turned on. I was staying with my cousin and my aunt for the summer months. I knew my aunt would be worried if I were late going home.

"Could you hold your questions?" I asked. "I need to go home. It's nearly curfew."

"Of course, of course. Why don't we meet tomorrow after your class? Please, tell your family that you'll be a bit late." Tor then added, "I really have many questions about your country."

"Okay," I said and shook his hand. As I moved to the bus stop, he entered a used bookshop.

The next morning as soon as I entered my first class, Krishna asked, "Where did you find the tallest foreigner in the world?" I did not like her tone.

"He is Norwegian. Naturally he is tall, not short like you and me," I said with slight irritation.

"Oh, oh! You're already defending the man. Are you sure you're not falling . . ."

I interrupted her and told her the whole story of how I had met Professor Rasmussen at the library and how grateful he was for my help. I did not mention anything about our meeting that evening. I thought of checking him out first before introducing him to her. Throughout the day I was reminded of another foreign man who had become my friend when I was only seven, although I had to admit that Mr. Rasmussen looked very different from Mr. Stein.

After classes were over I waited in front of the bookstore we had agreed on. I was wearing a dark purple cotton sari with a baize border, and by the end of the day, it had crumpled a bit. As I waited, I kept wondering if my attraction to the foreigner was only due to my early friendship with Mr. Stein, or whether there were other deeper reasons which I would never know. A brief honk interrupted my thoughts. I looked up to see Tor calling out to me from inside a shiny black car with a uniformed driver. He opened the back door, invited me in, and gave the driver an address. Within half an hour, we had reached the Grand Hotel on the busy Esplanade. After talking to the driver briefly, Tor accompanied me to the hotel lobby. Why a hotel? I became immediately cautious. Perhaps I should not have agreed so easily to meet in the evening. After all, I really knew nothing about the man.

Meanwhile Tor guided me across the lobby and went through a door onto the back terrace. There round garden tables were scattered. At one table, three Western women sat chatting, tea things scattered in front of them. Other than that, the place was quiet and pleasant. A breeze carried coolness from a sprinkler at one corner of the lawn watering a border of winter flowers. I was surprised to see such an oasis so close to the busiest part of the city. Tor pulled a chair out and invited me to sit.

"What would you like? Coffee? Tea? Something stronger?" he asked.

"Tea, please," I said after sitting down. Tor signaled a waiter and ordered. The waiter came back with a pot of tea, a plate of pastries, a tall glass of golden liquid, and a small plate of cashews.

After a few sips of beer, Tor stretched his long legs out in front of him away from the table and began his questions.

"First of all," he began, "do Indian women not drink alcohol at all?"

"It's not customary and is considered unbecoming for a girl of a good family to do so. Some may try it for fun once or twice," I said, adding, "Why would anyone drink bitter-tasting alcohol when we have such tasty tea available in India?"

Tor laughed aloud and stared at me for a few seconds. He then continued with his questions about India—its many cultures, politics, customs, and so on. I tried to answer as well as I could. Because his English was not that perfect, I felt less self-conscious and talked freely. In addition, I was flattered that a university professor wanted to know my opinions about serious matters. The pot of tea was nearly finished when I noticed the time. It was already after seven. I needed to get back. I was about to mention that when he suddenly changed the topic.

"Are you going to be married after your master's exam? Or will you go for a doctorate degree? By the way, what's your opinion about arranged marriage?

"I have a boyfriend," I said reluctantly. "If I marry after my exam, I shall marry him. I don't believe in arranged marriage. Besides, my plan is to try for a fellowship to go abroad—England or America for postgraduate studies. Of course, that will depend on how well I do on my exam. It's not possible to go to a foreign university without a scholarship," I said.

Tor put his hand inside his pants pocket and took out his wallet. "I too have a fiancée. Here she is." He took out a small passport-size photo and showed me. "Her name is Elisabeth, but everyone calls her Bee." He smiled tenderly at the photo. I saw the face of a Western woman who looked older than Tor. He put the photo back inside the wallet and the wallet back in his pocket. I noticed he held the wallet inside his pocket a few moments longer. This brief exchange moved our acquaintance to another level.

I felt an affinity with him despite our vast differences. This was the first time I had made friends with a man—a stranger—in such a short time. My connection to him had little room for romance, although in the beginning I felt intrigued by his invitations. I had mixed feelings when I first heard about his fiancée; I was disappointed yet relieved.

Outside the hotel, the black car was waiting. Once inside Tor mentioned that the car belonged to the Norwegian consulate, assigned to his friend, who was the consul general and his host in Calcutta. Since the friend was away on vacation, Tor had his home, car, driver, and three servants at his own disposal. It was a luxury—he added with a smile—that was not easy to get used to.

"In Norway we do all our household chores ourselves, including cleaning our toilets. Very few people can afford domestic help. Children are taught how to take care of themselves physically," he said as we began to pass crowds of people outside the frosted windows of the car. Everyone was returning home after work. Inside the air-conditioned car, I was separated from the world outside—the world where I belonged, which I was a part of every day. I directed the driver to Lansdowne Road where my aunt lived. I thanked Tor for a nice afternoon.

"I leave in a few days for Assam. Why don't you and your boyfriend join me for dinner one evening? Decide on a date and call me, I shall send the car." He scribbled a telephone number on a piece of paper and gave it to me. I put the paper in my handbag and got out of the car. I looked up and saw my aunt and a neighbor on the second-floor balcony, craning their necks to see who was inside the car. I climbed the steps two at a time.

"Who brought you home in such a shiny car? Where have you been?" My aunt's question was not totally innocent.

"A foreign professor is here to do some research. I was asked to help him. My teachers think my English is better than others because I went to school in a British company town," I lied to avoid further queries, and left for the bedroom to change.

Two days later I introduced Tor to Krishna. The three of us went to see a popular Bengali movie. We had tea afterward and answered more of his questions. He invited Krishna for dinner also. She declined, saying that her family would not allow such an outing. I was wondering about a good excuse to get out of it as well.

The next day I was at a neighbor's, chatting with a girl my age, when I heard a big commotion. I ran back to find my aunt behind the front door pointing toward the collapsible gate at the entrance. The hallway was too dark to see anything, but I could discern a tall figure behind the gate and, on this side, the maid standing in a puddle of dirty water with her mouth still open as if she were frozen by a spell. I turned on the hallway light and saw Tor Rasmussen standing at the head of the staircase with an empty bucket and a dirty mop at his feet. I immediately understood the situation. The unexpected appearance of a tall white man on the dark staircase had been ghostly enough for the maid to drop her bucket of dirty water and mop and scream, which had already attracted a group of neighbors.

"Haven't I told you not to appear at my aunt's house? You could have easily telephoned," I admonished Tor as I walked down the stairs with him. Tor looked surprised.

"I'm really sorry to have come without calling. I was passing by and thought, why not drop in and say hello to your family? I had no idea my presence would create such problems." He sounded embarrassed.

"You may never get explanations of such situations in any handbooks on India. I shall try to explain later," I said.

"Fine, come to dinner tomorrow. I'm leaving the day after." After this event, it was hard to refuse his invitation. The next afternoon at five, the black car came for me. Of course, I had to make up a convincing tale for my aunt. The dinner was supposed to be at Krishna's house. Fortunately, my aunt did not remember to ask for Krishna's telephone number.

The consul general of Norway had a beautiful bungalow in Mandeville Gardens, a fashionable residential area of South Calcutta. A patch of well-tended garden led to the front door. The living room was tastefully decorated with both Indian and Western art objects. In one corner stood a large bronze figure of the dancing Shiva on a mahogany pedestal. The opposite wall had a large oil painting by some Italian Renaissance painter I did not recognize. A uniformed bearer served a glass of orange squash. Sipping it, I remembered my friend and me trespassing in the garden of the English couple in Digboi when I was a teenager. Now, finally, my curiosity to see how foreigners lived was satisfied. This time I did not have to sneak in; I was invited. There wasn't anything unusual about the house except that an unfamiliar smell hit my nose—something like a mixture of cigarette smoke, perfume, and aftershave.

Tor appeared and sat down with his beer. I apologized for my behavior the day before and tried to explain why his presence had been such a shock to the women of the house.

"You see, I'm not supposed to have a male friend visiting me at home, let alone a tall foreigner. When I meet my boyfriend, he brings me home but leaves before the corner of the road leading to the house. A good Bengali girl of twenty does not have a male friend," I said.

"But I thought you were planning to marry the young man of your choice. Doesn't your family know about him yet?"

"True, that's *my* plan. No one knows about it yet. I shall introduce him after I finish my exam and at the right time. It's really complicated. Choosing one's partner for life is not considered the right thing to do, as you know."

"Even for someone who is at the university and already twenty? Well, good luck to you!" Tor looked at me briefly and left his chair saying, "Shall we eat?" He led me to the dining room. We had roast chicken with potatoes and vegetables and talked about many things. He was interested in Indian art and literature. I was impressed when he told me that he'd read Tagore's poetry in a Norwegian translation. He regretted that his comprehension of Tagore's songs was limited because he did not know Bengali.

After we moved back to the living room, the servant brought coffee in small cups. Tor got up and took out several bottles of various sizes and colors and put them on the table. He poured a thick golden liquid into two tiny glasses and handed one over to me.

"I'd like to make a toast to our friendship with this Scandinavian liquor. Do you mind?" He looked at me with a smile.

I took the glass from him thinking, "What's the harm in drinking a bit from such a tiny glass? Drinking for them is nothing but a polite custom, and I should respect that."

Tor raised his glass and said, "Here is to an unexpected friendship! May we meet again! Skoal!" and swallowed the whole drink in one gulp. Following him, I did the same. A sweet fire burned down my throat. I failed to taste anything special in the burning liquid.

Tor refilled his glass and said, "Let me tell you how this liquor is made. In the northern part of Finland a type of golden berries are grown, which are called cloud berries because they are shaped like clouds in the sky. This liquid is made from the extract of the juice of those berries. Shall I pour some more for you?"

"No, thanks." I jumped when I noticed the time. It was close to ten! I had never been out so late. I stood up and said, "It's really late. If I don't leave immediately, I will be in big trouble. Is there an antidote to the smell of the liquor? My aunt will have a heart attack if she smells alcohol on my breath," I said, gathering my handbag. Despite my desperation, Tor looked at me with a mischievous wink and laughed.

"There is a remedy that we used when we were young," he said and asked the bearer to bring a spoonful of tea leaves. "Chew and keep the leaves in your mouth for a few minutes before spitting them out. No one will know that you had this extraordinary liquor." He continued to laugh. I had no idea that tea leaves were so bitter, but that seemed a small price to pay for an interesting evening.

When I reached home, fortunately my aunt was busy with her guests and didn't pay much attention to me. I changed and washed before going to bed. I kept wondering about the vast difference between the two worlds I had just traversed within a span of few hours.

The next day, Tor came to the university to say goodbye. I gave him a parting gift of a record of Tagore's songs, along with my translations of the songs and a velvet purse for his fiancée. He thanked me and said, "I hope someday you and your husband will visit my country and be our guests. You'll meet my wife then." I carried a heavy heart around for a while.

HUNGER STRIKE AND FIRST MARRIAGE

In my second year at the university, it became clear that I couldn't cope with the living in the postgraduate dorm. I moved to a branch of the YWCA, where the conditions were more civilized, though quite a bit more expensive. The money from my scholarship was adequate, so when I wrote Baba about the move he understood. Also I asked Amitabha, my cousin and one of my local guardians, to write my parents about this necessary decision. His words were enough to convince my parents that I had to move.

The Y was quite a distance from the university. Soon after I moved in, a smart-looking young woman knocked on my door and said, "You've got a call. The telephone is in the lounge."

After I had finished talking to my cousin, she approached me again.

"Who was that on the phone?" she asked.

"My cousin, who is also my local guardian." We began to chat and learned about each other's background and family. After that, when we ran into each other in the lounge or cafeteria we would chat. One Sunday I saw her sitting with an attractive young man in the lounge. She waved and asked me to join them.

"Manisha, meet Samir, my cousin. Now you have to introduce your cousin to me. Deal?" she said with a wink. This is how I met the man who two years later would become my husband.

From my very first meeting with Samir, I was impressed by his personality and looks. He had a unique mixture of carefree manners and seriousness. I found out that he had just finished his master's in economics. A week after our first meeting, I ran into him in the corridor of the university as I was leaving the geography lab. It took him a few seconds to place me, but then he greeted me politely and asked if I had time for a cup of coffee. That afternoon we spent seven hours together having many cups of coffee and, eventually, dinner. When I came back to the Y late that evening, I knew something very significant had just happened.

Thus began the second time I fell in love, the first being my fantasy about Amalendu in high school. This relationship caught me off guard and took me through an avalanche of emotions—mostly the excitement of learning new things. Samir was a skilled conversationalist who could paint pictures with words. He opened the doors to a world that I was more than ready to enter—the world of ideas and passion. My twenty years had been spent in the world of books, imagination, and fantasy. Now I could live all these with someone who not only was open to the experience but also could talk about it beautifully. We met every day without fail, and it was clear to me that he wanted to be with me as much as I wanted to be with him. It was a fascinating journey of two years of new knowledge, new discoveries, and new passions.

He was a self-taught painter and musician. He introduced me to philosophers, artists, and scholars about whom I knew next to nothing—Karl Marx, Jean-Paul Sartre, and Bertolt Brecht among others. I sat in awe listening to him and slowly began to learn his language—to think and talk like him. I talked about him—how wonderful and learned he was—all the time to my friends. I even tried to convert them to his ideas. My friends were stunned by my rapid transformation, but I paid no heed to their comments. I thought they were jealous because I spent more time with him. I was intoxicated with everything he said and believed.

The freedom I had craved throughout my childhood and adolescence was right in front of me. I saw Samir as my liberator and savior. To me his ideas about life, women, marriage, and sex all were so fresh and modern that I wanted to live every bit of it as soon as possible. A strong desire to spend my life with him took root inside me, although there was one little obstacle to this dream. We never talked directly about marriage. I knew he did not believe in the formal aspect of the marriage ceremony. For him, it was only a demonstration of wealth to uphold a family's social status. Ultimately he had to succumb to the custom because of the pressure from our families.

My new love was a self-professed Marxist and a member of the Communist Party. I was sure that my bourgeois family, founded on generations of feudal tradition, would not approve of this choice, though this little "problem" enhanced my adoration for him. In the meantime, Mother had been busy looking for a suitable husband for me. I had one more year to go before finishing my master's. She said that she had waited long enough; I must be married as soon as I had the degree.

One day a gentleman arrived at the Y and introduced himself as someone Mother had sent. He handed me a letter from her. In the letter she urged me to be nice to this qualified and wonderful young man, who was willing to consider me as his future bride. The letter also mentioned his well-endowed family and his promising career as a civil servant of the central government in New Delhi. My mood rapidly changed from annoyance to anger. She was still trying to control my life.

I observed the young man in front of me. A man of medium height, he appeared quite innocent with his oily black hair parted in the middle. He looked at me with a shy smile. I tried to be polite, hiding my anger as much as I could. "It's really a bad time," I said. "I have to prepare for a test tomorrow."

"Will a couple of hours matter that much? It's good to take a break from time to time, don't you think? Let's just go for a walk in the park," he said still smiling.

"All right, just for one hour," I said and went inside to get my handbag. I decided to be totally honest with him and let him know my plans of marrying someone I loved. It was unfair to keep this nice man waiting with false hope. We walked along the road toward the park and saw a sweet shop still open at the corner.

"I heard that you love sweets. How about tasting a few? I'll also join you," the man said and led me toward the shop. "What would you like?" he asked after we sat at one of the small tables in front of a row of glass cases full of various kinds of sweets. I saw the perfect opportunity to scare him off. I pointed at every kind of sweet available—at least twenty of them! The shopkeeper brought a large plate full to the brim and placed it in front of me. "You must be really hungry," he said showing no surprise at all and sat opposite, watching me eat. I could not continue with the game. I told him that I had had enough sweets to last me a long time.

He smiled and asked the shopkeeper to pack the rest for me. I suggested a walk in the park, and we began to talk. After a few minutes of chitchat I said, "My mother must be impressed with you, but I've already chosen someone. I am really sorry. I have nothing against you," I blurted out. The man stopped walking. He seemed really surprised.

"Falling in love and choosing a mate in marriage are two different things. Not everyone can take the responsibility of a marriage. You need to think very carefully. I am in no rush and shall wait as long as you need to make up your mind."

"I know my mind enough to know not to keep you waiting. I mean it. Please believe me. I really do not like to be in the position of having to convince you that you are not the man I shall marry." I was surprised myself by such harsh words. The man kept quiet this time. I turned back toward the Y. He followed, and we reached the Y in less than five minutes. He joined his palms in greeting before leaving near the gate. I did not dare to look at him. I hurried inside and without wasting a second sat down to write a long letter to Mother. The message was clear. I told her that she did not have to worry about my marriage, I would take the responsibility. I registered the letter before mailing it the next morning.

Seven days later as I came in from my classes at the end of the day, the manager of the Y gave me a telegram. Worried, I tore it open to find a brief message from Father. It said: *Mother on hunger strike. Come home immediately. Airfare follows.*

I had no idea that the situation with the prospective groom she had sent would turn so dramatic, nor did I have any desire to fly nine hundred miles to argue with Mother. I had a lot to do in Calcutta. Apart from my studies, a new love took all my spare time and energy. It was not easy. Samir and I met every evening and wrote long letters to each other every night. I sent a return telegram with the message: *Impossible to leave now. Please tell Ma I'm not afraid of such threats.*

Two weeks later came a long letter from my uncle, Mother's oldest brother, the headmaster, who informed me that he and his wife had persuaded Mother to break her fast. The letter read, in part:

The purpose of your being in Calcutta was to finish your college and university degrees, not to waste time "playing around." Your parents are extremely worried about such behavior. You were one of the best students of the Girls' High School in this town and people here expect great things from you. As your uncle and one of your teachers I am particularly disappointed in you. Obviously you have forgotten your duties as a daughter of a good family and a good student of a renowned school. You have a certain responsibility to uphold the tradition of an educational institution.

I sent a brief response to him saying that I would explain everything when I returned home for the holidays in two months.

During the holidays, we had many closed-door sessions, excluding my siblings. The elders were careful that my younger sisters not become corrupted by my example. My uncle, whom both my parents respected and we children feared, presided over all these meetings. He had a habit of switching to English when he was angry and to formal Bengali when he was serious. He began the first session in formal Bengali.

"You were the ideal student of your school. Every day your teachers use your name as a role model for the other students. The definition of an 'ideal student' not only includes academic brilliance and qualities such as obedience, gentleness, and humility, but also a keen sense of duty toward one's family. We do not expect you to be a cause of your parents' disappointment. Do you agree?" I thought my uncle had ended his lecture in his letter to me. But no. He continued, "You moved to Calcutta barely five years ago. We would like to know how, in such a short time, such monumental changes in your character have come about?"

I tried to keep calm and chose my words carefully when I finally got my chance to speak. "I am nearly twenty years old and in a year shall finish at the university. If I am old enough to understand and digest complicated books, perhaps I am old enough to choose my friends. Is this fair—to dictate my relationships from a distance just because no one trusts my judgment? Or, is this not just an obsolete notion of obedience—to say 'yes' to everything my elders decide, including my future and marriage?" Ma was about to say something but Baba interrupted her.

"Well, we understand your . . ." He couldn't finish.

"We're not talking about friendship," Mother cut him short, "you went to Calcutta for higher studies with two scholarships. And now you are neglecting everything and going crazy over a man, calling it 'love.' What do you know about love? As your parents, we have some say about such major actions and decisions in your life. This is the result of overindulgence . . ." Throwing the last line at my father, she stopped and appeared as if she was about to cry.

Somehow I couldn't take her seriously. I looked at my father, who looked away.

I tried again, "I don't think you ever taught me that loving someone was a bad thing. I am so sorry that you are having a hard time watching me grow up. I am also sorry that I had to come down from the high pedestal of the 'ideal student' of my school." I addressed my uncle and looked at my mother directly before saying, "Ma, all my life, you've made all my decisions for me—what to wear, who to be friends with, where to go, what to read. Now it's my turn to decide to whom I shall be close. For the first time, I'm not asking your permission to do something." I was getting tired of all this talk.

"How dare you talk like that with me? I won't allow a scandal to spread all over the country. I sent an established government officer to meet you. You sent him back because he parted his hair in the middle." She could not continue on account of her anger, though Baba couldn't help smiling.

With that this meeting ended.

A few days later in another meeting, Mother surprised us all by saying, "Fine, if you're so determined about this young man, then you'll have to marry him immediately. I won't tolerate a full-blown scandal in my family. Though you may not care about society, we do."

I knew that she would like to control some aspect of my decision, no matter what. I held my ground. "A wedding now is out of question. I will not marry anyone before I finish my final exam," I said firmly.

"You chose the groom; we'll choose the wedding date. Before that,

I shall go to Calcutta and meet with this paragon of virtue. And then we'll write to his parents and proceed only after they agree. Everything has to be done according to the tradition and custom that is fitting to our position and status. You're not allowed to say anything about any details of the wedding—date, dowry, jewelry, guests. We'll consult an almanac and decide on an auspicious date." She got up from her seat and left the room, dismissing any possibility of objections from anyone. I did not see any point in arguing over anything further.

Things moved rapidly after that and behind my back. Ma was quite impressed by the looks and behavior of her future son-in-law. I knew he would win her over. The wedding date was in November, between my theoretical and practical exams. No amount of protest on my part had any success. I worked on my lab reports right up to the day before the wedding.

I knew she would try to avenge my independent choice of a husband any way she could. She went against our views totally and planned an ostentatious wedding that she wanted our town to talk about for a long time. By her choice she did all the shopping. Baba let her do it, because he knew how momentous this occasion of her eldest daughter's wedding was for her. On our front lawn, large tents were pitched to accommodate the wedding party of close to a thousand guests and relatives. Years later I wondered if, at the time, an astrologer had predicted that the chances of a successful marriage were slim, whether Mother would have gone all out in staging such an expensive wedding.

The morning of the wedding day began with many rituals, some of which involved symbolic bathing in sprinkles of cold water. Early in the morning I was given a light breakfast of yogurt, nuts, and dried fruit to be followed by an all-day fast. Older women sang wedding songs throughout the rituals, with lyrics about the love and hardship of married life in a husband's family. The monotonous tunes of these songs were hypnotic. Being the center of all attention, I began to feel very special indeed. In the afternoon, young married friends and cousins began working my long hair into a beautiful coiffure decorated with a gem-studded gold comb before adding makeup and jewelry all over. Sitting in front of the mirror, I saw myself transformed from a studious girl into an enchanting bride. The desire to be united with the man I had been in love with for two years added to the glow of my appearance. I was fascinated by the face in the mirror. I had never imagined I could look and feel like this.

The wedding began at sunset. I stood opposite the seated groom, who was dressed in a silk *dhoti* with a shawl draped over his long silk *kurta*. I sneaked a glance and saw how handsome he looked. I was led by two male cousins to circumambulate the groom seven times, and in the end he stood and we exchanged two fragrant garlands of jasmine flowers three times and looked at each other's eyes ceremonially in what is called an "auspicious stare." Then I sat opposite the groom as my father, who looked strained and serious, repeated after the priest the Sanskrit vows of giving his daughter away as he put my right hand in the groom's. Samir and I were asked to offer up flowers, yogurt, and ghee to the fire, the god of fire being the divine witness to Hindu wedding. The ceremony went on for a long time. The priest recited mantras, which were repeated by Father after him, and I became dazed, partly from fasting all day and from the smoke and the sounds of the mantras.

At some point, the priest tied one end of my veil to one end of the groom's shawl, and we were asked to circumambulate the fire together. Through the cheering of the crowd and auspicious blowing of the conch, the priest prayed to the god of fire to bless the newly wed. The wedding lasted for several hours, to be followed by a series of folk rituals throughout the night.

To my surprise, the experience of the religious ceremony of Hindu marriage moved me deeply. The sound of Sanskrit mantras mixed with the fragrance of incense, sandalwood paste, flowers, and fire created an atmosphere that lifted me to an ethereal world. In some ways that world was connected to the shrine where Mother kept her gods, the Durga *puja* of Father's family, the black stone near the pond of Grandmother's home, and the temple of Kamakhya. The same world also touched the stars and planets of the sky, the stories of the epics that I had learned by heart as a child from my grandmother, and somehow the human experiences of birth, illness, aging, and death as well.

I have experienced this transcendence from the mundane plane several times in my life. Whenever I was confronted with major tragedies or significant events, including brushes with death, I was privileged to enter the sacred world of gods, however briefly. Afterward, each time, even though life moved in its habitual track, I was never the same again. I wonder if our finite existence does not move a little toward eternity this way.

My wedding sari, which I still have—a weave of gold and red silk from Banaras—carries a faint perfume of sandalwood that reminds me of that evening and transports me to a sacred world.

GENESEE RIVER, LILACS, AND RON

In 1959, a year and a half after our wedding, my husband and I left India to pursue further education in the States. He was awarded a fellowship in economics at the University of Rochester in upstate New York—in a city that spreads out on both sides of the Genesee River and is where the Eastman Kodak Company is headquartered. Rochester is also famous for its lilacs, thousands of them in a park, which makes the whole city fragrant in spring. Tourists come every year from all over to participate in the Lilac Festival in May.

I was thrilled at the possibility of fulfilling my dream of going abroad for higher education. Accompanying the man I loved and adored in this new venture was more than I could have asked for. I was ecstatic. I was hoping to get a fellowship in the geography department. However, soon after my arrival, I found out that Rochester University didn't have a doctoral program in geography. I was reluctant to try another campus and be separated from my husband.

I decided to take a break from studies and devote myself to building a home for us in this new environment. We had to manage our household expenses with a meager fellowship of fifteen hundred dollars for an academic year. In the early sixties it was possible to live on such a small income and even afford a used car! Away from the support and scrutiny of our families, we were free to live any way we chose. The novelty of American culture kept me excited for months. It was a relief to be able to walk holding hands together on the street and to be able to show affection in public. I learned how to cook and experimented with new dishes. However, within a few months I began to feel lonely, since Samir had to spend many hours at the university. I decided to learn French and Spanish and began to use the university library, reading books in a variety of subjects. I was thrilled to occupy a comfortable sofa in the library reading room with a book while snow fell silently outside the tall glass windows. I read and discovered the French Romantics and the German Expressionists in both literature and art. Among the German authors I was strongly drawn to Thomas Mann. *The Magic Mountain* became my bible for a while. At the time I had no clue that a decade later I would end up in the country where the story was set!

I still remember the afternoon in November 1959, the first year we were in Rochester, when cotton-white flakes began to fall from a gray sky. The whole day was cold, gloomy, and quiet as if something ominous was going to happen. Then down came fuzzy flakes of the whitest of white snow, descending slowly, turning in the wind, and finally settling on every surface. I had never seen anything like this. I ran into the kitchen and poured some milk and sugar in a bowl, covered it, and put it outside, hoping to see ice cream in a few hours! I had no idea that ice cream was not a creation of nature. My husband laughed at my childish efforts. He promised to take me out to an ice cream shop where I could choose from many flavors. I couldn't explain to him that eating ice cream was only part of the excitement of making it outdoors.

The next morning when we awoke, I was enchanted by white silence and beauty everywhere. The dark branches of leafless trees were alive with snow blossoms, snow leaves, snow branches. The world was clothed in white purity. Even our secondhand car on the front road was buried under a foot of snow. As we got used to the long winter months of Rochester, we stopped marveling at the beauty of snow. Rather we complained about having to shovel it for four or five months.

As the novelty of discovering the new country began to wear off, I began to feel restless. Being a part-time student and a full-time housewife no longer held my interest. I decided to try getting admitted to a new field. Even though I had majored and done well in geography, I had never liked the subject that much. The only area in geography that I liked was human geography—a subfield that dealt with modes of human adaptation to specific ecologies. This was what Professor Bose had taught, and his knowledge and charisma sparked my interest in it. I discussed my plans with Samir. Together we decided that anthropology would be a close enough field. Luckily for me, Professor Bernard Cohn, the chairman of the anthropology department, specialized in India as his area of interest. He had just returned from extensive field research in India. He looked at my background and was willing to consider my case.

"Take these books with you," he said, "and read as much as you can. In a month we'll meet to talk about them. I'll decide then if you'll be able to handle anthropology." I was impressed by his unconventional method of assessing an applicant who had never studied the subject before. A month later, we met and he asked me some questions. I tried my best to respond critically and also told him there were many things in the reading that I could not understand. To my surprise, he let me into the graduate program in social anthropology with free tuition and a research fellowship. I was ecstatic and plunged wholeheartedly into my studies. I was determined not to let Professor Cohn down. It was hard work learning basics and at the same time competing with graduate students who had four years of training behind them.

Both Samir and I spent most of our days and half of our nights at the university. Sitting inside my assigned cubicle on the seventh floor of the library tower, I forgot the outside world. It was as if I had returned to my little room in Digboi, where at age fifteen I had discovered my love for knowledge and my desire to write. As I walked along the narrow paths lined with maples and sycamores, from one ivy-covered brick building to another in the university quadrangle, I felt I was on a pilgrimage. In my mind, an American university campus came close to the ideal place of learning that I dreamed of. I loved to listen to professors who treated the students as equals. Coming from the traditional British system of education, I was astonished to discover how democratic the higher educational system was in America.

Two years later, I got my second master's degree, this one in social anthropology, and decided to go for a doctorate. Meanwhile, Samir wanted to follow a Marxist economist to the University of Chicago, where this professor had been offered a better position. I was delighted because the department of anthropology there was one of the best in the country.

Our social life during these two years was restricted by our busy study schedules. Once or twice a month, we met with other married students for potluck dinners or took in campus films and concerts, which cost very little. I had always loved watching movies. Now my husband introduced me to the work of such giants as Ingmar Bergman, Akira Kurosawa, Federico Fellini, Michelangelo Antonioni, and of course the Indian director Satyajit Ray. Their creations touched my deepest feelings and moved me to want to create something new and beautiful. But I had no time then to do anything but study. I regretted having left my writing notebook behind in India in a trunk with my other books and papers. When summer holidays came and I had finished my exams, I longed to return to my secret world of writing. But I was too distracted and too busy enjoying my new life with my husband in a new land. I neglected my love of writing for years to come.

It might have been at a party just before the summer break when we first met Ron. Samir and Ron exchanged telephone numbers. Within two weeks of our acquaintance, Ron's generous warmth managed to win our hearts over as if we had known him all our lives. The only son of doting Jewish parents, he was a bit younger than Samir and a bit older than me. At the time he was living with his parents and taking a leave of absence from his law practice in California. He said he had gotten tired of the hazy sunshine of San Francisco. He needed this break to figure out what he wanted to do next. He had never been married, although he had had a string of girlfriends.

"The word *marriage* gives me sudden indigestion," Ron said. "I've kept away from it by shifting my alliance from one lady to the next. My parents expect me to get hitched and produce grandchildren someday soon. Right now, I feel great just goofing off and taking a break from both law and women."

In the meantime, my husband and I had promised a professor that we would housesit for him for the summer months. It was a fairly big house with gardens, and without pets. For us it was a convenient arrangement, since we planned to move to Chicago at the end of the summer. We gave up our rented apartment, packed our belongings, and moved to Professor Johnson's lovely Tudor-style home with three upstairs bedrooms. I was delighted to have a garden and a large kitchen in which to experiment with cooking. Ron helped us move.

"Lovely," he said. "Now you guys will be practically in my parents' backyard. I can visit you any time. Better still, why don't I move in as well? You've got so many bedrooms." He leaned against the piled up cardboard boxes with a beer can in his hand and a twinkle in his eyes. Over six feet tall and slim, a chain smoker with a pouting mouth, Ron could be considered attractive, if not handsome.

"This arrangement works perfectly," Ron beamed. "After a lunch of my mother's chicken soup, I can have your dinner of rice and curry." He put his arms around me as naturally as an old school friend. My husband entered the kitchen at that moment and smiled indulgently.

"How can you ever be ready for the responsibility of a wife and children?" I said half joking, moving away a bit and adding, "You behave like a child yourself. The whole world seems like a playground for you." Then I thought, *This playfulness is what attracts me to you.*

"You're like the god Krishna, who seduced hundreds of women with his flute. All you need is a bamboo flute in your hands to complete the picture," I said smiling. Ron was immediately curious about Krishna's story. He drew me by my hand and placed me on a sofa and sat at my feet.

"Tell me about Krishna, please."

I had to tell him all about the god of love and his mythology. He listened with rapt attention. It was late when I stopped. He left for his parents' reluctantly that evening.

Ron began to visit every afternoon and stayed through dinner. The three of us did everything together—shopping, cooking, eating, gardening, movies, and concerts. Soon the three of us were inseparable. Our acquaintances began to call us the Siamese triplets. These comments were no exaggeration. Ron's life became so intertwined with ours that we could not imagine a single evening without him. If he was a bit late coming, both my husband and I became anxious and looked out the windows every second. The sound of his car on the driveway lifted our spirits immediately and life flowed normally again. If he had to postpone his visit for some unforeseen emergency in his family, his voice on the telephone would be heavy with disappointment, and we would not know how to fill up the evening. A cloud of darkness would descend between us as if Ron's presence was essential for our daily existence.

When we were alone, my husband and I never talked to each other about Ron. One evening after a joint venture of cooking, the three of us sat down to eat. After the usual compliments on my culinary talents, Ron looked at both of us.

"Guess what? My parents are getting suspicious of our friendship. My mom asked me yesterday if I was in love with you, Manisha." He laughed and quickly added, "Guess what I told her?" We looked at him.

"I said, yeah sure. I'm in love with both of them. That's the truth." He looked serious, but in a few seconds he laughed again and said, "Come on. Are you scared? It's all very innocent and without demands. This love is perfect for me because neither of you will pester me about marriage." He said this in jest but looked pensive again as he added, "I don't even want to think what will happen when you two leave for Chicago." He pouted and turned to me, touching my shoulder with his head like a child who wants to remind his parents of their priority.

That night in bed I raised the topic with Samir for the first time. My talkative husband uncharacteristically had only a few words to say. "Why worry about it? It's such a beautiful experience for all of us. Why ruin it by analysis?" After that neither he nor I ever talked about Ron.

Ron continued to join us every day. Sometimes he even spent nights in one of the spare bedrooms when our discussions over a particular movie or book went on for hours, and it got too late, and he was too tired to go home. The summer flew by. As much as possible, I kept that reality out of my consciousness. Like my husband, I too did not wish to delve deeply into the mystery of this relationship lest I lose the intense pleasure of friendship and affection Ron had brought to our lives.

In spite of our pretending that the summer would never end, it drew to a close. The last Sunday before our departure—a beautiful day in late summer—we went for a long hike in the woods outside the city. After a while, we began to walk single file, and I slowed down, letting the two of them go ahead. They were too engrossed in their talk to notice that I lagged behind. I took a detour and discovered a narrow stream flowing gently, making soft music over rocks and pebbles. Dwarf clumps of fern growing along the water seemed to be looking at their reflections. I sat on a rock close to the stream. From somewhere in the depth of me tears welled up, and I let them come freely. I had a vague feeling that they were not just sadness for the eminent separation from Ron, but a sorrow much deeper and stronger. This sadness came from the very center of my soul. For the first time in my life, I felt a loneliness that I did not know was possible. Sitting alone near the gentle stream, I wept for myself until I heard them calling for me.

I washed my face in the cool water of the stream and called back, "I am here, I'm fine." Soon I joined them. Somehow it was not so hard to leave Ron after that.

Ron saw us off at the Greyhound bus station. With moist eyes he said, "I'll be there before you finish unpacking your boxes. How am I going to survive without you two?" He began to wipe his eyes. My husband blew his nose, and I wiped my tears. Ron kept his promise. He did visit us in Chicago one weekend before we were fully settled. My husband and I shopped all day and cooked his favorite dishes. We ate, talked, and laughed as before. But something was missing. The old magic had disappeared. The tightly tuned strings of the violin of romance had snapped. After that, our connections became sluggish and communication slowed.

I finally allowed myself to question my relationship with Ron. One day I stood in front of the mirror in our bedroom and asked myself, "Is it possible to have such an intense relationship that is not romantic? Is it possible that Ron came to our lives to fill a vacuum?" Samir and I had a marriage founded on modern values of equality and intellectual companionship, yet it lacked a deep instinctive bond, even though we'd fallen in love, or at least we thought we had. Otherwise, how could I explain Ron's stronghold on our emotions? His childlike spontaneity and warmth seemed to have opened the floodgates of our affection and we were ready to shower our love on him. Ron seemed to have occupied an emptiness that our childless marriage had created. For the first time in the five years of our relationship, I did not share these feelings with my husband.

Within a few months at the University of Chicago, I turned my concentration to my studies again. It was exciting to study with giants in the field—Clifford Geertz, Fred Eggan, Milton Singer, Victor Turner, and Mircea Eliade. However, I soon became increasingly disillusioned about academic anthropology, which seemed to be following the hard sciences in creating theories as yardsticks to understand human culture and behavior. Human beings began to disappear behind a wall of well-worded hypotheses. Although my passion for learning was contaminated by this disillusionment, I continued to attend classes with my habitual zeal.

DEATH OF A PRESIDENT

I was in the A&P, a neighborhood grocery store on the south side of Chicago, to pick up a few things. It was in the afternoon, around two or three on a late November day in 1963. As I waited in line to get to the cashier, I noticed several people with portable radios pressed to their ears, listening intently. I recalled a scene from back home in India: my youngest brother with a small transistor stuck to his ear, listening to the ongoing sports commentary at all waking hours during the cricket season. Perhaps some big baseball or football game was on, I thought. Then, within a few seconds, a big African American man ahead of me in the line removed the radio from his ear and began to cry loudly like a child, uttering something I could not follow. The only words I could understand were "the president, the president." His tears choked his speech. Within a few seconds several people in the store began to whisper while others stood paralyzed. Even the girl at the cash register stopped and looked at the crying man with blank eyes.

The woman next to me said, "The man is saying that the president is dead!"

I left my groceries at the counter and walked out of the store. The shock of the news gripped me as it did others. The air outside was chilly. The November evening began to fall rapidly. I had been in class all day and had no idea that the president had been shot in a Dallas motorcade. The big man and a cluster of women shoppers were out in the parking lot now. The women were also weeping. Others scattered and walked to their cars, all empty-handed, the groceries forgotten. I too walked back empty-handed to our apartment and turned on the small television set in the kitchen.

The broadcast came through again and again announcing the death of John Fitzgerald Kennedy, the thirty-fifth president of the United States of America. On the television, shots of the White House, faces of people in shock, and the hospital accompanied the announcement of his death by Vice President Johnson.

I remained glued to the television screen. That evening we did not cook any dinner, just had a few pieces of dry bread. I thought of another day fifteen years before, in another land thousands of miles away, when my parents told us that Mahatma Gandhi had been assassinated. I was too young to know or feel the impact of that information, but I remembered that we had cooked no food to eat. No Indian felt hungry that day. The mourning for Gandhi had continued for days, as it did that November of 1963 for Kennedy. I was surprised to feel the same sorrow I would have felt if I had lost someone close, and I kept thinking of the big black man in the grocery store, who had cried as if he had lost his father or brother. Later I understood that his sobbing came from the depth of his soul, because when President Kennedy died, African Americans lost something they had been promised since the administration of President Lincoln and had not yet gotten. This black man was not alone; all people of color and many others who were not mourned for days and months and years for a president who had understood and felt their plight and inspired them to hope and dream.

For days, weeks, months, and even years we all saw, and still see on every anniversary of that fateful day, the repeated images, captured as though in a home movie, showing the fatal motorcade. It passed crowds lined on either side of the road, with the close-up of a young woman in a white headband, and a few seconds later, President Kennedy moving his head on one side, and Mrs. Kennedy climbing up on the seat to help her husband in the open car. This film, of only a few seconds' duration, has been imprinted on the minds and hearts of millions of people, as the mystery of that assassination—"who killed JFK?"—lives on.

The night of the tragedy, and for several nights to come, my husband and I lay in bed talking about this awful catastrophe. I could not shake off the pictures of Mrs. Kennedy in a black veil walking to the cemetery, holding the hands of her two children, who had no idea of the monumental change in their young lives.

I too had no idea what was to happen shortly in our lives.

PLAYING WITH FIRE

One evening, my husband invited me to a celebratory dinner, saying, "I have a surprise for you." We sat opposite each other as he raised a glass of expensive French champagne in a toast. He continued, "Our marriage has reached a new stage. We're going to show the world that we, a young couple from India, can live like Sartre and Simone de Beauvoir, who never depend on each other and live separate lives, yet love and respect each other deeply." He took a long sip of his champagne and looked at me with a satisfaction that scared me. Puzzled, I tried my best to comprehend the meaning of his words. Paying no attention to my reaction, he continued to say many beautiful things, most of which did not penetrate my consciousness. I was already removed from the scene by a dark suspicion.

"In our marriage," he continued to lecture, "our love will flourish and mature in the freedom from the obligations of duties, responsibilities, and fidelity. We will be *free* to love, not *obligated* to love, not because we are bound by an outmoded institution called marriage." He poured more champagne into our empty glasses saying, "Let's toast to our new freedom. From today, we are free to have separate bank accounts, and we will be free from the responsibility of having to share everything." His eyes began to glisten as he raised his glass again.

"I don't know what you're talking about," I finally said. "All I feel is a chill along my spine. It sounds like playing with fire to me . . ." I couldn't finish. A mountain of sadness, of misunderstanding and loneliness, enveloped me and choked my voice. For the first time since I had met Samir, his dramatic oratory failed to carry me away. Every word felt like a weapon that had been sharpened to attack our existence together. A protest arose inside me, but I was helpless to stop this new game of setting each other free. My helplessness turned into enormous anger and stubbornness. All right, I said to myself, in order to prove some silly notion to the world, you're willing to risk our marriage! Fine, I too will play this game to the hilt.

As this "new stage of our marriage" began, the consequences loomed larger than either of us had dared to imagine. Once the game started, neither of us seemed to have the power to stop the sequence of events, as if we were directed by the invisible strings of a puppeteer.

What followed was beyond my husband's grand plans or my control. Hurt, insult, misunderstanding, and anger became our daily companions. Our marriage of determined love, immense intellectual adventure, and compatibility, which my friends and relatives had envied, became an arena of mutual destruction. I became reckless and had a brief stormy affair, which was the straw that broke the camel's back. My husband, who had delivered the lecture initiating our independent lives, now turned around one hundred and eighty degrees and became a possessive, patriarchal man, desperate to control his wife. A voice inside me kept whispering, *get out*. But I ignored it and kept playing a destructive game of deceit and hurt that grew out of a deep sense of having been betrayed.

Within a year of our stay in Chicago, it was obvious to both of us that the foundation of our marriage had collapsed. We were thinking of returning to India after the six years of our stay abroad. A flickering hope that India might cement our broken relationship motivated me to prepare for the trip back.

Ron came to see us off and talked to both of us individually, pleading with us to keep the marriage alive. He said that on some level he felt guilty, although he wasn't sure why. But neither Ron's nor anyone else's appeals managed to salvage our marriage. After seven years of life together, we filed for divorce in India.

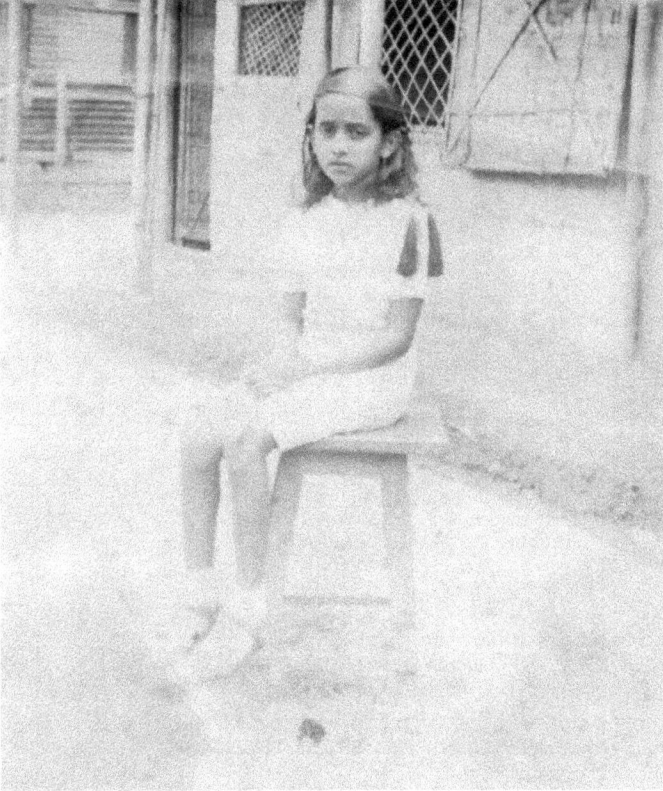

1943
The earliest picture of me, age 7,
visiting the military barracks where my uncle worked

1956
At age 20

1966
In my office at the Anthropological Survey of India
in Shillong, Assam

1967
During fieldwork in a village in West Bengal

1975
On the banks of the Limmat River in Zurich, Switzerland

1977
Traveling in Europe in a VW camper

1979
In a wedding sari of red silk woven with gold thread

1979
With Carl and the priest at our wedding ritual,
in front of fire as our witness

1980
Backpacking in the Alps

1984
My father tending his rose bush

1985
Back in America, in my garden in Wrentham, Massachusetts

1996
With Carl on the Atlantic Coast of New England

My Home

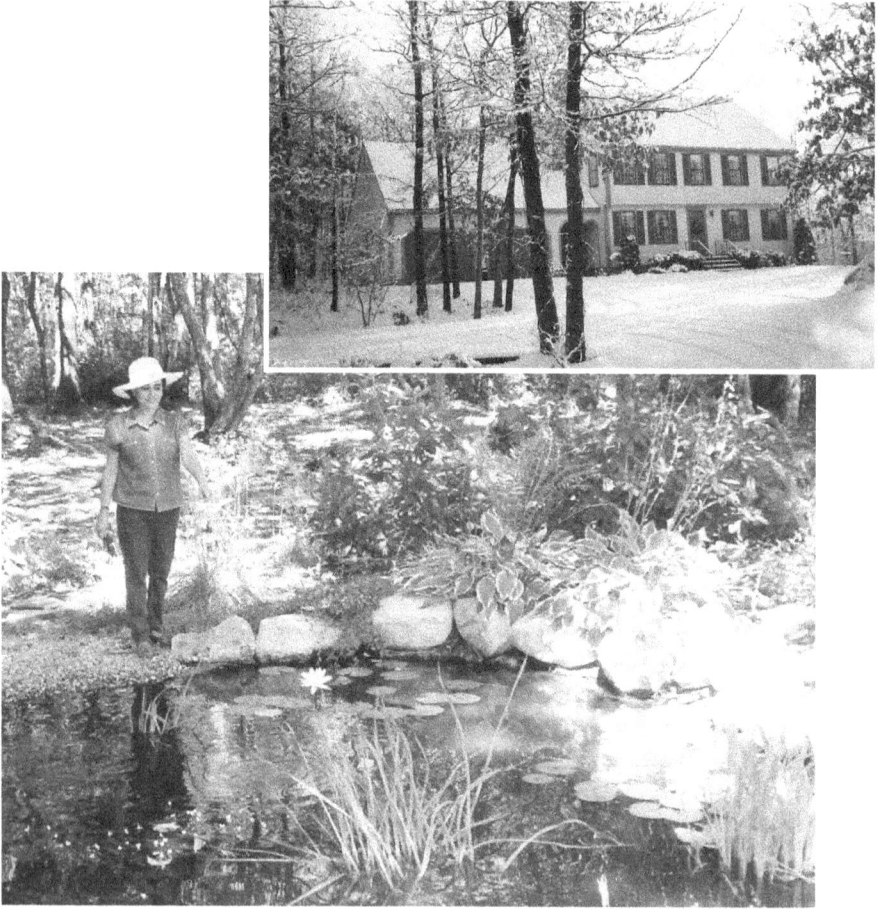

Our home and the water garden I created

THE FULL MOON ON THE MEDITERRANEAN

On the way to India Samir and I stopped in Europe for a couple of months. Five years before, when we were traveling the other way toward America, we had promised ourselves that we would explore Europe on our way home. The situation was not what we had anticipated. But the beauty and fascinating history of Europe made us forget our problems for a while, although the harmony did not last long. The pleasure of seeing new places soon dwindled, and it was clear that, at least for me, life alone would be more desirable than life together with someone who had become a stranger. I kept asking myself how I could lose such a strong attraction to a man whose manners, intelligence, words, and breadth of knowledge had swept me off my feet. Now I began to wonder if it had been love or desperation to find someone who would rescue me from my mother's control. As I pondered this, I recalled several incidences, which ought to have forewarned me.

When we first met, we began to exchange love letters that we had written the night before. One day, Samir praised me for my beautiful writing but added, "You've made one spelling mistake, however. I want you to write that word correctly a hundred times on this paper." I was astounded by this unexpected demand, and that evening, as I began to write the word on the paper he gave me, I had to suppress my tears. I not only choked back my tears but also any suspicion that was trying to surface.

Another incident took place right after our wedding. The day I finished the practical part of my master's exam, my new husband took me out to a restaurant to celebrate. He was pleased that I was now free to enjoy our marriage. After a drink, he said, "I've waited for you to finish your exam before I tell you something very important." He told me that he was in love with a coworker, a woman who was visiting from an Eastern European country. When he mentioned her name, I recognized it, because he had mentioned it a few times before. Watching my expression, he added, "Of course I love you more, and because of that I don't want to hide anything from you."

I was so shocked, I couldn't believe what I had heard. I sat speechless, in a daze. He waited a few more minutes before laughing aloud. "How could you believe this? You're really naïve." He grabbed my hand and kissed it. I was relieved and, again, did not allow myself to wonder why a newly married husband would joke about something so serious and watch his wife suffer even for a minute?

Then, years after the divorce, I heard from one of his aunts that, in response to her question as to why he had picked me out of many more sophisticated women around him, he apparently replied, "Manisha is made of soft clay; I can shape her as I wish." By that time, luckily, I was beyond his experiments.

Thus throughout our travels, I kept rehashing our lives before and after the wedding, and the new light of comprehension began to illuminate the dark corners of my ignorance. I could only blame my need to trust no matter what. I had ignored all the blatant hints that had looked me in the face. Seeing all of this, the shame of my own weakness was too much to bear. The only solution seemed another escape. I loved Europe, although every place we went, it failed to capture my full attention because of my preoccupation with my problems—the self-deprecating regrets and agony. I was sorry that I could not do full justice to such masterpieces as the cathedral at Chartres, the Sistine Chapel in the Vatican, the marvels of Michelangelo's art. I promised myself that some day I would return to appreciate the beauty of such creations. I loved the southern part of France. The small villages in the laps of hills and the Mediterranean coast invited me like a benevolent relative.

We were staying in a small and beautiful village on the edge of the hills facing the Mediterranean. One evening I took a walk alone along the deserted beach. An enchanting full moon on the horizon just above the blue-green water of the Mediterranean followed me. After a while, I sat on the sand, letting the gentle waves of lukewarm water caress my bare feet. A sense of warmth and peace enveloped me. The moon splintered into a thousand pieces and danced on the ripples of water. I recalled suddenly the quivering reflection of the goddess Durga in a pot of water. A similar feeling of something profound and sacred touched me again. I regained myself, feeling as I used to when I was alone in my little room as a teenager. The familiarity of the feeling wrapped me warmly like an old shawl. I sat there a long time and finally went back to the hotel. Now I was prepared to face my life and whatever awaited me. Two days later we reached Marseilles and boarded an Italian ship for Bombay.

Our families were happy to see us after six long years. Their love and affection kept us protected from any worry. The troubled reality of our marriage receded into the background. For a while we succeeded in seeing ourselves through the eyes of others as a happy and fortunate couple, just returned after successful years abroad. I breathed in the familiar atmosphere of my family

The location, however, had changed completely. After Father's retirement two years before, my parents had moved to Calcutta and built a small two-story house, much smaller than our house in Digboi had been. Everything was new to me. It was hard to retrieve my adolescent memories in this new space. It was like landing in a new country with old memories. But my family was happy to welcome us as they prepared for my older brother's impending marriage ceremony. Scores of relatives were coming and going, and the tempo of the wedding took over all our attention. I noticed that being separated from my husband—who was with his family most of the time—made it easier for me.

Gradually our problems became known to everyone. After the initial shock came questions, followed by judgments. Everyone was willing to give advice or air their opinions. For a whole year we tried in vain to keep the marriage together. Samir went back to a Canadian university to teach and to finish his degree, which he failed to do, although he kept this "little" bit of information hidden from his family and friends. I found out about it through a friend at the same campus in Canada where Samir was trying to finish his degree. The extent to which I had projected an adorable brilliant man onto him and his cultivated persona became clear. I could only blame the folly of youth and the naïveté of the act of "falling in love." However, I could not shake off the realization that I myself needed a lot more psychological exploration to understand my own psyche.

I tried desperately to avoid the questions and queries of relatives and neighbors and concentrated on finding a job. First of all, I needed to be financially independent. Within a month, I was offered a research position at the Anthropological Survey of India under the auspices of the government of India.

IN THE KHASI HILLS

Our marriage lingered like a terminal patient who survives longer than predicted by the doctors. Even the relatives and neighbors left me alone and stopped dispensing unsolicited advice.

At the Anthropological Survey I was appointed to write a monograph on the caste system in rural West Bengal, based on reams of data collected by a researcher who lacked confidence in writing. I invited Mr. Mukherjee, the researcher, to explain some of his data, and I suggested to my boss, Dr. Moni Nag, that it be a joint project. Mr. Mukherjee was grateful that I did not simply take over the material he had so painstakingly collected.

Our collaboration got off to a good start, but my other colleagues seemed determined to undermine my efforts from the beginning. Even though I had never worked for the government, I had heard many tales about the work situation in these offices. Several male colleagues came forward to introduce themselves and sat in my office over cups of tea, trying to find out about my personal life. In their eyes, I had been selected for the position only because I had an American degree. One man in particular spoke his mind clearly.

"You're young and new in this job. Obviously, you're not versed in the tradition of a government organization. It won't help if you work your ass off. You won't be promoted before the senior colleagues just because you have a foreign degree. The juniors and newcomers have to behave as we the old-timers advise them." He smiled maliciously before leaving.

I knew Indian society well enough to expect some of this behavior. I had been offered a well-paying job in competition with older male applicants because of my academic qualifications, even though I was only twenty-eight years old at the time. Men who had large families to support would naturally be upset. But nonetheless their behavior was not all that reasonable.

One of the pastimes in many such work places was to spread juicy gossip about single women, and within a couple of months, juicy gossip began to spread about me. Everyone wondered if I was married or not. If married, where was my husband and why didn't I wear vermilion on the parting of my hair—the sign of marriage for a Bengali Hindu woman? Perhaps one reason I was suspect from the beginning was because I did not go to the cafeteria for tea and snacks and to join others in gossip three times a day. I brought my lunch from home and had my tea in my office with whoever cared to join me. My colleagues saw this behavior as nothing but a snobbish gesture. One of my female colleagues, who became a good friend, used to report to me what she heard in the cafeteria. I told her to tell the gossipmongers to come to me and ask directly what they wanted to know. No one ever took me up on that offer. Eventually gossip subsides if one ignores it.

More disturbing for me was the hostile atmosphere which was definitely not conducive to serious work. I was looking for a way out of the situation and an opportunity presented itself. I had finished writing the monograph, and I was called for an interview for a higher position, which I got.

I knew that we had a branch office in Shillong, the second largest city of Assam, which was located in the Khasi Hills at an altitude of six thousand feet. My family had gone there a couple of times on our way to Father's ancestral village, and I remembered its cool air and natural beauty. I approached the director with my appeal to be transferred to Shillong. I wanted to take a break from Calcutta, from all the questions that well-meaning friends and relatives kept asking about my marriage and future. I had no answers for them, since they would not understand that a respite from my marriage was exactly what I needed. Luck was in my favor. I got permission to move to the

Shillong office, which was small with less than a dozen employees, as the second highest administrator and research scholar.

As soon as I landed in Shillong, I loved it. I got a small apartment with a piece of land in front and domestic help—an elderly man from Bihar named Ram, who could cook a little and was willing to help me with the garden and chop firewood for my fireplace in the winter months. I was assigned an office with a view of the pine-clad mountain slopes. Under my desk, I warmed my stocking feet on a charcoal brazier. I liked the friendly atmosphere of the small office and concentrated on my work immediately. I had always wanted to work among the hill tribes of Assam and, being a government officer, I now had the opportunity to do so. In this position, I had the benefit of authority and the help I needed, including a jeep, a driver, and an assistant. I began to plan my field research.

In the evening when I locked up my office and walked back to my little apartment, I had enough daylight to work in the garden. Ram helped with the heavy work, hoeing or uprooting a tree stump. Later, I would light a fire and sit near the fireplace and feel very cozy with a cup of tea. Ram managed to learn to prepare a few dishes for my dinner. By the time I went to bed each night, I thanked the gods for such fortune. I began to feel good about my life and work, and for the first time in many months I saw the possibility of being content with my life.

There were three of us officers, one my superior and the other my subordinate. The gentleman under me—Mr. Gupta—also had a master's degree and was competent. He often came to my office for signatures or to discuss issues and decisions, and I often asked him to join me for a cup of tea. We exchanged pleasantries, and he gave me tips about where to shop and how to find good poultry or fresh fish. I knew that in government offices ranks determine the code of conduct, which I did not like and obviously did not bother to follow in being more democratic in my behavior with my colleague.

One evening I stayed late in my office finishing a book. I was so engrossed that I did not notice the time. Mr. Gupta came in without a knock and closed the book, which was on the desk, saying, "All work and no play will ruin your health." Astounded I looked up. I never liked anyone coming into my office without knocking, and I myself try not to do that to others.

Without noticing my expression, he said, "There is a good Bengali film showing at the downtown cinema. I've bought two tickets. I'm going to take you to the movies tonight." He began putting my books and papers in a pile. I pointed at the chair on the other side of my desk and asked him to sit.

"You shouldn't have bought tickets for a movie without asking me first if I'm available." I tried my best to control my annoyance but added, "Or have you presumed that you can decide for me how I should spend my time? I don't recall giving you such a message. I'm going to spend some time in the office and finish this book. I hope you'll find someone to join you for the movie." I picked up the book and opened it.

Now it was Mr. Gupta's turn to be astounded. He stared at me for several seconds, then spoke. "If you work so hard, you may get sick. You're alone here in this town away from your family. As a Bengali gentleman and colleague, it's my duty to look after you. You'll feel a lot better if you get out of here and breathe some fresh air."

"Obviously, you haven't heard what I've said. Let me decide what's good for me. If you don't mind, I have work to do. So long." This time I didn't try to hide my irritation. He pushed his chair back with a loud noise, got up, nostrils flaring, and walked out.

Then began his rebellion. Whenever I needed to talk to Mr. Gupta about anything official, he refused to see me on various pretexts. I decided to wait and let things cool off.

One Sunday a couple of weeks later, I was harvesting the first lettuce of my garden while Ram held the basket for me. He seemed a bit uneasy. I asked if everything was all right with his family.

"My family is fine, madam. But, I have to tell you something. Gupta sahib from your office came yesterday and asked me many questions about you—Who comes to visit you? Who are your friends? Things like that. He even offered me money for such information. Memsahib, he is not a good man. Please be careful." He looked really worried. I thanked him for his honesty and tried to hide my concern. The next day I went to our boss and told him the whole story. He listened to me quietly as he doodled on the blotting paper of his desk.

"You see, in this small office, only three of us are officers, responsible for the whole operation." He paused, still looking at the blotting paper and still doodling. "If two out of three have problems, it is not good for running the office. I suggest you call him and make up by asking his forgiveness." He looked up for the first time and a faint smirk turned his lips a little. "He is a man. Most possibly, you've hurt his ego without realizing it. After all, he wanted to protect you . . ." I did not wait to let him finish.

"If a man's self-respect is so brittle, what about his manners toward a superior, no matter whether she is a woman? I have been courteous to him all along. Does that give him the right to treat me with such familiarity and ownership? Besides, how do you justify his using my servant to spy on me?" I said, without even trying to hide my irritation.

"You've been abroad for several years. Perhaps you've forgotten the social system in this country. Even if you are his superior, you are a woman and a gentleman is obliged to take care of a woman. If you allow that a bit, everything will return to normal." He pulled his hefty structure out of the chair, indicating the end of our meeting.

Despite my mounting surprise, I still tried. "Do you think you could give him a warning not to go to my home and talk to my servant behind my back? If this continues, I shall have to inform the director in Calcutta." This last statement got his attention.

"I'll see what can be done."

I came back to my office, closed the door, and sat for a long time. Looking at the peaceful pines outside my window, I asked myself, "Am I really a misfit in my own country?" Then I consoled myself by thinking that in a month I was to go into the field, and I would be away from all this. Thank goodness.

Although I never got a response in the affirmative to my letter to the head office in Calcutta stating that I wanted to go to the field alone, I presumed my request had been accepted. About a fortnight before my departure, I received a memo from the Calcutta office with some instructions about the trip that shocked me. It was addressed jointly to Mr. Gupta and me, so I asked the bearer to call Mr. Gupta to my office. He took ten minutes before arriving at my door, looking like a villain from a Bombay movie with his open leather jacket and defiant stance. I hardly recognized his new style.

"If you've something to say, be quick. I've got many things to do before going to the field." He stood with legs stretched and eyes on the ceiling.

"I called you in to tell you that you are not going into the field with me. You must know that you need my permission to do so. That's all. I just wanted to remind you of the rules." He shrugged his leathered shoulders and walked out without a word.

I had little time to waste. After I talked to our boss briefly, I telephoned the Calcutta office and told the director everything. I tried to get across that having Mr. Gupta as a partner in research when I was alone in the remote countryside would be unsafe. "I'm afraid he is not behaving rationally. You're not in a position to guarantee my safety from Calcutta," I ended my plea.

"All right," the director said, "I'm sending another memo immediately, asking him not to join you. Why hasn't someone already let me know that the situation had gone this far? I'm awfully sorry. Please be prepared to go into the field alone," he said.

"I did send you a letter a couple of weeks back explaining the situation and asking your permission to go alone. It appears you haven't received that letter," I said.

"I never received any letter. Anyway, you don't need to worry about it any more. Good luck!" he ended the conversation. I could not shake off a nagging feeling that perhaps Mr. Gupta had something to do with the misplaced letter.

A week before I was to leave for the field, my boss informed me that Professor Bose was coming to Shillong to attend a meeting with a minister in the state government. He relayed the message that if I cooked him a meal with my own hands, Professor Bose might consider finding a couple of hours to have dinner with me. I was delighted by this unexpected honor. I couldn't believe that he even remembered me from my university days some eight years back. I found out later that he had heard about my problem with Mr. Gupta from the director in the Calcutta office and decided to meet with me.

I cooked all day and was very proud that Professor Bose had volunteered to be my guest. I invited my boss and his wife also, but they had another engagement. After dinner we sat down with maps of the region, which Professor Bose knew like the palm of his hand. He drew lines in red pencil over dry riverbeds to show me which could serve as roads and which could not. He gave me the names of villagers who could be of help, including a local priest whose mother would be happy to put me up for the first few weeks. He also gave me useful tips on many things. Just before leaving, he mentioned Mr. Gupta.

"I don't think he'll bother you again. The director showed me the letter he wrote to him. I'm sorry all of this has happened to you." He paused and added, "By the way, don't forget to take a few paperback novels, a bottle of aspirin, and a short-wave radio with you into the field. And don't drink anything but tea." I took the dust of his feet and touched my head in respect. He put his palm on my head in a gesture of blessing and said, "No matter how tired you may feel, don't neglect to write your day's notes before going to bed every night. The Khasis are good people—you'll like them. Be careful." I was deeply touched by this caring warmth.

IN THE FIELD

One foggy morning I climbed into the jeep, the trusty Nepalese driver Bahadur on my left, my Khasi interpreter Tom on my right, and a cook in the back, with enough provisions for six months, along with other necessities. I was as excited as a teenager going for a first rendezvous with her beloved. The prospect was thrilling, yet not without unforeseen perils. But my zeal never wavered, even after such hardships as five- to ten-mile walks along rough terrain or bumpy jeep rides on dry riverbeds. Despite monumental exhaustion every evening, I typed up my notes, collapsed on the canvas bed, and fell sound asleep. I often had nothing but coarse rice and a piece of wild ginger for meals. Still, for me, here was an enchanting world waiting to be explored.

Clusters of tin-roofed houses huddled together in the valleys, interrupted by waves of blue-green hills. We saw Khasi women like dots walking slowly up the hills, going to their fields and gardens or to the next village on the other side of a hill. The interpreter told me a bit about the social system. The Khasis were one of the few matrilineal tribes left in the world. Their property was handed down through the female line, and the youngest daughter stayed in her parents' home with her husband and family looking after the property.

Barely five feet tall, these women were bent by the weight of conical bamboo baskets on their backs tied by belts around their foreheads. Along with other things, they carried their babies in these baskets or transported an occasional old and invalid in-law to a relative in the next village. Women worked hard to take care of the property they owned. They used a slash and burn technique for farming, sowing, hoeing, and harvesting their crops all by themselves during the day and coming home at dusk to prepare the evening meal for their family. Sometimes their husbands helped them in the fields with heavy work, but as a rule the men liked to sit around. They lacked the motivation to work on their wives' properties.

I was interested in the fact that the Khasi women were already liberated, in the sense that they did not mind doing the hard work—usually done by men in other societies—because it secured their property and the well-being of their families. Not surprisingly, the men seemed more discontented. They sat around in tea shops talking politics and drinking home-brewed rice wine.

I had planned to study the political unrest between the Nepalese and the Khasis, the latter being exploited by the former, who were technologically more advanced and politically more astute. But I was drawn to other things, the so-called soft data about the Khasis—the captivating beauty of their land, the strength and resilience of their women, the frustration and despondence of the men. I recorded these feelings and observations in a journal that I kept alongside my scientific notes. It was a brief glimpse into what real anthropology was about, at least for me. Years later that journal formed part of a book called *The Reckoning Heart: An Anthropologist Looks at Her Worlds.*

My first round of fieldwork turned out to be more than an escape from the problems in the Shillong office; it opened the door again to my secret world of writing. Scenes, events, and people that I encountered in the field offered me treasures far more valuable than the scientific data I set out to gather.

When I got back to Shillong six months later, I found out that Mr. Gupta had come by the day before my return and offered a hefty amount of money to Ram to keep the front door of my dwelling un-locked at night. Despite the temptation, Ram could not bring himself to betray me. His voice heavy with concern, he told me, "Memsahib, you may like to report him to the police. He's a bad man. If he comes with a weapon, what will we do?" I did not want to show him my nervousness and pretended that nothing had happened.

"Thank you, Ram, for telling me this," I said. "I'll take care of it. He can't do anything." This time I was more afraid than angry. Had the man really gone mad? I remembered reading about stalkers in Amer-ican newspapers who would even go so far as to kill their victims. Would an educated young man from a middle-class Bengali family do that? I had no way of knowing. The enthusiasm that I brought back from the field began to disappear rapidly. I tossed and turned all though the night and, just before falling asleep, reached a decision.

The next morning I went to the post office to pick up my mail, which had been held for me while I was gone. The man at the counter told me that Mr. Gupta had collected all my mail. He showed me a typed letter, forged in my name, authorizing him to do so. I was stunned. I realized that this was his revenge for excluding him from the field trip and that perhaps he would not rest until he drove me out of my mind.

My boss showed little concern. His tone was more accusatory than sympathetic. I had no choice but to write to the Calcutta office again, this time for a transfer. Already informed of the situation, the director believed me when I wrote to him and agreed to give me permission for a transfer provided that I organized the field data and wrote a monograph within three months. He also added that the future of my job would be uncertain. I knew that a central government position could not be terminated without extremely convincing reasons. Per-haps the director was at his wit's end about how to protect a woman who did not behave like all the other single women. He also asked me not to let anyone in the Shillong office know about my transfer.

Within a week, I told my landlord that I had to leave for a while and took off with a suitcase. I gave Ram three months' salary as sev-erance pay and all my kitchen things, and I gave Bahadur, the driver, all the firewood. Bahadur took me to the bus station in the same jeep we had driven together into the Khasi Hills. It was not just a vehicle—it had been part of our life in the field.

When we reached the bus station, Bahadur, a man of few words, took the suitcase down and looked at me. "Memsahib, if you had told me your troubles, I would have finished him off with this." He touched the scabbard dagger hanging from his waist. Anger narrowed his small eyes. I took out a hundred rupee bill, quite a sum at the time, and offered it to him.

"Take it for your children." I got on the commuter bus and hid my tears from the driver. All the way to the airport, I felt sad for my little house, my garden, and people like Ram and Bahadur. I had received respect and love from two men who had nothing in common with me. As I thought of the sequence of events, I had to smile at the irony of it all. I'd come to Shillong to avoid the petty politics in the Calcutta office and find some peace and quiet in this beautiful hill resort. Yet, within a year, I was compelled to flee this place and return to the same big city and big office, where the employees behave in small petty ways. I had to ask myself, was it only me, or was it impossible for a single woman in India to work with dignity in a mostly male environment?

An embellished version of my problems with Mr. Gupta had traveled back to the Calcutta office before I arrived there. It offered perfect material for juicy gossip for months to come. The debate in the cafeteria was: Had I ordered him to my bedroom, or had he seduced me first? One version even spoke about how poor Mr. Gupta had had to escape my clutches in order to save his job and his self-respect. As his boss, I could do anything I wanted with him. I tried to close my ears and concentrate on writing the monograph.

I told the irate female colleague who reported this to me that I had no intention of dignifying such fabricated stories by any kind of response. "Some day I shall write about this, so that the harassment of a single woman is recorded in our social history. A woman in India breaks the cardinal rule of life when she leaves the protection of a husband, no matter for what reason. *She* is the culprit. It's a real shame that in a country where such great men and reformers as Gandhi, Tagore, and Nehru worked all their lives to bring them dignity and respect, women cannot live and work safely." I walked away quickly lest she see my face. I was ashamed to show my tears of frustration, even to another woman.

NEW RESEARCH

By now it was clear to me that for a single young woman to survive in the work world in India, she would need other kinds of protection. Economic independence was not enough. Tarashish Mukherjee, the man whom I had helped earlier in my job by organizing and writing a monograph based on his research data, was grateful and offered me any help I might need in return.

"If you ever want to do research in a village, you are welcome to stay with my family," he said. A man of totally different character than Mr. Gupta, he was always a perfect gentleman. I had already sent in a letter of resignation and had come to the conclusion that it might be better to conduct my own research with the money I had saved this past year. I took Tarashish up on his kind offer and set off for Tamluk, a town sixty miles west of Calcutta, surrounded by rural areas. He accompanied me and introduced me to his parents.

The Mukherjees lived in a big, old two-story brick house. Moss-covered stones lined the walk leading to the front entrance and the verandah with its high columns. A circle of coconut palms and mango trees around the house protected it from the sun and the outside world. A faint memory of my ancestral home in East Bengal floated back to me. Mr. Mukherjee Sr. welcomed me warmly. "Any friend and colleague of my son is my child as well. Consider this your home. From today you are part of our family." Inside and upstairs, Mrs. Mukherjee immediately made me feel comfortable. She showered me with affection like a mother and always prepared my favorite dishes. We became very close.

Staying with the Mukherjees—an established and wealthy family of the town—made my introduction flawless, and no one dared ask any personal questions. I was free to wander around and meet people of both genders and all classes for the purpose of my research. I realized that in India what is questionable in one context could be acceptable in another. As long as I was part of a family, I was protected from gossip and questions.

Fortunately for me, the people of Tamluk were familiar with anthropological research. Among others, the anthropologist Dr. Ralph W. Nicholas of the University of Chicago had spent time in the area researching Bengali kinship. In fact, the man who assisted him was also willing to help me. Every morning my assistant and I went out with umbrellas over our heads and notebooks in our hands, negotiating several miles through dry paddy fields to visit and talk with people in the surrounding villages. By noon, the scorching sun drove us back. After a refreshing bath in cool water drawn from a deep well and lunch, I took a nap lying next to Mrs. Mukherjee (whom I called Mashima, "aunt") in her big bed. After a couple hours' rest I went up to the roof terrace, where I could touch the fronds of coconut trees. There I was served tea and puffed rice with date sugar—my favorite snack. I sat with whoever wished to join me and talked until the sun went down behind the big pond in the back of the house.

I spent nearly six months in Tamluk and gathered pages of data. The cool and dry season was nearly over. The scorching sun now felt oppressive even in the morning. Working outdoors became impossible. I awoke before the sunrise and went up to the roof terrace and walked barefoot on the cool moss-covered terrace. I thought about my research and noticed how the original plan had shifted focus from the caste system to the roles of women within an extended family. Women seemed eager to share their thoughts and feelings with an outsider who understood their language. They poured out their hopes, pleasures, frustrations, and disappointments. Many women in their advanced years craved spiritual fulfillment, whereas others did not. They remained steeped in the mundane details of their families and created problems for others and themselves. I still had no idea how I was going to use all this information.

One morning I packed my reams of field notes in my suitcase and said good-bye to the Mukherjees. I had no language to thank them for their hospitality and unconditional affection for a stranger.

Back in Calcutta, I began to look for a job again. My savings were nearly depleted. Hoping that my old professors might be favorable, I applied for a lecturer's position at Calcutta University. Acknowledging my qualifications, they told me to come back ten years later. At age thirty-one I was considered too inexperienced! I also applied to the department of sociology at Jadavpur University, which had been founded much more recently. Age was not a problem here, but a few young professors raised serious questions about my eligibility because of rumors about my personal life. As I left the campus, the reality of the situation hit me hard. I wasn't sure how long I could survive this kind of antagonism.

In the meantime, Samir had returned from Canada. I went to Delhi to meet him. We planned to spend a holiday in Kashmir, unconsciously hoping for some miraculous rebirth of our love for each other. Even the heavenly beauty of Kashmir failed to prevent the final demise of our marriage. We agreed that there was no point in dragging this on any longer. After returning, we met with an attorney to begin the process of legal separation. The reactions among the members of both our families were open and blatant. The news hit my mother the hardest. Refusing to talk to me, she went to Samir and asked him for the details. I tried to explain things to my father and brother. Even though they tried to grasp the situation, they did not have the courage to go against Mother and show me any support.

Father finally said with a sigh, "If only you had waited five more years, the scandal would have not hit our family so hard. In a few years people might get used to the idea."

"But Baba, it's you who has always taught me to think independently. Surely you don't wish me to live in an unhappy marriage. The Hindu code bill allowing divorce was passed in 1956, and now it is 1967," I said desperately. I wanted to tell him that I did not want to bring so much sadness on my family. The same mother who had been so against my choice of a husband was now adamant that I stay with him.

<hr>

SEARCH FOR A JOB AND LIVING SPACE

"I hope you don't mind my saying this . . ." the bearer of a court notice addressed me as he handed over a large envelope with a government seal on it. I was about to open the envelope but stopped and looked up. The man continued, "Apparently you've been abroad and are highly educated—why are you doing this? It's a shame, please make up with your husband. The marriage of a daughter is the parents' dream that is realized with so much money, effort, and hope . . ." he trailed off. Stunned, I did my best to control myself from giving him a piece of my mind. Looking away, I opened the envelope and read the content—which was a date for the first hearing—signed it, and put the form back in the envelope before handing it back to him.

"Here, take it, and good-bye." Even the ordinary bearer of a letter now had the audacity to lecture me on my duties. It was always automatically assumed that I was at fault, because in a marriage, as a rule, it was the woman's responsibility to keep the marriage intact. Even some of our friends who were close to both of us began to take my husband's side and start rumors about me. Only my father and elder brother bothered to ask me what really had happened.

I tried very hard not to let public opinion dampen my spirits and kept busy with job hunting day and night. I was allowed to stay downstairs in my parents' home, paying a small rent until I found a job. What hit me hardest was not the gossip and scandals, but Mother's cold treatment. At night in bed I went over the situation again and again trying to understand why my inability to adjust to my husband was such a major crime and such a concern for everyone. Many of the novels I had read as a teenager from Mother's library dealt with the problem of a woman's inability to break away from an unhappy marriage because of the fear of society's punishment. Now I well understood the price a woman has to pay for the security, honor, and protection that her tradition offers.

I applied for a position as a student adviser at the Calcutta office of the US Educational Foundation of India. One of the qualifications specified a degree from an American university. I was offered the job without any inquiry about my marital status. I was relieved that now I had enough money to rent a place of my own. I found a small but clean apartment in a respectable neighborhood not far from my parents' home.

"Why don't you come back tomorrow with your husband so that you both can sign the lease with the advance deposit," the landlord said as I was leaving. I stopped in my tracks.

"I shall be staying here by myself. I'm prepared to sign the lease and pay the advance right now, if you like," I said.

"Oh, I'm so sorry. I made a mistake, I thought you were married. Please forgive me." He looked at his wife, who was standing by his side without having said a word so far.

"No, you haven't made a mistake," I said. "I'm married, at least for now. We have filed for divorce."

Now the landlord's wife stepped forward and looked at me from top to bottom and said to her husband, "I don't know what's got into you. Don't you remember—I gave my word to another couple yesterday?" Both her husband and I looked at her with surprise. I realized I had just lost the apartment to an imaginary couple. I had a hard time accepting that an educated working woman had no right to live alone in the fourth largest city of the world, just because she had no man by her side!

Meanwhile I encouraged my youngest sister Anu to leave her in-laws, come to Calcutta, and return to school. She had been married three years ago, before she finished college, and her husband had died suddenly. She was twenty-three years old and had two children. I couldn't imagine that her whole life would be over just because she had lost her husband. When I fought with her husband's family over this, some of my relatives were furious and accused me of trying to break all traditions and customs. One relative said, "You're trying to change this country into America, where no family values or morality exists." Traditionally, Hindu widows were expected to live under strict rules of conduct. They were, and still are, not expected to re-marry but to live with their in-laws and remain in their household as dependents or glorified servants.

Initially, Mother objected to this plan, but when she saw her two beautiful grandchildren, she acquiesced. She devoted herself to bringing up her grandchildren and trying to forget the tragedies of one daughter being widowed and the other divorced. In my case, forgetting was more difficult for her, since I was leaving a husband I had chosen myself. Also, I had failed to present her with any grandchildren during eight long years of marriage.

A friend told me about a retired army officer who owned a group of apartments, which he rented out only to single working men and women. I liked this stranger immediately and went to meet him with an application and a deposit. The rent was a bit high, but the security was good, he assured me. I arranged to move in the next day. I told

Mother the news and added that she no longer needed to be embarrassed on my account.

She was, of course, furious. "Where on earth will you be going? Now you have full liberty to behave as you please. What have I done in my past life to deserve this!" I knew that her angry laments camouflaged her real feelings of pain and the insult that her daughter wouldn't stay with her.

I liked my new place. One small bedroom overlooking a balcony, a tiny sitting area next to a kitchenette, and a bathroom were just enough for one person. Within a week, Father, Sundarkaka, and an aunt (their sister, who lived in another town) all came with boxes of sweets to see how I was. I was deeply moved. My father's side of the family never criticized me for what happened. They wished me well and said I should move on with my life. They had faith in my abilities and determination.

"Your aunt asked me to invite you to come and have lunch with us every Sunday or even on weekdays after work. We're on your way to work. Promise me you'll come!" Sundarkaka said before leaving. I smiled and agreed. I couldn't help noticing Father's drawn face showing his sadness that his daughter was not welcome in his own home. That night I cried in my bed, both in gratitude and sadness.

Soon my life fell into a routine. I spent most of my day at work, after taking long bus rides back and forth to the office. On my way back, I would pick up some vegetables and fish or eggs and prepare a simple meal and go to bed early with a book. I did keep my promise to my uncle and aunt and went to their place most Sundays for lunch. They were both extremely generous to me.

Since childhood I had been my uncle's favorite niece. This was the uncle who, during the war, had taken me to his construction sites in the jungle of Assam. His wife had showered her affection on me ever since I had met her. They lived in a two-room apartment but were always hospitable. My uncle, who had made a fortune during the war from his construction business, now lived hand to mouth. He had always been altruistic and had shared his fortune with whoever needed it. Along the way, his best friend and partner in business had cheated him out of all his fortune, but he never once criticized his friend or blamed his fate for being treated so badly.

During these lunches, we talked about old times. My uncle told his children about me, how brave I had been at age seven to accompany him to the jungle and how I had made friends with Mr. Stein, an American military officer. The children listened with rapt attention. I was taken back to that time and place when life was uncomplicated and full of dreams. For a short while I was able to forget the recent years of heartbreak and hardship. When we are young, I thought, we never imagine the price we will pay for a cherished adulthood.

One evening I awoke in the middle of the night. Someone was banging on the door. The clock on the bedside table read one a.m. Who would come at this hour! It must be bad news. I left my bed in a hurry and was about to open the lock when something stopped me. I asked, "Who is it?" A garbled male voice came though the closed door.

"Open the door. I want to spend the night with you. I know everything about you. I know who you are. Don't be coy, open the door. You'll see, we'll have a lot of fun. Do you know how many women are dying to have me?" More banging. Then he introduced himself, and I was shocked to hear the name of a renowned author whose books I had read and admired. Now I remembered that he was supposed to be living in one of these apartments. His wife had thrown him out because of excessive drinking and womanizing.

I went out on my balcony and yelled for the night guard several times. No one responded. The banging on the door continued. I gathered all my courage and spoke through the door, saying firmly, "Please go back to your apartment right now; otherwise I shall call the police." After a few more minutes, everything quieted down. I couldn't sleep the rest of the night. The humiliation, insult, anger, and frustration all mixed together and penetrated my skin like a thousand knives. *No single woman can survive in this city!* was my last thought before I fell asleep around dawn.

The next day, when I talked to the manger and wanted to know where the night guards had been, he averted his eyes before speaking. "I've heard what happened. People from other apartments have also heard. I shall investigate where the guards were. I'm sorry that this happened. Of course, we can't really take a drunk seriously. You know what they say about the drunk and the mad . . ."

"If you don't say anything, I will," I interrupted him. "You're asking me to ignore it as drunken gibberish? Since you're unable or unwilling to do anything, then just watch. Please call him. I'm sorry that I believed all your big words about the security here. One more thing, I'm giving a month's notice to terminate my lease. I don't feel safe staying here." I took a few deep breaths to control my anger. The manager left the office and came back after a few minutes with the famous man. He entered with his head down and didn't look up as he spoke.

"I ask your forgiveness. Please believe me, I don't remember anything I said or did last night. I must have had too much to drink. If you kindly accept my invitation to have a cup of tea with me, then I'll know that you've forgiven me," he said with his eyes averted.

"You may not be able to remember what you said or did last night, but you knew exactly what you were doing when you climbed up the stairs and walked to my door and banged on it for fifteen minutes, spouting obscenities," I said. I took a deep breath before continuing, "And now you've got the gall to invite me to tea as if nothing, nothing at all had happened. You talk about the deplorable injustice to women in your wonderful novels. How would you like your readers to know that you don't hesitate to humiliate and insult a woman just because she is alone?" I waited a few seconds. The famous author said nothing. I left the manager's office.

A FRIEND IN NEED

A month later, after several failed attempts to find another place, I agreed to move in with Bela, an old colleague and friend who had been by my side through all these struggles. Both she and her husband were kind people and did not mind sharing their small apartment with me as long as I needed to stay. They cleared a small storage space on the top floor of their apartment, which had a tiny toilet next to it. Before I moved in, I convinced them to take a modest amount of money for rent and food.

The room was barely eight by six feet, most of which was occupied by a single bed. The first evening, my friend's husband hammered a few nails on the brick walls to hang my mosquito net. I kept wondering where they had moved their boxes and trunks to make this room available. I smiled to myself remembering the transformation of another storage area seventeen years before in my parents' home in Digboi. The circumstances then, however, had been quite different. As I lay on yet another new bed under the mosquito net that night, I tried to examine the events of my life as calmly as I could.

In societies such as India, economic independence was not enough to empower women with dignity. Women must learn to walk a thin line not to usurp traditional values and expectations. I knew that had I behaved like a helpless victim and begged everyone for help, people would have been more sympathetic. I was being punished for my self-reliance and independent attitude. No one feels pity for a woman who not only leaves a husband but also dares to challenge the expected codes of behavior. In the eyes of a traditional society, such a woman does not need compassion and help.

In India, the ideal woman is expected to be gentle, obedient, and self-effacing. However, neither my mother nor grandmother fit that image. And I did have the good fortune to meet a woman like my friend, who, with her husband and many others, was not hesitant to help a woman who dared to go against traditional expectations. I knew that many of my relatives lacked the courage to flaunt tradition and come forward to help even if, secretly, they ached for me.

As I was about to fall asleep, a sound of *tik, tik, tik* cut through the threshold of consciousness. I put my hand outside the mosquito net and turned on the light switch. Defying the law of gravity, two plump geckos were scurrying around on the ceiling. I had always been slightly afraid and mostly disgusted with anything that looked like a lizard. But tonight, compared to all the other problems of my life, their proximity evoked no disgust or fear. Their presence made me aware of something simple yet significant: I was not alone.

RETURN TO AMERICA

Every morning I rode to work in an overcrowded bus, where I held on to an overhead handle. I clutched my handbag close to my chest in order to protect both the contents of the bag and my upper body from groping hands. The same feat was required on the return journeys. I scrubbed myself with sandalwood soap in the shower every evening after coming home to cleanse myself of the grime and fatigue of the day. After dinner, I wrote a few letters, read, and went to bed. The next day I faced the same struggle—heat and dust, Calcutta traffic, groping hands.

My social life was minimal. In addition to the students I advised at work, and apart from brief encounters with my friends downstairs and Sunday visits to my uncle's family, I saw hardly anyone. One day I decided to break the boredom of my routine and ventured out to visit Buddhadev and Pratibha Bose, the famous Bengali authors whom I had met in Chicago and to whom I had become close. In their living room, as always, were gathered several guests—mostly writers and poets, plus some foreigners. There I met the Chicago professor and Indologist Edward C. Dimock again. I had known him briefly while we were in Chicago. He was shocked to hear about my situation and advised me to return to the States, where I could do better than taking a crowded bus every day to an administrative job with little future.

I knew I could not stay in my friend's attic forever, living a life of seclusion, harboring anger and frustration against my family and society. But in order to go back to any American university, I not only needed enough money to travel but also adequate financial assistance for survival.

The next Sunday I sat at my portable typewriter—one of the few possessions I dragged around with me and my only constant companion which had witnessed all I'd been through for the last decade. The same instrument produced many academic papers and my occasional outpourings—a journal that I kept off and on during my fieldwork and in hard times. That Sunday I composed half a dozen applications for fellowships at various American universities. I also wrote to my old professors in Rochester and Chicago for letters of recommendation. It felt good to have started this process. Within a month I heard from four universities that were willing to offer me admission and fellowships for doctoral programs in anthropology.

I chose the University of California in San Diego because they offered the best financial support. I began to save as much as I could from my salary for the airfare. I was grateful to all my gods for the opportunity to escape my current life. However, I was not able to celebrate with unadulterated joy because I had a feeling that if I left now, it would be forever. The sadness of rejection from Mother and judgments from others still burned strongly inside me. It would be years before I would be able to overcome these feelings.

Six months passed before I had enough saved for a one-way fare to California. I took leave of my good friends and moved back to my parents' home for a week before my departure. Ma was against my going back to America. Baba was not happy about it, yet he understood that under the circumstances I could not stay in India. His judgment was tempered by the fact that I had been offered a fellowship for higher studies. My uncle and his wife supported me in the decision, possibly hoping that returning with a doctorate would be reason enough for the relatives to forgive me.

On the day of my departure, I went upstairs to say good bye to Mother. I took the dust of her feet and touched my head in the usual gesture of *pronam* and turned to go. She followed me to the staircase.

"Why must you go so far away? If you go this time, you may never see me again," she said and looked away. Her voice was thick with anger and grief, tears rolling down her face.

We began to walk down the stairs, with Mother several steps above me. The only source of daylight was through the front door below. The staircase was in shadow, but I was close enough to see her face. We could hear the children of the downstairs tenant playing hopscotch in the lane outside. But it felt as if we were removed from everything, the family upstairs and the noise of the world. We were trapped in this vertical space facing each other.

I wanted to respond and say many things, but I couldn't. At that moment it was not possible to tell her that one reason I was leaving had to do with her lack of support when I needed it most. Mother came down a few steps. We were barely a foot apart, yet neither of us crossed that small distance to embrace the other. I never had another chance to do so. Three years later, at age fifty-six, my mother died. She must have known somehow.

WELCOME TO CALIFORNIA

I wanted to go to the University of California partly to avoid the winters of the Northeast and Midwest. When I changed planes in San Francisco, the landscape began to transform from misty green to brown and purple. From the air, the dwarf shrubs hugging the canyons of dry hills looked pale purple. As we approached the airport in San Diego, the decorative palms reminded me of the tropics, nothing like the America I had known. I thought this environment would help me to leave behind the old life and memories of Rochester and Chicago. I was enchanted by the natural beauty of La Jolla, the neighborhood on the Pacific Coast where the San Diego campus was located. I also liked the fact that San Diego was only half an hour's drive from the Mexican border.

When I arrived in the airport I looked around for Mrs. Wallace, who was there to receive me. The Foreign Student Hospitality Organization of the university had found a family to be my host for the first week. I was grateful to have a bed where I could collapse after a twenty-two-hour flight from India. Mr. and Mrs. Wallace were wealthy Americans with a ranch-style home of ten rooms, a two-car garage, and a swimming pool. When I awoke next morning, I found Mrs. Wallace totally naked in the kitchen preparing breakfast. Mr. Wallace, however, was fully clothed in suit and tie, reading the newspaper and sipping coffee. Jennifer, the seven-year-old daughter, and her twelve-year-old brother John—also fully dressed—were playing with their cereal in cold milk. No one showed any sign of anything unusual happening around them!

"Good morning, everyone," I said averting my eyes from the kitchen.

"Good morning," Mr. Wallace lowered his paper and said. "Have you slept well? Welcome to California!" He went back to his paper. A few minutes later, everyone got up from the table and left the house for work and school.

I'd heard a lot about the difference between California and the rest of the country. But I had never expected to see proof the very first day of my arrival. In the late sixties California was going through a cultural and political revolution. Perhaps for women like Joyce Wallace getting rid of clothes symbolized opening up on all levels, keeping nothing covered. In my brief stay with her, I found out many secrets of her life, including her marital problems. The boundary between the public and the private realms seemed quite blurry.

The day before I was to move to my apartment, Joyce organized a pool party in my honor and invited a group of her friends. I wasn't sure if she had chosen the date intentionally to coincide with a time when Mr. Wallace was out of town. After she explained what a pool party was, I told her that I would like to have a swim in the morning rather than later with two dozen people. She and I went to the pool as soon as the sun was up—I in my one-piece suit, she in nothing, of course. After a few laps, we both stretched out on a couple of plastic deck chairs. She moved hers into the sun, and I moved mine to the shade.

"Don't look now; a pair of eyes is staring at us from behind the fence. This neighbor is always staring, as if he has never seen a woman swim before. One of these days, I might just invite him in to join us," Joyce said.

"This man may not have seen any woman swim naked before," I said smiling. Joyce shrugged her wet shoulders and got up to dive in again.

The guests began to arrive in the afternoon. Some were already in their swim trunks or suits. They also brought large plastic bottles of fruit juice and big wooden bowls of green salad and finger food. The men walked in with six-packs of beer and large bottles of wine. Joyce had already put out a spread of carrot and cucumber sticks with yogurt dip and other kinds of raw vegetables on poolside tables.

"Hello, there." A blond man with a dark tan came toward me. "I've always wanted to swim with a saried woman. Now is my chance. Come on; let's see how you swim in this long material. Or, maybe you're going to drop it before jumping in. Give me a warning, I want my camera ready." He laughed loudly at his own joke. Joyce appeared and rescued me, saying she needed me in the kitchen to help her make an Indian dish.

No one seemed interested in any conversation. By the end of the evening, they all moved to a carpeted room with dim lighting and lots of oversized pillows to "feel and touch and be open with one another." I sneaked out before anyone explained the game to me. Later, I peeked in and saw a lot of exposed flesh mingling and touching. I decided I had had enough of an introduction to the Southern Californian lifestyle. Thank goodness, I would be moving to my own apartment the next day.

Joyce had helped me find a studio apartment only a few minutes from the ocean. The rent was seventy-five dollars a month. Although small, the apartment provided a view of the Pacific through a glass wall on one side. There was a lime tree out front, and every morning it dropped a couple of limes on my doorstep. I began my day with a glass of warm water mixed with lime juice and honey. I was delighted to find a place so reasonably priced and so beautifully located. The only problem was the distance from the campus. I would have to have a car. I settled in and looked forward to my first class at the university. I was to be part of the first batch of ten students in a new department of anthropology with eight professors. I soon felt at home with the familiar university atmosphere. India, with all my problems there, seemed very far away.

WHITE DAISIES, RED ROSES, YELLOW WATER LILIES

"Here you are, an Indian woman—are you sure you can be objective?" an American man asked me. I was standing among a group of Asian and American students. The topic of conversation was American foreign policy in South Asia.

"Of course my opinions are from an Indian point of view. To judge American foreign policy in South Asia, or any other country for that matter, you need someone like yourself, an American, and someone else from there. Otherwise, we hear only the American president, the American press, the American point of view," I said to the group around me, but particularly to the man who had questioned my objectivity, and who had made a few trite remarks about Asian politics earlier. It was Saturday, and I was at a party for the international students being given by a retired American couple who had lived in different countries as diplomats for many years.

Usually I spent my Saturdays in the library catching up with my reading, and in the evening I might go to a foreign film on campus. One of the reasons I avoided big parties was the cigarette and marijuana smoke. I got a headache from them. I had been in La Jolla for over a year by now and had made only a few friends. One of them, a Brazilian student, had urged me to come along to this party.

"There'll be Latin music, and I can show you the steps of the rumba. Let's go. You study too much, everyone needs a break. Okay?" Orela insisted and drove us both to the party.

All graduate students worked hard the whole week and looked forward to the weekend for fun and relaxation. The weekend began with a TGIF party at the Institute of Oceanography, which was not far from the campus, and Saturday evenings were usually reserved for dating and partying until the early hours of the morning. Most students slept until noon on Sundays. On Mondays the routine began all over again.

Before the American man I had addressed could respond, another student with curly reddish hair pushed himself into our circle and began to argue with me. It was clear to everyone that he was talking simply for the sake of arguing. From his accent, I guessed he was from Europe, but I was not sure from which country. When I was not persuaded by his aggressive and irrelevant words, he changed his tune.

"Would you like another drink?" he asked with a smile, fixing his eyes on me.

"No, thanks. I'm about to leave. It's too crowded and smoky for me." I began to look around for Orela.

"I was thinking exactly the same thing. In these parties it's impossible to talk with anyone seriously. Moreover, there is hardly a chance to get close to a beautiful woman. Have you noticed the man/woman ratio? And now, if you leave, it'll fall even further," he said in mock sincerity.

The man not only talks too much, he also is a flatterer, I thought. "I have no desire to be part of your statistics. You're aggressive enough; you shouldn't have any trouble getting close to someone," I said and moved to the other side of the room, looking for Orela. He followed me.

"I'm glad to hear that you have such confidence in my ability. Thanks," he said happily.

When I failed to attract Orela's attention from my corner, he turned around and, like a street urchin, put two fingers inside his mouth and whistled loudly. His tactic worked. Orela turned and saw me, but she refused to leave so soon and urged me to stay one more hour. Reluctantly I agreed to wait and stepped outside for some fresh air. The western sky was red. I stood for a few minutes watching the sunset.

"Smart idea," the man spoke from behind me. "It's too noisy inside. I thought you were leaving." Again he had followed me.

"I wanted to. But my friend wants to stay longer," I said, folding my arms and shivering slightly from the cool evening air. He immediately took his sweater from around his neck and draped it around my shoulder.

"I'm Martin, from Switzerland." He put out his hand. I shook it as I introduced myself and tried to return the sweater saying that he must be cold, too. He said, "No, not really," and added, "I think I'll be leaving soon, I have to check on an experiment in the lab. I could drop you if you wish." Then, raising his right palm to his chest, he added with a smile, "And I promise I won't utter a word on American foreign policy."

"Are you sure? Thanks. I live on Prospect Street; it may be out of your way."

"Not at all. I like to rescue women who are deserted by their drivers and who may get headaches if they stay long in noisy and smoky parties." The way he said it, I couldn't help laughing. I went inside to tell my friend that I had gotten a ride.

"I'm sorry, the heater doesn't work in my car," he said as he started the engine of his Volkswagen Beetle.

"I'm fine, really. In October one has to expect cool evenings," I said as I took the seat next to him. The sky was still light, although the sun had set a while ago. A light fog began to gather on the ground; it was hard to see where the car was heading.

We exchanged only a few words. I found out that he had also been in the States one year and was studying for his doctorate in physics.

"I don't like this country—its politics and many things, but I love living close to the ocean. Being mountain people, we Swiss dream of oceans." His voice was softer than before.

"I was born in the hills also, on the northeastern border of India, close to Tibet and Burma," I said. We reached our destination. He opened the door on my side. I gave him back his sweater. I knew that the customary thing to do was to invite him in for tea or something. But I wasn't ready to do so. I shook his hand, thanking him for the ride and the sweater, and walked down the steps to my apartment. I heard him say, "It was my pleasure."

It was already nine, too late to do any serious work. I regretted having gone to the party; it had ruined the whole evening. On Sunday, my usual routine was to spend most of the day on housekeeping—shopping for the week, cooking for the week, cleaning, and doing laundry. It was also the day when I wrote letters home and took a long walk near the ocean. In the evening, I studied for Monday's classes.

The next Friday, I noticed that my car was slow to start. I ran into an Indian friend, an engineering student, in the campus cafeteria and asked for his advice. He was kind enough to ride with me to a garage he knew. The car needed new spark plugs. Grumbling about this extra expense, I thanked Prabhakar and promised to cook a meal for him. I got home late, took a shower, and was sitting down with a cup of tea when the telephone rang.

"A great jazz group is playing in San Diego tomorrow. You must love jazz. I managed to get two tickets. Please say yes." From the accent I had a vague idea who it might be. The voice added, "I am Martin."

"I do love jazz. But I shall go with you on condition that I pay for myself."

"Fine. I'll come to pick you up at six."

I sat down to finish my cold tea and wondered why this arrogant Swiss suddenly was interested in going to a jazz performance with me. More important, why had I agreed to go? I did not feel like searching for the answers, though.

On Saturday at ten to six Martin knocked on my door. He was wearing a lavender striped cotton shirt and on his shoulders the same brick-red sweater that he had lent me the week before, its sleeves tied in a knot at the front. He immediately turned to my glass wall and looked at the ocean.

"What a wonderful view you have! I'm jealous. My apartment right next to the landlord's garage overlooks his parked car. You're really fortunate." Then looking around the room, "You've decorated beautifully. Are these from India?" He picked up a couple of bronze horses from the bookshelf.

"Thanks. Yes, all my friends envy me for the location. Would you like something? Tea? Fruit juice?"

"Thanks, but we really should go. I'm sure there'll be a big crowd. We may not get seats if we're late."

I picked up my handbag and a shawl and closed the front door after us. When I asked him about the price of the ticket, he smiled and said, "A friend got two tickets for free. I have no idea what the price is."

"Sounds like you're fortunate in your friends if not in your apartment."

"Yes, I depended on that luck before I dared to call you."

"Am I that scary?"

"Who knows? I've heard a lot of tales about Indian women . . . Besides, why shouldn't you be formidable? Your prime minister is such a strong and brave woman. By the way, your dress is beautiful. It is called a sari, right?" He looked at me briefly.

"Thanks for the compliment on both counts," I said.

That evening, the tunes and melodies of the saxophone, my favorite instrument, entered every pore of my skin and moved my soul to the core. I was in another world. The concert ended around ten. Martin asked if I wanted to have a cup of coffee. I declined, saying that if I had coffee this late I wouldn't be able to sleep. Inside the car, the atmosphere was heavy with the lingering feelings of the music. Neither he nor I seemed to feel any need to say anything about the performance, or about anything else for that matter. After awhile, I began to feel uncomfortable with the silence of a talkative man.

"You were a different man last Saturday. Now you're very serious," I said.

"Actually I was thinking of the concert. Such wonderful music, the Californian evening, and the company of an exotic woman—all that made me speechless, I suppose." We had just reached my place. "And here we are," he said, as if relieved that he could change the topic. Before getting out, I waited a few seconds.

"I don't have coffee, but I can offer you the best Indian tea," I said, partly to be polite and partly to return the favor of the gift of a free concert.

"You're right. Tea is the best idea you've offered so far." He smiled at me and followed me down the steps to my apartment.

Once inside, Martin led me gently to my bed and sat me there, saying that he was going to make the tea. Ordered to say and do nothing, I watched him with surprise—how easily he found his way around my kitchen. "I'll take care of things and serve you the most delicious cup of tea you've ever tasted. Be comfortable, put your legs up, and watch." He began to open drawers and cupboards looking for utensils.

I didn't know how to react. No man—Indian or foreign—had ever served me this way before. This simple gesture of caring hospitality as if I were in his little place—not the other way around—touched me deeply.

In ten minutes, he brought a tray with tea things and placed it on my bedside table, moved the table between the bed and the chair, and sat on the chair, the only one I had. He poured two cups of tea from the teapot and served one to me after asking whether I wanted milk and sugar.

"Now tell me if my tea is to your liking."

"It's just right. Thanks." We chatted about different things—our families and countries. Around midnight, he got up from the chair, arranged the empty teapot and cups on the tray, and took it all back to the kitchen counter.

"I'm leaving the dishes for you to do tomorrow. Now you must go to bed, you look really sleepy." He put his sweater on and moved toward the door. I got up from the bed and walked to the door with him.

"Thanks for a wonderful concert," I said.

"Thanks for the tea. I'll see you around," he said. I gave him my hand to shake; he came forward and left a tiny kiss on my forehead.

That night I slept badly. It must be the tea, I thought. I awoke late on Sunday and opened the door to look for the limes on the step. I saw a small piece of paper folded and pierced with the stalk of a single daisy. A sudden joy enveloped me. I picked it up, came inside, and put the flower in a small glass of water. I had no idea then that this simple white flower was going to usher in the most complex chapter of my life. I opened the folded paper to find only a telephone number on it.

After breakfast I went to the ocean to examine my feelings. I couldn't ignore the truth that kept encircling me, yet I couldn't find any answers as to why this arrogant young man was slowly but surely making a link to my soul. In my lonely life of the previous five years, I had had a few male friends with whom I had come close to romantic involvement, but no one had been able to pique my curiosity in such a short time. Was it because of his European manners, his full attention when I was with him? I had noticed how easily he could break through barriers and step close to a stranger. I concluded that in a demanding and hard student life it's difficult to ignore the possibility of such tender friendship. The sun was high in the sky, showering a thousand pieces of silver on the ripples of the ocean water, dazzling my eyes. I turned back. When I got home, I picked up the small piece of paper and dialed the number. It rang a long time before he picked up.

"Hello? I thought you were upset with me. I waited for your call all morning, then went out to buy some groceries. The phone rang before I could open the door and in my rush I dropped the grocery bag, breaking the eggs. Before you say anything, would you have dinner with me? I'm a good cook. Do you eat everything?" Martin finally stopped talking.

"Yes, I eat everything except snakes and people. May I bring anything? When do you want me to come?"

"Come now, bring nothing. My address is 16 La Jolla Shore Drive. Can you find it?"

"I can't make it before late afternoon. I'll see you then."

It was easy to locate the street on the map. It would take twelve or fifteen minutes by car to get to his place. I needed to finish some reading before I went out to dinner on a Sunday evening, something I'd never done before.

I sat at my desk with a book but was unable to keep my eyes on it. The ocean through the glass wall seemed far away, as was my concentration. I had a desire to move to another world where a different set of rules, or no rules, operated. I was wrapped in a net of loose knots, and I failed to gather my scattered mind into a neat bundle of duty.

No definite thought was around, just a vague sense of pleasure and inevitability that floated in and out of my consciousness. I did not want to think about it clearly.

With a dozen eggs and four limes from my tree, I knocked on Martin's door at six in the evening. Martin welcomed me with two kisses on each cheek and accepted my gifts with a laugh. "Very thoughtful of you," he said as he led me inside his apartment, which was indeed smaller than mine.

A bed covered with a light blue linen cloth occupied most of his room, which had only one window overlooking the landlord's driveway. Delicious smells of cooking came from a tiny kitchenette in one corner; beyond that was the bathroom. In the middle of the room, next to the bed, was a table covered with a white tablecloth, which had two place settings. In the middle of the table, three fresh daisies looked up from a small glass of water. The fourth one was still fresh in my room. On the wall above the bed was a large print by the Swiss painter Klee and on the other wall a bookshelf, possibly recently installed, full of books.

Martin had prepared coq au vin, small new potatoes, boiled and buttered with dill, and a green salad. A bottle of Bordeaux accompanied the meal; it ended with slices of fresh peaches in cream. Finally we had espresso in tiny cups. My generous praise with every bite pleased him.

"I had no idea that a student of physics could cook so well and serve so beautifully," I told him as we went for a walk near the ocean afterward. The feeling that had distracted me in my room earlier now enveloped us both. Martin suddenly stopped and turned toward me and kissed me deeply. I lost myself in the freedom of total surrender that swept me away from all my plans and duties. I was carried away by the lawlessness of our universe.

The next morning when I awoke, the first thing I saw was the painting above Martin's bed. I jumped out of bed and looked at my watch; it was ten o'clock! This was the first time in a whole year that I had missed my first class on Monday morning. I looked around for Martin. He wasn't there. I could hear the sound of water in the bathroom; he must be in the shower. I dressed quickly and scribbled a note on a page of his notebook, "Shall call later," and left.

The daylight outside made everything seem unreal. I couldn't recognize myself in the rearview mirror of the car as I backed out of his driveway. As I approached my apartment, I realized that I had never noticed that the office of the gas station on my road was painted bright yellow. At home I took a long shower and, after a cup of tea, went to bed, my own bed, which had not been slept in last night. It felt cold.

Tears welled up inside me and poured onto my pillow like the rains of a monsoon. All the struggles and scandals, pain and suffering of the previous five years were washed away by this flood of emotion. It took a stranger's caring love to free my body and soul from this burden. The memory of Martin's touch enveloped me as ether encircles the earth. My skin, my hair, my lips had all been infused with a new sensation, a new energy. Gradually I floated into a deep sleep.

It was almost evening when I awoke again. A pang of hunger pushed me out of bed. I quickly ate some food and called Martin to thank him for the dinner and the evening. He said he had been quite worried by my sudden disappearance.

Days, weeks, and months passed in frenzied happiness. I lost all count of time. The rhythm of our love did not always keep step with everyday routine, yet this very rhythm turned every moment of that routine into music. My life moved between two poles—the university and Martin. Nothing else mattered.

But in such a universe nothing remains the same for long. The price that my all-consuming love extracted from me was high.

I was summoned to the office of my academic advisor. He was shocked by my performances of the previous semester. He got to the point directly.

"Who is the lucky guy? Who has stolen your mind? If you continue to do so poorly, your fellowship may not be renewed. Consider this a warning." I was stung and left his office, determined to rectify the situation. The midterm test was only three weeks away. I told Martin what the professor had said and that I had to pay more attention to my studies.

"We can't meet everyday, but we'll talk on the phone as often as we want. It's only a matter of three weeks. Besides, a little separation may be good for us," I said, quoting from a famous romantic lyric of India, where the god of love himself realized the increased depth of his feelings after a long separation from his beloved. Martin was disappointed but finally acquiesced.

I mastered all my strength to return my attention to my books again. The old habit wasn't hard to retrieve. I began my preparation for the midterm in earnest. Every day, Martin and I talked several times on the phone. I managed to digest the tough theories of tribal politics and social systems, but only if I could hear his voice every day.

A few days after I finished my exam was the anniversary of our first meeting. I decided to mark our reunion with a celebration of the date. I called Martin early one morning, but he wasn't home. Perhaps he'd gone to the ocean for a swim. After several attempts, at ten o'clock I finally reached him. He accepted the invitation and said he was very happy to hear from me but was busy and couldn't talk right then.

On the day of the celebration, I spent all morning shopping for Martin's favorite foods and all day preparing a meal that he would love. As I worked in the kitchen, I smiled to myself with the anticipation of our reunion after three long weeks, which seemed like three eons. I wondered if he still remembered my smell and touch. How could he forget? I remembered every single thing about him. His smallest gestures—how he tilted his head slightly when he looked at me, how he smelled of the ocean all day when he went surfing in the morning. Telling myself that I would see him very soon, I tried to stop weaving such reveries. The pleasure of that anticipation was the highest blessing I could ask from all my gods.

I had just finished dressing when someone knocked. Martin had a key, so it couldn't be him. Who would come now—a few minutes before I was expecting my beloved? It was Martin standing at the door with a bunch of blood-red roses and a smile. I was about to jump into his arms but stopped. The roses were next to his chest obstructing my eager embrace. I took the flowers from him and put them in a vase. He held me from behind and hugged me tight. He took me by the hand and led me to the bed. Sitting me there, he sat on the floor.

"I have a problem," he said. "Right after I talked to you, I got a call from a friend. Three of my classmates from college are due to arrive tonight from Switzerland for one evening on their way to Hawaii. They want to go to a nightclub with me. What do you think I should do?" He squeezed my hands before adding, "I know how much work you've put into making this dinner." He looked uncomfortable and avoided my eyes for a few seconds.

"Your old friends have come from such a distance only for one evening. Of course you'll go. Why don't you spend as long as you like with them and come back here. We can eat the dinner tomorrow; Indian food is even better next day," I said.

"Good solution. As usual, you're brilliant. It may be very late. Men's night out, you know. Please don't wait up for me. I'll call you around midnight." He stood up from the carpet and turned toward the door. This quick gesture of relief hurt me more than the news of his going away for the evening. I wanted to see or hear some sign of disappointment.

"Today is the date when we first met six months ago. Remember we have been celebrating this date every month? Let's at least have a toast." I was embarrassed by my voice, which sounded desperate. He stopped, turned back, and grabbed me in a hard embrace.

"I'm really sorry. I'd forgotten the date; please forgive me. Consider the roses your anniversary gift until we meet again—soon." He left in quick steps and disappeared through the door. I remained transfixed where I stood, as if someone had frozen me with a spell. I looked at the bunch of roses. Something about them stopped me from going near them. I had a visceral sense that something far more shocking would be happening.

One by one, I stored the cooked food in various containers and put them in the refrigerator. I drank a glass of warm milk and went to bed. When we were together, Martin always warmed the milk and stirred in a spoonful of honey before giving it to me. Tonight, instead of honey, my tears mingled with the milk. I was very tired and fell asleep.

At about two in the morning I was awakened by the telephone ringing. But I was dreaming. The telephone on my bedside table was silent. I remembered that Martin had said he'd call after midnight. I dialed his number—once, twice, a third time. No answer. Worry and fear pushed me out of bed. What if he had had an accident! I put a raincoat over my nightgown and went out with my car key. I was not sure where and why I was going. Something moved me with great strength. At this time of night the roads were empty of traffic. I reached his street in a very short time. The apartment was dark, and nobody answered when I banged on the door several times. I went back to the car, turned off the engine, and waited.

The cold of this hour was bone-chilling. In my rush I hadn't thought of wearing anything warm. I do not know how long I sat like this and shivered. So far, I hadn't felt anything clearly—anger, sadness—nothing registered yet. Then I saw a dot of light reflected in my rearview mirror. Martin's car came closer. The sound of its engine was as familiar to me as my own heartbeat. Martin stopped his car behind me, got out, and came to the side of my car. He looked genuinely surprised. I got out and slapped him across his face as hard as I could and continued to beat him with my bare hands as much as I could. He did not resist. When my palms began to burn and ache, I stopped. He caught me in his arms as I was about to collapse.

Martin picked me up and took me inside. "You're so cold, you're freezing; how long have you been out there?" He kept repeating these words again and again, as he rubbed my hands and feet. He put me in bed, gave me a glass of warm brandy, and covered me with all his blankets and coats. At some point, my sobbing stopped, and I fell asleep.

I awoke early and saw Martin on the floor, sound asleep in a sleeping bag. Looking at his sleeping face, I knew that my right to sleep in his bed had ended. I wanted to leave before he awoke. But I needed to hear his side of the story, knowing well that it would enhance my suffering. I went to the kitchen and heated water for tea. He got up a few minutes later and prepared breakfast. I asked him several times to tell me what had happened last night.

"I'll tell you everything. First, please eat something. How are you feeling? I hope you haven't caught a cold." The same good old attentive Martin, I thought. Oh you cruel lover!

We had just started breakfast when someone knocked at the door. Martin opened the door and went out. Hearing a woman's voice, I looked out the window and saw a young Japanese woman standing with a bouquet of red roses. I overheard Martin whispering, "I'm a little busy, I'll call you later. Thanks for these." He came in with the flowers in his hand.

"I see both of you are fond of red roses," I said and picked up my raincoat and went to the door.

"Wait, please wait. Let me tell you everything. She is no one important. Please let me explain, please." He sounded desperate.

"I don't need any explanation. I have just seen what I needed to see." I went out of his little apartment where for several months I had found my home.

It took me several days to get over the shock of betrayal. I disconnected the telephone. Martin took the hint and did not try to reach me. The silence of the phone haunted my life. One single stroke of behavior from one single person had turned the colors of the landscape of my world into a barren gray desert. I ceased to feel anything, not even pain. Then gradually and slowly I began to ask questions—hundreds of them—just like we ask when death suddenly takes a person we love. Why? What could I have done? Was I too eager? Too possessive? Too demanding? The questions led to anger—anger with Martin, anger with all men, anger with myself. At age thirty-four, how could I have been so stupid? In a short span of six months, I had given myself away so totally that now I had nothing left to hold on to.

I saw the rows of books staring back from the board and brick shelves Martin had helped me put together. I ran my hand over them affectionately and asked forgiveness for neglecting them all these months. My books would save me again from the abysmal pain of love.

Once in a while Martin and I ran into each other. We even went to a few parties together. These occasions brought mixed feelings of pleasure and pain, serving as a confused transition to letting go of old expectations. Once I invited him to an Indian classical dance performance by an Indian woman who had a foreign last name. At the end of the performance we went up to the stage to congratulate her personally. She introduced us to a distinguished looking man, Dr. Carl von Essen, as her husband. I remembered then that this gentleman had been staring at me through the whole performance! On the way home Martin made a prophecy. "You mark my word, I think the husband of the dancer is interested in you." I laughed and said, "He's not only married to a talented dancer, he may have five children and ten grandchildren, for all I know!"

Three months after my breakup with Martin, I received a letter from my youngest brother with the unexpected news that, while visiting him away from Calcutta, Mother had died after being in a diabetic coma for a couple of days. Even after I had read the letter four times, the news remained outside my consciousness. How could it be possible? She was only fifty-six years old. She had had diabetes, but the doctors had never said it was serious. In a foggy state, I ran to the ocean. I had heard many times that in grief one goes to nature for help.

I sat on the sand near the water for hours. The gentle waves of low tide touched my bare feet every few seconds. Hundreds of events, words, and moments encircling my mother came floating into memory. The pain that had begun three months ago now mingled with a limitless grief. I entered a dark abyss where nothing was available to measure the depth of my sorrow. My tears fell into the salt water. I felt a primordial connection to the vast ocean. I lay on the sand and looked up.

A few stars peeked out from a cloudy sky. As a little girl, I had heard that when people die they become stars. Perhaps the brightest star over there was my dead mother. A shooting star fell from the sky at that moment. I began to think.

Where has the shooting star gone? Has it been lost because it moved from its place? Stars are born in the emptiness of the universe and shine from the same emptiness forever, unless they fall as shooting stars. We humans are born of parents, live in the care of a family, a culture. Yet, all existence is empty, no matter how secure we may feel.

I looked at the brightest star and prayed, "Ma, when you were in this world, we fought over everything, and we never had a chance to make up. Now you are gone. Please bless me so that I am somehow able to accept this limitless grief."

As the night fell, the air became cold. I was cold and hungry and had run out of tears.

When I returned to my place, I telephoned the only person who would understand my pain. Martin came immediately and prepared food for me and made me eat. He held me in his arms through the night. We were bound again by an innocent bond, which had no promises or demands. With this, he occupied a corner of my heart forever.

The next day Martin bought a plane ticket for me to go to Philadelphia, where my youngest sister Kamalkoli and her second husband

and two children had settled only a year before. I needed to be with her, to weep with her. The day before I was to leave, Martin invited me to stay with him. He would take me to the airport the next morning. I packed a small suitcase and went with him. He cooked a simple meal and fed me with the care of a mother. After dinner, Martin left saying that he had to go out for a while. I noticed with relief that the possibility that he might be going to see a new girlfriend did not send a knife through my heart. I went to bed. This was the first time I had fallen into a deep sleep since the arrival of my brother's letter a week earlier.

The light of dawn awoke me. I saw Martin sleeping by my side next to the wall. As I turned to my other side, I saw three yellow water lilies floating in a basin of water next to the bed.

I remembered a Sunday afternoon four months before. Without saying where we were going, Martin had driven us to the botanical gardens in Los Angeles . I had told him once that my favorite flower was the water lily, which grew wild in many parts of India. As a child, I fell in love with this exquisite flower of white, yellow, and pink—which floats on the water, blooms with the sun, and closes as the sun goes down. I loved the yellow ones the most. Martin had driven two hours that Sunday afternoon to show me the blooming lilies in Los Angeles, tens of thousands of miles away from my country.

"If I ever want to bring you your favorite flower, I may have to drown. These flowers have long and tangled roots deep in the mud," he had said.

"There is a folk tale in Bengali," I had said, "which tells about a man who rowed a boat to the middle of a lake to pick a few water lilies for his beloved. As he pulled at them, their long stems pulled him down into the depths." I had looked at him and added, "Please don't ever try to pick them."

"I've already been pulled into the depths by my love for you. I don't need any water to drown," he had said before kissing me.

I realized with surprise that Martin must have gone to the botanical gardens in Los Angeles last night to steal my favorite flowers!

With a flicker of smile in his eyes, Martin said, "The night watchman almost caught me; I was in waist-deep water. Fortunately I had my trusty Swiss Army knife with me. In your enormous grief, I hope these flowers will console you a little."

I lowered my face to the basin—into the half-open flowers. Their tender touch opened the floodgate of my tears—tears for my mother, tears for our lost love, and tears for Martin, who was so loving even when he did not love me.

An hour later he took me to the airport and kissed me good-bye for the last time.

MY FIRST BOOK

As time passed my mourning for Mother and my lost love transformed into a ferocious zeal for work. I worked hours at a time to finish my degree as soon as possible and leave California, where I had experienced the most unprecedented joys and the most wrenching pains of my life.

In June of 1972, three years after I had come to La Jolla, and two months after my mother's death, I finished my doctoral thesis and defended it. I was awarded a postdoctoral fellowship from the South Asian Studies Department of the University of Chicago for a year. The University of Chicago Press had already accepted the book resulting from my thesis for publication. A year's residence in Chicago made it very convenient for me to make the necessary revisions to the manuscript, which was titled *Bengali Women* and was published three years later. The chairman of South Asian Studies, Professor Edward C. Dimock Jr., who had encouraged me to return to the States five years back while visiting Calcutta, was a well-known scholar in Bengali language and literature, and he agreed to write a foreword to the book.

That year in Chicago was a hallmark in my career. I made friends with extraordinary people—scholars, writers, and wonderful human beings. I had the opportunity to teach the great Indian epic *Mahabharata* with Professor A. K. Ramanujan, a poet and scholar. Raman—the name his friends used—was one of those rare individuals who combined creative intelligence and striking intuition with human warmth. He had already published his translations of the earliest Tamil poetry of India and had written several volumes of poetry himself. It was an honor to assist him in teaching. Thanks to his unique style, I rediscovered the epic which we had known since childhood. The University of Chicago in those days was a mecca for outstanding teachers and students. I sat in on Mircea Eliade's and Victor Turner's classes and enjoyed the scintillating discussions of their original ideas on religion, philosophy, anthropology, and related fields. It was wonderful to be reacquainted with my anthropology professors—Bernard Cohn, who moved to Chicago and joined the anthropology faculty there, Milton Singer, McKim Marriott, and others.

Many evenings we gathered at Edward Dimock's home and discussed books, films, politics, and literature until the hour was late. One of my friends would walk me home, and we would conclude that in the final analysis all great ideas and creativity must serve humanity and nourish human soul and relationships, especially friendship. I shared an apartment with a Bengali postdoctoral student in physics, a young man I had known in La Jolla. Amitabha was a kind friend to share one of the rooms of the apartment with me despite the unconventionality at the time of living in the same house with a woman who was not a girlfriend. That year was not only an exciting time for me intellectually but also healing emotionally. I made close friendships that lasted for years to come. But like all good things that year, too, had to end. I was offered a teaching position at the University of Colorado at Denver. One morning in September, I left Chicago for the Mile-High City.

IN THE LAP OF THE ROCKIES

The moment I landed at the Denver airport, I had a premonition that this was not a place I would feel at home. As far as I could see, the landscape around me was dry and barren, ending at the feet of distant mountains which were covered with large boulders. These mountains were totally different from the waves of blue-green hills of my childhood. The Rockies were indeed aptly named.

Within a few weeks, I realized that teaching at a state university was quite different from studying at a university like Rochester,

Chicago, or California. At this campus, as a junior professor, I had to teach nine to twelve hours a week, including carrying out some administrative responsibilities. My disappointment in my first job dampened my idealism and enthusiasm. My year in Chicago had been so interesting by contrast that I kept missing the university and my friends there. In this somewhat lonely existence I looked forward to occasional telephone calls from Carl von Essen whom I had met in La Jolla a year or so before I left for Chicago, although he had not shown any interest in me until the day I left for Chicago.

CARL VON ESSEN

I need to step back a year to tell this story. The day I was leaving La Jolla for Chicago, Carl von Essen telephoned me in the morning and asked if I had a minute to spare; he had something very important to tell me. It took me a few seconds to place him. I told him politely that I was busy packing, winding up my household, and that sparing any time was not possible; he could tell me on the phone what was on his mind. He insisted that I give him just a few minutes—he must talk to me in person. Slightly annoyed, but curious, I agreed. I could use a break from packing, I told myself. He suggested we take a walk near the ocean.

Hesitantly and slowly he said, "The first time I met you at my wife's dance performance two years ago, I was attracted to you. You seemed to have a deep center inside you which I couldn't resist. I know that I am a lot older and have a very different life. I hoped this attraction would pass. But I couldn't get you out of my mind. Now I hear you're leaving for good. I needed to tell you that I am in love with you. There, I said it; it's up to you now." This was the last thing I expected to hear from a man whom I had met only a few times and paid no attention to whatsoever. All I knew about him was that he was a doctor and a married man with an established career. Perhaps he had a big house full of children as well. I knew he had a sailboat.

About a year before, soon after I had met him and his wife at her performance, Dr. von Essen had invited me to join him and a visiting

South African doctor, who was also an anthropologist, for an afternoon sail. Although I feared seasickness, I accepted the invitation, thinking it would be fun if Martin came along. I asked if I could bring a friend, and he said yes. Martin was interested in sailing enough to agree. To my surprise Carl's wife was not there.

On board the boat that afternoon, Carl von Essen took great care in showing Martin various tricks of sailing while I talked with the South African doctor. Fortunately for me, the ocean was calm, and I enjoyed the picnic and the sunset that brushed the horizon with all shades of red. On the way home, Martin reminded me of his earlier prophecy and said, "He has invited you in order to check you out." Although at the time I laughed again, later I marveled at Martin's intuition.

Now Carl von Essen and I were standing side by side looking at the Pacific. I had just heard him declare his love for me. "I hardly know you," I said to this man who was eager to hear what I had to say. "I thank you for telling me your feelings, and I am flattered. But I don't know what to say. What about your wife and children?"

"Yes, I'm still married, and I have three children and a complicated life. But all this is irrelevant right now. Things can change. I just wanted you to know how I feel before you leave," he said looking at the ocean. His voice was calm.

"I really need to get back to my packing, please," I said as I turned away.

More than a year later, Carl von Essen resurfaced in my life at a time when I was at a loss as to where I stood regarding my career. He had written and called a few times during the past year without putting any pressure on me. I had to admit I was impressed by his undemanding persistence. But I did not have a strong urge to respond to him positively. He did not seem to possess either the virtues or the vices of the men who had attracted me in the past. Yet it was hard to dismiss him. He had a calm gentleness that offered me a resting place after passing through a tumultuous storm. It was hard for me to deny the lure of peace after years of struggle and suffering.

But the road to this peaceful haven had its share of obstacles. Even if I believed him when he said that his marriage had been dead for many years, it would be hard for *me* to be the reason for him to leave his wife, who was also Indian. Born of Swedish parents and brought up mostly in California, his background was worlds apart from mine. And ten years' difference in age was not insignificant in terms of ideas and views. Although my own parents were eleven years apart, ten years can make a big difference, I argued with myself. Besides, I always believed that falling in love without reservation was the best start for a life together. Yet, I couldn't deny the glaring fact that my failed marriage had begun with a convincing love that both of us had felt was enough.

I still couldn't bring myself to say yes to Carl's offer of a relationship, but I agreed to remain open to getting to know him, although meeting him often was difficult since we lived at a distance of almost a thousand miles. "I really don't know where I stand. I'm confused, and I need more time to sort things out in my life," I told him. I mentioned my quandary with my job and my dislike about his leaving his wife, even if their separation had little to do with me. Carl understood and, in his characteristic fashion, said he was not in a hurry.

Meanwhile, my discontent with the university, which used junior professors to perform duties that had little to do with teaching, kept mounting. One afternoon the members of our division, which consisted of all the departments of social sciences, received a memo asking us to gather for an emergency meeting. The meeting was to decide what to do about a pipe leaking in a bathroom of the building. After more than an hour's heated discussion, we were asked to vote on several suggestions coming from various departmental heads.

I was at the end of my patience. I raised my hand and said, "Why do we need a meeting wasting everyone's time for this? All we need is a plumber. Couldn't someone at the top make this simple decision?"

"We have to do things democratically," the dean of the division informed me with a sting in his tone. I got up and left, knowing well that this gesture would go against my overall performance.

On another occasion, I organized a team of teachers from different fields to give a series of lectures to the first-year students on the topic of women. Those were the days of emerging feminist literature on everything from sexual politics to gender identity. Each professor was asked to present a specific point of view. The course was a great success. However, there was one problem. I was summoned to the dean's office to explain why I had given a failing grade to an African-American student.

I was quite surprised. I asked if I was being questioned on my academic judgment. The dean explained to me that it was not politically correct to fail a black student. Besides, the university received a substantial federal help to fund the newly emerging black studies program. I had to be careful before I made such decisions, which might have grave consequences. I was stunned. Without realizing that I was trying to defend a position that I saw as academic, not diplomatic, I argued with her for a long time about legitimacy and academic integrity, without success.

That day I came out of the dean's office enraged and disappointed. I might have been naïve in being idealistic, but why work so hard to be part of a noble profession if one had to cater to the prevailing political view over and above learning itself? Moreover, the dean seemed not to notice that when her skin color became the primary criterion of her academic performance it undermined the student's sole purpose of coming to a university.

Amid all this, I had a hard time sleeping. I rented an apartment on the ninth floor of a high-rise building in the middle of downtown Denver in order to be close to campus. Some nights the police and ambulance sirens kept me up for hours. I realized that I needed to be close to nature and decided to move further west to the university town of Boulder, to find a place near the mountains. After asking around for information about how to find a cottage at a higher elevation, I was told that one of our colleagues in the Philosophy Department had such a place and that she might be able to guide me in the right direction.

DISCOVERING CARL GUSTAV JUNG

Sometimes a serendipitous event turns life around. When I met Linda Leonard for lunch to find out how she had found a cottage on the mountain, I had no idea what was to come next. As we sat down at a table in a café near the campus, she put a pile of books on the table.

The one on the top was a paperback titled *The Portable Jung*, edited by Joseph Campbell. In graduate school, I had had to read a lot of Freud's theory as it might or might not apply to other cultures. Jung was never mentioned. I asked Leonard about him, and she immediately offered to lend me the book.

"I have a lot of books to carry home. You may borrow this one and reduce the weight of my pile. You can find out for yourself who Jung was," she said. I thanked her and took the book. I found out that Linda had also just joined the Philosophy Department after her return from Zurich, Switzerland, where she had been training to be a Jungian analyst. Although she had gone to Zurich to study her favorite philosopher, Heidegger, she had ended up training to be a Jungian analyst. I asked her what a Jungian analyst was, and she told me a lot about her experience in Switzerland. Later I realized that I hadn't remembered to mention the mountain cottage even once.

That evening after dinner, I opened the book in the middle of an essay by Carl Jung titled "Answer to Job." I began to read. I finished the essay and continued. I spent all night reading the book. I could not put it down. For the first time in my life, I was reading a scholar who dared to question an ancient scriptural morality with astute and honest psychological inquiry. He also substantiated his hypotheses carefully with experience. His concepts were illuminated with deeply felt intuition, and his conclusions resonated with me on a level that was beyond the cerebral. In a strange way, Jung's writings reminded me of Rabindranath Tagore, whose work I adored. Although Jung's prose lacked music, like Tagore he was successful in preserving the beauty in the exploration of the mystery of the psyche. He could invite his readers to experience his ideas at a gut level of feeling, thinking, intuition, and imagination.

In the early hours of the morning, when I was tired from the sleepless night but inspired with new energy, a decision was born in the depths of my soul. Something told me that Jung was a psychologist who could help me to explore myself. I needed to understand my passion and drive, which had so far led me to the heights of success and happiness as well as to the depths of failure and despair. Never before had I felt such an urge to know myself—why I do what I do, why I fall in love with men who betray me, and what really makes me tick.

Before going to bed that morning, I called Linda Leonard and asked how I could go to Zurich to study Carl Jung.

As with every strong desire in my life, the path to achieve this latest dream was strewn with hurdles. Linda suggested that I begin with a query letter and gave me the address of the C. G. Jung Institute in Zurich. The response was not what I expected. They let me know that I couldn't expect any financial help, no matter what outstanding academic merit I possessed. I also had to show the Swiss government a bank account of at least ten thousand dollars before I could expect to get a visa, even if I received admission to the institute. Then there was the unlikely possibility of my getting a leave of absence from the university after only two years of teaching.

My desire to go to Zurich to study Jung was so definite and clear in my mind that I was determined to try everything I could. But I had to be realistic. With an annual salary of twelve thousand dollars, to be able to save ten thousand was a goal that no amount of determination could achieve. I put a want ad on the campus notice board for a studio apartment; the rent must not exceed seventy dollars. The next day I got a call from a woman who recognized my voice. She said she was one of my students and asked why I needed to rent such a cheap place; when she heard why, she was more than willing to help me save from my meager income for such a good cause. She said that she and her husband had an unheated basement with a bathroom but no kitchen. It would be illegal to rent it but I could stay there free if I wished. I immediately accepted her offer.

I moved in soon afterward and began the most spartan life style I could imagine. I made simple meals in their kitchen. My landlady helped me budget my expenses to the last penny. However, I needed six blankets on the bed that summer, and when winter came, I bought a space heater. I asked Mr. Pryor to put a latch on my door to keep their friendly dog out, but had I been a dog person, he could have kept me warm in bed.

With the possibility of escape in front of me, I felt lighter about my teaching load. And to my delight, my application for a year's leave of absence was granted—but without salary. The way things began to fall into place, I had a feeling that I might not be far from achieving my goal. I also began analysis with Linda, the only Jungian analyst in town, to prepare myself for the exploration of my psyche.

Meanwhile Carl von Essen had been visiting me once in a while, and I made several weekend trips to Los Alamos where he was working at the nuclear research laboratory. Along with other medical doctors and physicists he was trying to find a way to use atomic particles in the treatment of cancer. He had been legally separated from his wife for over a year, and our relationship was going through its early phase of romance. Yet I had doubts whether I was ready for a commitment, just three years after my breakup with Martin. And Carl was struggling with a furious and uncooperative wife who was not willing to end their marriage of twenty-six years. But he was confident that everything would work out in the end.

FROM THE ROCKIES TO THE ALPS

In September of 1975, after two years of teaching at the University of Colorado in Denver, I boarded a charter plane for Luxembourg, where I took a train to Zurich. This was the cheapest way to reach my destination. As the train approached the hills at the Swiss border, outside the train window I saw a landscape obscured by early morning darkness and mountain fog. An otherworldly sensation enveloped me. The urge that had made me take every risk to prepare for this unknown journey of more than seven thousand miles was beyond all practical reason and beyond my control. I had no idea what the future held, what kind of game my fate intended to play with me. The irony of going to Martin's country after our relationship had ended was hard to overlook. Perhaps our meeting was the beginning of this mysterious journey after all.

However, this was not my first trip to Switzerland. On our way back to India in 1964, my ex-husband and I had stopped in Zurich to visit Thomas Mann's grave. We had heard that Mann had spent the last few years of his life in Zurich and was buried there. No one had any idea where his grave was, and after a lot of asking around, we finally found a taxi driver who took us to the neighboring town of Rüschlikon, where we found a simple unadorned grave in the town graveyard. It was a freezing, sunless November day, and I was so tired and disappointed that I had said to myself I would never set foot again in this cold and unfriendly country. Now after a decade, I was back in the same country in search of something more personal and profound. I could not help marveling at the unpredictable twists and turns of my life. I looked out and saw the sun slowly trying to filter through the fog, as the train entered the main station of Zurich.

After some searching, I found an attic room on the fifth floor of an old building above a laundry, about fifteen minutes' walk from the C. G. Jung Institute. There was no elevator, but the heat of the laundry kept the stairs and the landings warm. My room was small but compact, with a narrow bed, wall cupboards, a desk, a table with a hot plate, and a sink. Linens and kitchen utensils were included. I shared a toilet and a shower—which were not heated—with four other tenants on the same floor. I began to keep track of every franc I spent and settled down in my new life. Apart from the classes at the institute and intensive German lessons, I began analysis with two analysts—a woman and a man—twice a week.

The classes at the institute ranged over a large spectrum of subjects, such as the history of medicine, comparative religion and mythology, anthropology, fairy tales, and various creative expressions, such as music, literature, and art as connected to neurosis. Then, of course, there were core courses on dreams, psychopathology, psychiatry, and so on. In spite of many years of study of human culture and behavior, I began for the first time to see the unconscious foundations of cultural traditions and social systems. Without such deep roots, cultural institutions could not have survived for centuries. I also saw the deep connection between unconscious factors and the personality formation of individuals in a specific time and space.

Jung's concept of the archetype—allegedly borrowed from Plato—to me is a profound idea that explains both psychological phenomena and the connections between desires, motivations, and emotions of everyday life and dimensions larger than life. These connections that happen through a person's emotional realization of symbols from the unconscious also create the ground for healing. In all my years of faithful learning in different universities on two continents, I had never been so excited as I was now in discovering the intimate relationship between learning and experience, including the emotions and feelings. Learning was no longer just an intellectual exercise, it was an emotional adventure.

What I learned in the classes and seminars came together with my experience in analytic sessions, where I could use the concepts and terms to examine my past behavior. It all began to make sense within a network of linked meaning. Although I began analysis with two analysts simultaneously, it soon became evident that this format was untenable. I ended up picking one of the two, Dr. Adolf Guggenbühl-Craig, a Swiss psychiatrist and Jungian psychotherapist, to do more intensive analysis.

The more I went inside myself and learned to explore my unconscious through dreams, the more I discovered the dark faces of myself which had been hidden from my conscious scrutiny and projected out onto others. Coming face to face with these ugly and unacceptable parts of me was the hardest work of all. The pain and shame of recognizing aspects of myself that were just like the people I had disliked, criticized, and denied all my life were hard to bear.

I have always disliked people who lacked discipline and were indulgent about their compulsive habits and addictions. I myself enjoy drinks mostly with meals occasionally. One night I dreamed that I was one of a group of drunken women who kept dancing in a frenzy. Later I understood the drunken women to be like the maenads, worshippers of the Greek god Dionysus who represent madness, intoxication, and death. I realized with a shock that I too possessed these traits in potential, which I could never consciously imagine myself having. Another example was my disdain for overweight housewives who never try to do something worthwhile for themselves and waste time gossiping most of the day. I used to avoid them with a sneer. It took me many hours of analysis to see that I could easily become one of them. Over time, life brought me close to some women who were like this, and gradually I could see that often these women had very little choice in the matter. I saw how hard they worked to keep the family together. I began to appreciate their plight and the multitasking they all did. I felt ashamed to have judged them. Around this time several of my dreams showed me being helped and taken care of by a few housewives I knew in real life. Their behavior toward me made me aware of their goodness and generosity, and I felt ashamed of myself.

In analysis, I realized how limited our self-image is and how narrowly founded our self-esteem can be. The latter is often nourished by whatever is praised and accepted by the family and valued by society. Our fragile ego can only survive by claiming the "acceptable" virtues and projecting the negative qualities out onto others, as I describe above.

However, this neat arrangement does not work for long. Denial of such a big part of oneself extracts a heavy price. We develop neuroses, that is, compensation for an unlived life. Without neurotic suffering, human beings might never wish to know themselves deeply. Within a few months of analysis, and many painful hours of wrestling with myself, I realized that I had to come to terms with my dark side before I could even begin to live life fully. Surprisingly, this realization and honest reckoning with myself released me in a way that I had never thought possible. I began to heal.

My dreams guided me to the most painful memory of my life— my complex relationship with my mother, which had ended abruptly with her untimely death, depriving me of the opportunity to reconcile with her. As a matter of fact, I wasn't sure that we could ever have reconciled even if we had had another fifty years together. I had to do the reconciliation internally. Dream after dream appeared with her and me in various situations and events. Sometimes I felt she was sitting with me in analysis, where we both had to face our shadows in order to free ourselves. It took me five long years of analysis to finally let go of the pain of her rejection, insult, and betrayal. Knowing and accepting myself more deeply and unconditionally resulted in a new tolerance of myself.

The excitement of this exploration, I was afraid, would have to end in a few months. My leave would be over at the end of the year, my savings would be depleted. I had spent three times more money on analysis than I had on board and lodging. The thought of going back to teach at the University of Colorado at this point was unthinkable. But I had to if I wished to keep my job. Meanwhile, my book *Bengali Women* was published, and to my surprise, the University of Colorado promoted me to an associate professorship in my absence. I wrote a personal letter to the provost saying that I needed another year of leave. I added that otherwise I would come back and join other unhappy teachers, which would not be in his best interest.

Again to my surprise, I was granted one more year of leave, on condition that after this, I would return for a year and decide if I wanted to continue in my job or not.

Now I had to find a way to replenish my depleted savings. I called the anthropology department at the University of Zurich and asked if they had any part-time jobs available. The chairman—whose specialty was South Asia—was surprised to hear my name, because he had just finished reading my book! Of all the incredible coincidences, this was the most astonishing.

"I have a bit of extra money that I need to spend by the end of this year. If you want, you may teach one course this coming semester. The semester, by the way, begins in two weeks," Professor Loeffler said.

"In two weeks! I have no books or notes with me. How can I teach on such a short notice?" I said and immediately regretted having said it. I needed the job.

"Why don't you teach something you can teach without any notes and books? We've a good library," he persisted.

"All right," I said. I was reminded of my old professor Bernard Cohn at the University of Rochester, who had been just as unconventional in giving me a chance to be a student in his department. I am very lucky to have had such mentors.

I taught a course entitled *Women of the World*. It was the first course ever given at the University of Zurich on the issue of women and drew a large number of students, especially women. In a country where women had not been able to vote until 1971, a university course on this topic was more than welcome. Switzerland was at least a decade behind in any active women's liberation movement. I knew by then that, bit by bit, situations and events were contributing toward my staying in Switzerland longer than I had thought possible.

In 1977 I went back to Colorado to teach for a year as promised. I could see the impact of my two years of intense analysis and study of analytical psychology on my teaching and my life. Everything in everyday life seemed to have shifted its relevance and context. The change was subtle, a matter of sensing myself, rather than being clear or obvious to others. I even enjoyed my teaching in a different way. I did not feel obligated to justify observations of human cultures with established theories. Instead I felt drawn to show my students the meaningful connections of human culture and social structures to unconscious energies and tendencies symbolized by archetypes. I coined a term *cultural archetypes* to mean that each culture has its specific symbols couched in its tradition, history, and ecology which are used by the archetypes to be realized in human life. All human creativity in all fields is expressed through these cultural archetypal symbols. It felt good to be able to share my newly acquired knowledge with my students, and I felt free not to be bound to outworn academic expectations.

However, despite this satisfying teaching experience I knew that by the end of the year I would have to make the most crucial decision regarding my career. If I wanted to stay in my teaching position, I would have to leave my analytic training. Leaving the university job meant saying good-bye to an academic career. My colleagues, my old professors, friends, and relatives were all against my resigning from the teaching job. I sat alone with this dilemma waiting for the decision to surface. Deep down I knew I would have to sacrifice my academic ambition to fulfill my desire to finish the training, which was essential for my soul work—something I had just begun. But it was not an easy decision to make. At that moment I did not know that I would be offered a visiting professorship by the University of Zurich.

At the end of the year—in spite of nightmarish fears—I sent in my resignation and packed my books to leave Denver for good. I trusted my instinct and took the plunge.

MY NEIGHBOR MARIA

When I first came to Zurich, my neighbor on the other side of the staircase in the attic was an old lady who always wore a small white apron over a navy blue woolen skirt, a white blouse, and a cardigan with a lace collar. She was thin and small, looking frail, perhaps in her late seventies or early eighties. She had a thin layer of white hair resembling goose down on her head. Her face reminded me of dried dough, but her blue eyes, though cloudy, had a smile in them. The day I moved in, I saw her standing in front of her door, watching me go up and down with my bags and books. Finally, she came up to me and introduced herself in High German, saying, "I do not speak any other language—no English, no Swiss German or Hindu."

"It is Hindi, not Hindu," I said and told her that my German was not good, but I was happy to have an opportunity to practice it with her. She smiled and craned her head like a bird to peek inside my room. I invited her in. She looked around the room at my unopened boxes, a pile of clothes in hangers on the bed, and a bag of groceries on the chair, perhaps wondering where I would put all my stuff. She left and came back ten minutes later with a small tray covered with a clean starched piece of linen, a teapot, and two cups and saucers made of old china. She placed the tray on the small desk and poured some tea for us, taking a few biscuits from her apron pocket. She cleared the bed and sat. I cleared the chair—the only one—of the grocery bag and sat. It was good Darjeeling tea, already sweetened, without milk.

"It's delicious tea. Thank you," I said. She smiled, showing a broken incisor and a row of uneven yellow teeth. After tea she showed me how to use the outside window ledge to keep my vegetables and fruit fresh. I was entitled to use half a shelf of a small refrigerator that stood in the foyer for everybody's use. I kept my eggs, milk, and butter there. Maria offered me part of her shelf in the refrigerator in case I needed more space.

This first tea was followed by a daily tea party over delicious, sweetened Darjeeling tea without milk. Gradually Maria began to invite me for an occasional lunch of soup and a small salad or a roasted chicken leg. Her room was a bit larger than mine but seemed smaller because it was packed with old and heavy furniture, lamps and ceramic plates, decorative vases and knickknacks. I liked to be in her room, sitting on one of her antique stuffed chairs and listening to her tell me about her past, about Germany when she was young. A devout Catholic, Maria went to church every Sunday. She told me that even though she had little money she had no complaints, because she had her God. She believed the pope was her father as he was father to many others.

I tried to understand her German and gathered together the bits and pieces of what she said to make a picture of who she was and what her life was like. Listening to her talk about her life was like reading about a country in a book that was old but full of interesting information. I had the impression that she enjoyed talking to me—a foreigner and a stranger—who came from such a different world. I was impressed by her simple hospitality. Whenever I was in my room, I looked forward to our afternoon tea.

Maria was an orphan and had been brought up in various orphanages run by Catholic churches. She had a few distant relatives who visited her and took her out sometimes. She was never sent to any school, but she learned to read and write from the kind nuns. As she grew older, she taught herself to read more complicated books. She told me that she had read Goethe, and she even recited a few verses from *Faust* for me. The nuns had also taught her how to knit and make lace. As a young woman, she had earned a living by working in rich homes as a maid.

In one such household, a young man, the son of her employer, liked her and shared his books with her, helping her to understand them. And the inevitable happened: they fell in love. "I was quite pretty in those days," she said smiling and straightening her skirt. "Can you believe I had long blond hair down to my shoulders?" She showed me the length, touching her right shoulder with her hand. The young man was called to fight in the war in 1914. Before leaving, he had promised he would come back and marry her. Maria waited for him and knitted sweaters and scarves for her future husband and made fine lace for her wedding dress. When the young man returned, he told her that he was going to marry a nurse he had met when he was wounded.

"I promised myself then never to have anything to do with men as long as I lived," she said without anger. "And look at me now. I am living a lot longer than I thought, but I'm happy without a husband," she added with a smile. "What about you? Do you wish to be married?"

"I was married once. I was young and foolish. It didn't work. I am single now," I said.

"Good, you are better this way. Men are trouble," Maria said.

Some evenings after dinner, she invited me for a brandy, and we chatted about her life and mine. She would put a blanket on my lap and a footstool under my feet. I would sit comfortably in her warm and crowded room, totally at home, as if I were visiting my own grandmother.

Once in a while I bought a cake or a piece of veal for her. She always shared it with me. Sometimes I watched her cook on her hot plate using limited utensils, a saucepan, a frying pan, and a spatula. She cut her vegetables and bread without a cutting board, holding them in her two hands. She rarely washed her vegetables and never peeled the onions. Yet everything tasted wonderful. She urged me not to cook for myself; she would be happy to make food for both of us, she said. I couldn't tell her that I needed my privacy and needed to taste my own food sometimes. I did offer her my dishes sometimes, but she didn't like spicy food. Once I asked her how, on her meager pension, she managed to feed me. She shrugged and said that she knew how to stretch her money. I never heard Maria complain about anything.

One afternoon when I returned after my classes, I saw that her room was dark. I called her name, and she answered in a teary voice. I asked if she was well. She told me that one of the older nuns in her church had died that morning. She wept like a child, and I did not know how to console her. She then asked me if I would go with her to her church to attend the Easter Mass the following Sunday. "I told my friends and the nuns about you, and they are all eager to meet you," she said, wiping her tears.

"I would be happy to join you for the Easter Mass. Thank you for inviting me," I said.

On Easter Sunday, Maria dressed in a clean woolen skirt, a white silk blouse with a lace collar, and a lavender cardigan. She put on a pair of once white pumps—now a dull yellow with age—and a navy hat and silk gloves. She also suggested what I ought to wear. She had a beautiful broach on the upper left side of her cardigan. I complimented her on it. "It was given to me by my boyfriend when we were in love," she said. "These diamonds must be costly, but I couldn't sell the broach, not even when I needed money badly. I wear it only on special occasions." Did I see a flicker of pleasure and sadness pass over her wrinkled face?

The chilly morning was flooded with sunlight. We could hear the church bells sounding all around us. Maria's church was a short walk away. Inside, it was filled with people. I was struck by the musty smell of incense, flowers, and molten candle. After the service, Maria led me to the altar to receive communion. I was not sure I was supposed to do so but just went along. For me, all religious rituals are interesting. Here I watched what others did and proceeded to do the same. The woman ahead of me looked at me and said something to the priest in the Swiss dialect, and the priest stopped short. Maria came forward, and the priest asked if I was with her.

She said yes and demanded that I receive the host and the wine. When the priest refused, saying that I was not a Christian, Maria told him that I was. She threatened that she would complain to the bishop if he denied me communion. I tried to interrupt the argument, telling Maria that his refusal was perfectly all right with me. She would not hear a word of it. Meanwhile, the row of people behind us began to whisper and ask questions. Maria stormed out of the church, dragging me by the hand, and went behind the building to the rectory to find someone to complain to. I stopped her and coaxed her to accompany me to lunch in a nice restaurant. She was furious over the priest's behavior. At lunch, I tried to tell her that I was not offended. After all, I was not a Christian.

"But you are more Christian than that priest, I can assure you," she said. I thanked her for her goodness and open heart.

"Maria, you are a true Christian. You love everyone. Not all people can be like you," I said in admiration.

"I don't love everyone. I love you, and as far as I am concerned, you are a Christian," she insisted.

It took another occasion for me to discover a side of Maria that surprised me. She had often talked about going to the circus as a child and how much she had loved it. She would love to go again if she could. I decided to take her to the Swiss National Circus, the Circus Knie, when it came to Zurich that spring. Maria was overjoyed when I got two tickets for us. One Saturday afternoon, I held Maria's hand tight in mine and entered the huge tent on the park of Bellevue Platz. The usher, a tall African man, took our tickets and showed us to our seats in the makeshift gallery. Suddenly Maria began to shiver. Her palm inside mine shook uncontrollably, and she said something under her breath, which I could not follow. After we were seated, I asked if she were sick. Would she like some water? She still shook a little and stuttered. All I could understand was "the black man, the black man."

Astonished, I asked if she had ever seen an African before. She said no and again murmured something negative about blacks that I could not fully understand. I pulled up my sleeve and showed her my arm. "Maria, look, my complexion is not as white as yours. But you have no problem becoming my friend, and you love me as I love you. He is from Africa, where the sun is very strong and makes the skin burn." I could not find any other way to tell her what I wanted to say.

"But, you are Manisha, and I don't notice your skin," Maria said very simply. I was relieved to notice that she had recovered from her shock.

Several years later, after I had finished my studies at the C. G. Jung Institute in Zurich and returned to the States, I received a letter from a nun, in care of a Catholic church in Zurich, telling me that Maria had died that spring at the age of eighty-nine. The letter also said that Maria had left a few things in her will for me—a diamond broach, a small carpet, and a copper vase. Would I let them know how they could ship them to me? The letter ended: *It might be a good idea for you to come in person to pick up the broach since it is quite valuable.*

ANALYSIS, DREAMS, AND THE UNCONSCIOUS

An important part of Jungian analysis is to interpret dreams and to discover the connections between dream images and real-life situations, conscious feelings, and understanding. These connections are essential in order for a person to expand self-knowledge and to feel emotional security. The images from the unconscious are not always understandable by intellect alone because they embody symbolic representations. These images bring new information from the depths of the unconscious. In order to become more complete human beings, we need to integrate this information.

The more I became aware of my unconscious, the more I felt connected to a larger-than-life existence. My limited personal experiences became part of a universal perspective on eternal life. Its finite boundary expanded and became part of an infinite space. It was a painful journey on which I encountered dark and unacceptable aspects of myself, which had so far been projected onto others, as I have described earlier. Once I acknowledged these emotionally, to my surprise, a new source of creative energy was released and became available. Dreams were the bridge that connected me with my larger self and eternal life. Memories and events of life became more meaningful as I delved more deeply into my psyche.

For the first time, I had an understanding of the source and the meaning of my otherworldly experiences. My encounters with the black stone in my childhood, the Kamakhya Temple in my teens, and the Hindu wedding ritual in my youth all were archetypal encounters expressed through my cultural heritage. Moreover, certain important dreams appeared to tell me the purpose and significance of specific events which had puzzled and shocked me. Early in analysis I had a dream that explained why I never had children.

I'm in a waiting room with a group of pregnant women in what appears to be a maternity hospital. One by one women go in and after a few minutes come out with a basket in which a newborn baby wrapped in a white blanket sleeps. When my turn comes, I enter the office of a woman doctor. When I leave, I too am given a basket. I go out to meet my husband, who has come to take me home. I show the basket to him, and instead of a baby we see a beautiful bluish white dove that is ready to fly.

It appears as if the unconscious offered a peaceful solution to compensate for my inability to be a mother in the biological sense of the term. In its place I was given the gift of imagination, peace, and sacred purity—some of the qualities a white dove symbolizes. I was entrusted to give birth to these possibilities, which had already been born in my unconscious; now, with this dream, I was conscious of them. This dream and the associated feelings explained my lack of motherhood and at the same time guided me to a profound realization that childlessness was no longer an issue. It was imperative that I *give birth* to something different, no matter how intangible. After many years of teaching and analyzing the unconscious of other people I now know that mothering can take many forms.

Another dream that came two years after the maternity dream was also crucial in my journey to the unconscious world and to my real self.

An ordinary woman from a simple background is cleaning the
mud floor of a hut to prepare an eating area for guests. As she
wipes the floor with a rag, she notices that inside her two palms
all ten fingers are studded with silver jewelry embedded into her
flesh. In the dream she knows that this embedded jewelry can
also scratch the faces she would touch to connect and comfort.

When I awoke from this dream, I could not shake off the vivid image of the fingers studded with silver jewelry, yet I failed to see any connection between this strange yet stunning image and my conscious life. This image pursued me persistently. I had to draw it on large pieces of paper to see if any associations would appear. Several weeks passed but I could not link my dream to anything meaningful. I lived in a state of suspended irritation and disorientation. I could not get rid of the image; it followed me everywhere.

Around that time I became seriously ill with a bad cold and fever. I had to stop all my activities, including going to analytic sessions, and took to my bed. One night, in the middle of a feverish sleep, I suddenly saw a vision of the goddess Durga, whom I had worshipped as a child in my father's ancestral village. It was the same glorious figure I remember from childhood, standing on a lion, about to attack the buffalo demon with the shining weapons held in her ten arms. With this vision, I broke out in a sweat and the fever subsided. I jumped out of bed and dialed my analyst's number to tell him that I now knew the meaning of the dream. The ten fingers of the woman in my dream were miniature forms of Durga's ten hands, showing the miniature weapons embedded in the flesh. Then I noticed the time on my clock and put down the receiver. One did not call a Swiss at three in the morning, even if it was a breakthrough realization.

It was hard to contain my excitement at this discovery. The goddess I had known and worshipped as a child was still in my unconscious and appeared after all these years—albeit indirectly—to give me a valuable message. Those powerful weapons were diminished in size in order to fit a human scale. They remained etched in the flesh of the simple woman of my dream, a version of myself, with the capacity to fight, to subdue the demonic forces, but here they took an attenuated form. The message I took from this dream was that I must never forget the power I inherited from the goddess to fight the demons within us. At the same time the miniature weapons studded inside my fingers can scratch faces I want to touch.

What appears to the naked eye and what is explicable by rational thinking is not always the truth about oneself. Sometimes our real nature may be hidden in our history and religious symbols, especially if it is associated with our childhood. Of the thousands of my dreams, many offered these symbols back to me as if to remind me who I really was. Carl Jung dared to say that we human beings must reconnect to these hidden aspects of ourselves. Otherwise we risk neurotic symptoms or worse. The more deeply I delved into my unconscious, the more I was convinced that I needed to take this painful yet rewarding journey to reach the goal of a balanced and creative life.

LOVE AGAIN

My relationship with Carl von Essen moved toward a committed one with various constraints, including the distance between us of seven thousand miles. In 1976, he came to Switzerland to spend a sabbatical year working at a laboratory in Lausanne in the French part of Switzerland, and we lived together for that year in the beautiful Swiss capital, Bern. Every morning we left Bern from the railway station going in opposite directions—I to the east to Zurich, and Carl to the west to Lausanne, perhaps a daily pilgrimage for both of us before we could begin a life together. We met again in the evening at the station before going to our small apartment. Carl was still in the process of getting his divorce, and neither of us had much money. But with the money he got from selling some of his assets, he bought a Volkswagen camper in Germany, which took us to many beautiful places in Switzerland and other countries.

It was an intensely romantic year for us—living in a city where we knew no one and playing at housekeeping in a studio apartment without furniture. On weekends we took off in our Volkswagen to explore various places where we camped and took long walks in the valleys of the Alps. We hiked on the slopes along the manicured pastures bordered by evergreen woods. I carried a botanical book and tried to learn the names of alpine plants and flowers. After a picnic lunch we would rest in the camper. Some afternoons we encountered herds of cows with large metal bells hanging from their necks that rang through the fog to alert their owners to their whereabouts. The farmers milked their huge udders, filling large cans with frothy milk. They always poured some in a cup for me when I asked. The milk was warm, sweet, and creamy.

Besides being an excellent sailor, Carl is also an avid angler. He is more at home in the wilderness than in an urban atmosphere. I, on the other hand, have always been a product of the city, though as a girl I loved to walk in the hills of our little town. Still, I had never had an opportunity to camp or to be in the wilderness for days at a time. Carl opened up an entirely new world for me. I told him that my fishing adventures had ended when I was seven years old with a few attempts in the front pond at my grandparents' home. Our great-uncle taught us how to fish with a bamboo pole with a thread tied to it, ending with a hook on which we girls put a tiny ball of rice and the boys put worms. Carl laughed and said that he would get me a real fishing rod and teach me how to cast a line in a swift river. What he did not tell me was that I would have to get *into* the river before casting. My fishing efforts were brief, and after several attempts Carl gave up on his lessons. But I loved to accompany him on those trips.

It was on one such fishing trip in the rolling country of Pennsylvania—early in our acquaintance after I decided to be open to his overtures—that I was first drawn to him. It was early autumn. The trees were still green with touches of yellow and red. We stayed in a small hotel near a stream where guests were allowed to fish. After lunch, while resting, I fell asleep. When I awoke, it was late afternoon and Carl was not there. I went out to the stream looking for him and saw his silhouette against the western sky, filled with the last light of the day. A row of trees stood along the river.

It was totally quiet except for the occasional hissing sound of Carl's casting line. I was able to see the line only because it caught the light of the setting sun for fractions of a second. Everything—the dark water of the river reflecting the shadows of the green trees on its bank and the red and blue of the sky—framed him tenderly. If I had not seen him there, I would never have known that such a perfect blending between a man and his surroundings was possible. At that moment I knew that I *had* to get to know this man, to be close to him. Perhaps he could teach me how to be part of such magical peace.

Although I never learned how to cast a line, I came to enjoy nature. We traveled all over Europe in our simple camper without air conditioning and spent nights in the middle of silent woods, in sudden electric storms, and near thunderous waterfalls. I enjoyed cooking freshly caught trout on the open fire and improvised dishes from wild garlic and fiddlehead ferns. But I was always envious of Carl's ability to feel at home in the wilderness. I had to undergo a few dangerous experiences to realize how different our upbringings were.

One spring day Carl took me to swim in the Aare, one of Switzerland's major rivers which flows through Bern. The river was full of cold snow-melted water that rushed past its banks with great force. Floating downriver with the spring flood was challenging, a popular sport for young people. The older people lay on their reclining chairs watching children play on the bank. Some swimmers were dressed in wet suits and some of them used tires for floating. The laughter and frolicking made me relax even though the sight of the force of the water worried me. Carl told me that he would hold my hand the whole time; all I had to do was go with the current and not panic. "You'll love it, it's more thrilling than anything you have ever experienced," he said. Knowing his abilities, I tried to shake off my fear.

With the sun above us, the water did not feel so cold. But the strong current made it impossible to stand even in shallow water. Ferocious waves broke over me. I thought I would break into pieces. One such wave pulled me so hard that I lost my grip on Carl's hand. I tried to float, but the spray from the turbulent current blinded me, and I panicked. Then I saw a red iron post in the water close to the bank. With all my strength I tried to reach it so that I could grab hold of it. A big wave pushed me within a few inches of the pole. Miraculously my head was not bashed against it. With both arms I held on to the pole like a hooked game fish, the currents splashing over my body.

Saved from disaster, I started crying. I was furious with myself for listening to a man who had nothing in common with my upbringing. But then I became worried about him. Was he all right? In a few moments Carl rescued me by pulling me to shore. He had no idea why I was crying. I wondered if my trusting him so fully was not too much of a responsibility for him. After all the bitter experiences with men in my life, I still seemed to have unlimited trust in a man's ability. I ought to have listened to my instinct and stayed away from the ferocious river. But I had not learned my lesson yet.

One morning, six months or so after the event in the river, Carl suggested that we go to Lucerne for the weekend. I was immediately ready to visit that beautiful town with the large lake surrounded by mountains.

"Sounds like a great idea, but why Lucerne?" I asked.

"I have always wanted to climb the Pilatus, which is one of the mountains near Lucerne," he said with enthusiasm.

"How high is this Pilatus? I have never heard of it."

"Close to two thousand meters, I think. Even you'll find it possible to climb."

"Oh, no. I'm not going to climb Pilatus or anything else for that matter. I would be quite happy walking around town and by the lake. I've heard there are ferryboats with good restaurants. Let's do that. It would be fun, don't you think?" I said.

"I thought you were born near the foothills of the highest mountains in the world. You cannot be afraid to climb such a small mountain," Carl dared me.

I ignored his provocation and moved to another topic. I was determined not to fall into his trap this time.

In Lucerne we stayed in a cozy hotel. The windows opened to a magnificent view of the mountains. The next day, early in the morning, we dressed in our hiking attire and trusty Swiss boots to take what I thought would be a leisurely walk. With some nuts and chocolate bars in our backpacks, we headed for the lower plateau of one of the mountains. It was a beautiful day in late spring. The sun warmed the cool air quickly. We walked for a couple of hours on fairly level tracks. Then we sat on one of the trailside benches and looked down at the city.

"How beautiful it looks from here! Look at the red tile roofs around the twin spires of the cathedral . . . and the lake over there looks like a mirror reflecting the patches of clouds and the sky," I said in rapt admiration.

"It will look even better from higher up," Carl said and began his hike again as he bit into a chocolate bar.

"What's the need to go any higher? The view is perfect from here," I mumbled as I followed him, although I did not think he heard me. After a while he looked back and smiled.

"See, you are already climbing, but you have not even noticed. You are a pro. Imagine, when we reach the summit, and you sip your hot tea as you look down on the world below, what a thrill that will be!" he said and kept walking.

From his words, I knew now that he really meant it when he told me earlier about climbing to the peak of Pilatus. I was upset but kept quiet partly because, so far, I was enjoying our gentle climb. We climbed another hour and noticed that the trees were gradually being replaced by dwarf shrubs and bushes. Then those too disappeared from sight. There were only rocks and stones. I slipped a few times, and the trail began to grow narrower and steeper. Carl stopped, opened his backpack, and took out a bundle of looped rope. He tied one end around his waist and the other end around me, making sure the knot was secure.

"You go ahead of me, I'll follow. Nothing to worry, if you slip I am here to catch you," he said casually.

Now I realized my stupidity in believing that we were out for a leisurely walk. I was afraid to look down or look ahead. One of my feet could slide at any moment, and the two of us would disappear into the abyss. After all these years of hard work, struggle, and waiting, were we doomed to this end? I could not think any more. Chanting the name of the goddess Durga in silence, I proceeded to climb slowly, putting one foot in front of the other. I have no idea how I managed to climb another thousand feet to the summit.

Once we reached the top, I was about to say something harsh to Carl when he put his arms around me and said, "You have to admit, the view from here is out of this world."

"Please don't pull me into your adventures again. Getting to know and love you is more challenging an adventure than climbing a mountain," I said as gently as I could, and I added, "Exploration of the inner world is my challenge. I leave the outer adventures to you. Please don't forget I am a woman from India, where people do not climb their mountains because they believe the gods live there." Carl listened to me quietly. On the way back down, we took the cable car.

MY SECOND MARRIAGE

Carl had been offered a position by the Swiss government to direct a research department on nuclear medicine under the auspices of ETH, the famous Swiss Federal Institute of Technology in Zurich. Finally, after seven years, we could be in the same location. We could settle down as a married couple. We flew back to the States to be married.

On July 14, 1979, we were married in the rose garden at the home of my sister and her husband on the outskirts of San Francisco. Carl wanted a Hindu wedding because he had not been brought up in any Christian tradition. Our Hindu ceremony was condensed and simplified. It was a small wedding with only forty close friends and family attending. Father sent a letter from India blessing us. I wondered what Mother would have done if she had been alive. Could she have been happy for me?

My experience of this wedding was different from the first one. The ceremony felt like a ritual marking a culmination—a union that had been going through a journey with ups and downs over a long time.

I still wonder if I could have married Carl, and lived as I have for thirty-five years together with him, without my self-exploration and the understanding I gained of myself. I was grateful for my years of deep analysis. I needed to understand my own motivations and complexities, as well as my past attractions to the kind of men who made me feel special yet could not sustain a commitment. I needed to know what I had been looking for in those relationships. I needed to understand which traits and qualities of my own character needed to be brought into balance within myself. I began to realize that I had been neglecting parts of myself to achieve my academic aspirations. I needed to learn to sacrifice ambition. I had to be self-sufficient emotionally, not just economically.

Carl was not only supportive and respectful of my efforts to complete this inner journey but also helped me find my way back to my real self by being who he was. My first husband had swept me off my feet with his dazzling oratory and took me by the hand to a world that was intellectually stimulating and challenging. But he also took me out of myself and enticed me to become someone else. I recall how, when we first started dating, he criticized me and called me illiterate because I never read Karl Marx. He insisted that I read *Das Capital*, and every week he quizzed me on each chapter until I finished the book. His unrealistic and crazy idea that we imitate the lifestyle of the French existentialist philosophers Jean-Paul Sartre and Simone de Beauvoir was another example of his efforts to change me into someone else. I have always felt comfortable with Carl because he loved me patiently and left me alone. His only attempt to change me was in the area of physical activities, which, after a few near disasters, I resisted. We both had the benefit of being older and of having gone through previous marriages and relationships.

We moved to Brugg—a small town halfway between Basel and Zurich—located near the linear accelerator that Carl needed to use for the research in his new job. We found an apartment in a new building next to the river Aare. I took the commuter train to Zurich every day for my analysis and teaching at the university. I kept my little room in Zurich as an office where I began to see clients under supervision. I still had the chance to have tea with Maria once a week.

The Aare near our apartment building was the same ferocious river that flowed through Bern where I had nearly drowned a year before. But the Aare in Brugg, many miles downstream, was gentle and contained within its banks. Ducks swam on this river with broods of ducklings trailing behind. In the mornings, I jogged along the river. Our apartment was small but cozy, with a balcony and a fireplace. I liked to cook tandoori chicken on an iron grill in the fireplace. On the balcony, we planted small pots of flowers, tomatoes, and chili peppers.

I had been single since my divorce fourteen years before. It was not easy to adjust to married life again. In those fourteen years I had gone through a lot of pain, pleasure, and struggle—struggle to understand my life, myself. So much of my life had been spent in search of freedom—an ideal that was clear in the beginning but became more elusive. It was no longer a question of freeing myself from my mother's authority or the motherland's restrictions. In this marriage, our languages, histories, family legacies, educations, and religions were different. Yet, in the depth of our souls, we were alike. We both wished to create a life of creativity, peace, and tranquility. Carl at age fifty and I at forty began this new journey with a few advantages, as well as a few disadvantages, in having lived nearly half of our lives.

MY LAST QUESTION TO MY FATHER

In 1982, after six years of studies and practical training, I was awarded my diploma in analytical psychology. Carl and I decided to stay two more years in Switzerland before returning to America. I got affiliated with a clinic and treated patients and continued to teach at the University of Zurich. Carl tried to wind up his six years of research and find a suitable successor for his position. In our last year in Switzerland, he was invited by the World Health Organization to spend six months in Sri Lanka to train young radiotherapists there. He has already spent several months in Zimbabwe, Africa, in a similar capacity, training young doctors. I visited him in Zimbabwe and spent a week in Cape Town, South Africa, to give a few lectures. I was struck by the paradox of the natural beauty of Cape Town under an ugly control of the apartheid government. It was interesting to have met with some of my colleagues there. I was happy to accompany Carl when he was sent by the WHO to Sri Lanka, that beautiful island—a tropical paradise that was going through hell at the time due to severe ethnic strife. Despite the turmoil in the country, we loved our stay there and somehow managed to avoid being killed by terrorists' bombs.

The year was 1984. On our way back from Sri Lanka, we stopped in Hyderabad, India. Since my mother's death Father lived there with Dadamoni and his wife. Father had invited us, as he wanted to spend some time with Carl, whom he had met only once and liked. I suggested to the family that we all come together to celebrate Father's eightieth birthday by traveling to a place none of us had seen. Everyone in our family loves to travel. Father himself had traveled all over India as a young man and had been to the States twice. We rented a small bus, and all sixteen of us, including spouses and children, traveled for ten days across South India to Goa on the West Coast. Father encouraged each of us to keep a diary during the trip as a birthday gift to him. When we returned, we read aloud what we had written.

An engineer by profession, my father was a secret lover of literature. It was he who inspired his children to read and write as a hobby. When I visited him in India after Mother's death, I found him so distraught that it broke my heart. "Baba, you have always told us to write to express our feelings. Why don't you write now about your life with Ma, your memories? It may help," I told him. He began to write a memoir. He lived thirteen more years and wrote hundreds of pages during that time.

When we met him he looked frail. Remembering Mother's sudden passing away, I decided not to lose this opportunity to talk to him openly. I had a feeling I might not see him again. One morning I found him on the roof terrace, sitting with the newspaper. My brother and Carl had gone to the market and my sister-in-law was in the kitchen downstairs. Father smiled as I approached him and offered me a stool to sit on. It was always easy to talk to him. He had the wonderful capacity to make even a stranger feel welcome.

"Baba, I wanted to ask you something. I have thought about this conversation many times but have never had the right opportunity before." He looked at me, still a faint smile on his lips. I continued, "When I broke up with Samir and came back to our house to stay, Ma rejected me. I expected you to protest, because since childhood I have known how much you valued honesty and justice. Not only that, you have always put love and affection before anything else." I paused. Part of me hated doing it, but I needed to finish what I had to say. "When I needed my family's support most, it failed me. Twenty years have passed since then, and I am not angry anymore. But I need to know from you why you could not offer me the shelter and support I needed so badly."

Father listened to me quietly. His eyes now lost the smile. I felt miserable about bringing old pain back to him. All his life, my father tried to avoid conflicts in order to maintain peace. That was his nature. I needed to know, not only to hear the explanation of his behavior but perhaps to understand if a particular situation can relativize the judgment between right and wrong. I think I was unable to accept a weakness in a man I loved and respected so deeply. My father kept quiet for several minutes before speaking. His eyes were unfocused, as if he was looking at something far away.

"My dear, your question is just. I hope you believe me when I say that my heart broke when your mother objected to your coming to stay with us. I admit I lacked courage to stand up to her. You know how impulsive she was. But don't for a second believe that she was at peace with the decision. She suffered immensely. Your mother was very tender inside, but her outward expressions were often the opposite. For some reason, which I never understood, she could not show her loving side directly. Because I had been aware of this conflict within her, I should have helped her to show her loving side to you. But I failed, because I did not dare go against her decision. I took her side and was unjust to you." He looked back at me before adding, "Please forgive me if you can. I am grateful that you brought this up today. I admire you for your courage to stand up against injustice and ask questions when you are not satisfied. I hope you always walk with your head up and fight against wrong."

I lowered my head and took the dust of his feet and touched my head in *pronam* to show my respect and gratitude. Father put his palm on my head in blessing. I was proud to see one more time that, despite his weakness, my father was an honest, humble, and above all a loving man.

NEW ENGLAND

In October 1985, we returned to the States and settled down in Wrentham, a small village forty miles south of Boston. We bought a house with some land, and finally I was able to create a garden, something I had wanted to do all my life. I had never lived in New England before and was deeply moved by the beauty of the spectacular autumn colors. Soon after our arrival, I was driving to Boston to attend a reception at the C. G. Jung Institute. Carl was with me. At a point where the highway divided and I was supposed to take the right fork, I became momentarily disoriented and felt as if I would faint. Fortunately, the traffic was slow, and I could pull off the road. I stopped the car. I told Carl to take over. I had an uncanny feeling that something significant had happened somewhere.

That evening I went to bed feeling uneasy and was awakened by the telephone in the middle of the night. My sister called from California to tell me that Father had passed away that morning. I calculated the time difference and realized that he had died exactly when I became disoriented while driving the evening before. I wept remembering our last meeting and a thousand other memorable times with him. I do not know when I fell asleep again, but I dreamed that my father came to see me. He looked nice in white Indian clothing. "I came to say good bye," he said and disappeared. I saw him clearly, tall and handsome, as I remembered him in his forties. Meeting him in my dream made his death more tolerable.

Six months later I went to India to be with my family. The house felt quiet and lifeless. I remembered how the house in Calcutta had felt after my mother's death. We were like a family of robots—everything was as before but something central and crucial was missing. This time I missed Father's presence everywhere. He had filled every room in my brother's house with life and warmth. Whenever I visited him, at eleven in the morning, after a cup of hot Horlicks, Father used to rest on his bed and call me to chat with him. I would lie next to him and tell him all about my life. In his advanced age he behaved like a friend to his grown children. His beloved son—my older brother—held his hand as he peacefully died.

My brother showed me Father's journal. On the front page he wrote, in his beautiful hand, "I leave these pages to my children and grandchildren if they want to know what I have to say." When I returned to America I brought the journal with me and went for a retreat to a cloister in Kentucky. For a week, I remained silent and went through the pages of my father's journal. I was totally absorbed in the pages, which described his observations and impressions about culture, society, people, and the beauty of nature. I was astonished to see how keenly he observed everything around him. For an engineer, he had the mind of a social scientist and the soul of a poet.

As I read his writing, I discovered how much I was my father's daughter in my thoughts and imagination. Like my father, I too try to discover the extraordinary in ordinary situations. Like him, I try to go to the depth of experience to find meaning. But I could never be as pleasant and loving to every living thing as my father was.

I went back to India two years later and, together with my two brothers, sat down and edited Father's diary into a book titled *As I Remember*. We published it and gave a copy to all the members of our extended family. This book records not only Father's impressions and observations but also gives the reader a slice of the history of his time.

Back in New England, I realized for the first time what it was to lose both parents. It was a sense of being alone yet also of being a more responsible adult. I became very busy with my practice as an analyst and with teaching and training students at the C. G. Jung Institute in Boston. As usual, I worked extremely hard in my double profession, along with keeping a large house and tending a garden. I received invitations from different countries—Europe, Australia, India—to give lectures and seminars. I traveled from one end of the world to the other, riding high on success. One of my friends used to compare my life to a South Indian temple façade, where not an inch of space is left without an intricate design. Carl, busy with his own profession, never interfered with my work and travel plans. The decade between 1984 and 1994 was the busiest and most fulfilling time of my life and career. But in the big scheme of the universe, nothing remains the same for long. Hubris is followed by a nemesis.

SHOCKING DIAGNOSIS

In September of 1993 after a routine mammogram in the hospital where Carl worked, I was told that there was an abnormality in the X-ray film. A needle biopsy showed a tiny malignant tumor of a rare kind in my left breast. This brought down the world around me. When Carl told me the result of the mammogram I kept telling myself that there had to be a mistake. It could not be. But I could not remain in denial when, along with several lymph nodes, the pea-sized tumor was surgically removed. Fortunately for me, the cancer was localized only in the tumor. For prophylactic purposes, I had to undergo radiotherapy for six weeks.

Early each morning I went to the hospital, where Carl was the chief of the radiotherapy department, had the treatment for ten minutes, and took the train to Boston to my practice and teaching. In the evening, I returned and took walks. I did not join a support group as was suggested by the doctors. I did not have time to sit around and talk about my illness, either to vent anger or to ask for sympathy.

After the initial shock of the diagnosis, when I found out that the cancer was localized, I behaved as if nothing had changed. As the wife of a radiotherapist, I trusted fully in the power of modern medicine. I knew that I would receive the best treatment available. Nobody except my closest friends and immediate family knew that I had had this trauma. I was proud that I did not stop working even one single day. Now, looking back after more than two decades, I realize that fear of death kept me from facing the trauma of the real experience of my disease and its consequences. Obviously this life-threatening disease was not enough to slow down the high-speed lifestyle I had created for myself and was proud of.

MY HEART, MY DEATH

It was October of 1994, a little over a year after the diagnosis of breast cancer. All the trees of New England had changed from green to yellow, red to rusty brown; their leaves played in the liquid gold of the autumn sun. I watched my favorite season in delight as I planted crocus, daffodil, and tulip bulbs in the already cooling soil of my garden. Every fall I planted these bulbs until my gloved hands froze. The hope of seeing the colors bursting through the thaw of early spring was enough to entice me. I became distracted thinking, how soft and golden, like the autumn, this season of my life was.

For a few days I had been noticing a sharp pain in the middle of my chest when I walked or did any exercise. It came suddenly and disappeared after a few seconds. When I told Carl about it, he showed no concern and said it could be indigestion. However, he suggested I call my doctor and get a checkup. When I called my primary physician and described the symptoms, he asked me to go to the hospital immediately. There I spent most of the day undergoing tests. The observations during a stress test led the cardiologist to conclude that one of my coronary arteries might be blocked.

The same day they sent me to the Lahey Clinic, a famous clinic for heart-related problems. I was to have an angiogram the next morning. "It will be over in half an hour," my doctor assured me before I was put into an ambulance.

I was distraught from having had to cancel five patients that day. Suddenly I was plucked from my normal life and placed in a hospital, spending the night in a strange bed. I was given light food and various medications. A resident sat near me with a portable EKG machine and kept recording my heartbeat. It was impossible to rest or sleep. In the middle of the night, I began to feel intermittent sharp pain in the chest. Early the next morning a nurse woke me and asked me to shower and put on a robe.

"Your angiogram is scheduled at seven. Does your husband know when to come to pick you up?" the nurse asked.

"Yes, he will be here soon."

In the bathroom I looked out the window. It was still slightly dark. I saw the red branches of a sugar maple moving gently in the breeze. There was no sound except the hum of the air conditioner. I stood under the hot shower. I had a vague sensation that something important was about to happen. It was a feeling of neither fear nor hope—it was as if I were separate from my body and somewhere beyond this reality. I do not know why I thought of the morning of my first wedding thirty-seven years ago. That morning I had had to take a ceremonial bath in cold water before being made ready for various rituals. This morning in the hospital bathroom, I was getting ready for something special as well.

Outside the door the nurse was waiting. She gave me an injection and put me on a gurney before rolling it to the operating room. The doctor explained the procedure and said that I could watch my heart on the television monitor if I wished. I watched as a dark liquid entered the arteries around my heart, which kept throbbing on the screen. Soon after that I felt sleepy, very sleepy, as if I had been waiting to fall asleep for many years. It was a feeling of enormous contentment and peace. When I awoke, ten hours had passed!

I opened my eyes to find four or five clocks on the wall in front of me. I wondered if I was in an airport going somewhere. I looked around, and a woman in white bent toward me and asked, "Are you awake?" When I tried to respond, I could not. A thick nylon tube in my mouth obstructed my words. I found more tubes coming out of my chest and abdomen. I was totally puzzled. Then I heard Carl's voice. He and my sister stood on one side of the bed and a friend who was also a medical doctor stood on the other side. The nurse held a black writing board in front of me and gave me a marker. I raised my hand with great effort.

"What happened?" I scribbled.

"You have had a coronary bypass," Carl said.

"How many?"

"Five."

When I heard this I closed my eyes. My fatigue and grogginess from the anesthesia were not over. But the news of a quintuple bypass brought back my consciousness fully and with it came the discomfort and pain. Two days later they moved me from the intensive care unit to a private room. I could see the red and yellow trees outside my window. A large amount of medication kept the pain at bay, but it took a long time to gain enough strength to walk without help. After ten days, I came home and was bedridden for another eight weeks. It was a major project to brush my teeth, to shower and change. I lay on a bed in the downstairs den among my familiar books and paintings and did nothing but stare at the bare ceiling. This was the first time in many years that I was unable to do anything at all. It was my first long vacation.

Lying in bed and staring at the ceiling I thought sometimes of the only dream I remembered while I was in the hospital. I was on a sandy beach; my date book with all my appointments fell into the sand and disappeared. The message from the unconscious was clear. I had to cut down on my appointments, reduce the activities of this busy life. In these long hours of rest, I had no strength to do anything. I was too tired to think, to talk, to read, or to watch television. The only thing I was able to do for a short time was to listen to my favorite music, Tagore's songs, on a cassette player a close friend gave me in the hospital. My sister stayed for several weeks and helped Carl manage the household. My friends helped in my recovery every way they could.

I knew that I had come back from the door of death because of the prompt attention of skilled doctors. Thanks to Western medical technology, I had been given a second lease on life. I needed to understand the significance and purpose of this rebirth. If I had died, it would have been a pleasant death. I recalled the peaceful sensation I had felt when I had my heart attack during the angiogram. Yet the moment I awoke from the long sleep of anesthesia the pain of life began. Living brings pain and pleasure intertwined.

These two months of convalescence were my opportunity to find out why I was still alive. I knew that I could not continue the way I had lived the previous twenty or thirty years. A change had to happen. But I was too tired to think. The limitless fatigue pushed me to a place where I saw and understood nothing. A vast cloak of darkness enveloped me from all directions. I lost any desire to live.

A friend who had had bypass surgery a year before came to visit me with flowers. When I told him how I felt, he immediately understood. "At times I felt suicidal, too. All the medication you are taking can bring on depression, but more importantly, it's the heart trying to heal from the violation of surgery." He continued, "When I was at the end of my endurance, one morning I woke up and received a parcel, a box of long-stem roses from an old friend. The note in the box said, 'May my love help in your recovery!' That did the trick. I saw reasons to live. I am sure you will find the light when the time is right. These dark days will pass, I assure you."

His visit helped. I knew from my experience of treating depressed patients that if I had the strength to stay with this despair, it would pass and bring renewed energy at some point. Carl asked me if I wanted an antidepressant, but I refused. Slowly and gradually, out of the dark and fog, I could hear a faint voice inside saying, "Wait, and you will know why you did not die." I held on to this voice and was able to endure my depression.

It was already December. One day I opened my eyes to a sunny morning. Ribbons of light fell on the carpet of the den. I raised myself up and looked outside. The old snow on the deck glistened with the new sun. Little birds jumped over the snow, sliding and bobbing their small necks back and forth looking for some food. Somehow the scene struck me as funny. I smiled. I was alone in the house. It was very quiet. I turned back and looked around the room. There were the four Navaho paintings on one wall, familiar books on the other, a large print of the cave painting of northern Sweden above the fireplace—all called me in, welcomed me back to my own home. A peaceful enthusiasm whispered in my ear, "Everything will be all right."

The realization that stayed with me all that day and all the time since was that in the grand perspective of this universe my life and death are irrelevant, even more miniscule than the fractions of a grain of sand. Yet, my miniscule life is also as beautiful as those tiny winter birds sliding on the snow touched by the morning sun.

A few weeks earlier, a patient had sent me a small package of molding clay and a note wishing for my recovery. "You have helped me to heal; I hope this will help you to regain your energy by shaping things with your hands," the note had said. As I touched and molded the clay in my hands, I suddenly had the urge to shape my heart. I wanted to make the repaired arteries healthy and durable. I am not a sculptor, yet a strong creative energy grabbed hold of me. As I tried to shape a heart, to my wonder, I saw a female figure being born. She was majestic like a goddess, and the arteries looked like serpents encircling her body. I baked her in the oven and named her the *Heart Goddess*. She sits on my writing desk and reminds me every day that my heart is a goddess. I worship her as a way to make up for my lifelong neglect of her. I had for too long been busy pursuing the goddess of learning and my career and had not listened to my heart.

I had not forgotten the brief dream I had in the hospital. I cut down my practice and my travels around the globe. I felt grateful for my heart attack, because it took me back to my original love—my writing. I had been too busy teaching, lecturing, and publishing academic work and had basked in the glory of applause. Now I write for the love of writing. Surprisingly, years of intellectual work in anthropology and psychology seem to inform my imagination in creating my fiction, which I wanted to write desperately when I was a young girl of fourteen.

I take long walks along the Charles River and watch the migratory ducks and geese fly over. I watch the students jog and row. I feel fortunate to be alive in a part of the world where the beauty of nature and culture mingle in a magnificent blend. Here in New England, I go through every season, feeling the heat and cold on my skin, enjoying the riot of fall colors. Like nature, my life rotates from one phase to the next and back again. My husband, my friends, and my family—and above all my writing—keep me alive. I try to love the people around me without the expectations that bind us to one another without respite.

Clay sculpture of the Heart Goddess

Two decades have passed since I first wrote this manuscript, in which I depict a diagnosis and cure of a stage 1 breast cancer followed by a major heart attack and bypass surgery. Thanks to modern medicine these calamitous events gave me a second chance and catapulted me into a new orbit of activity, soul searching, and the rekindling of my initial passion to write fiction. During the long recovery from bypass surgery, it became clear to me that I received a second chance so that I could realize this neglected dream. My ailing heart survived and guided me to bypass the *logos* and delve deep into heart matters. So began my new journey of learning to write from the heart in my mother tongue, Bengali, a rich and lyrical language. This renewed interest in my language would turn out to be one of my companions on my journey back to my deeper nature and culture, my inner home.

Although my first creative writing notebook disappeared at some point during my many moves, I have never forgotten the work of my fourteen-year-old self. I have come a long way since then, but my desire to write fiction has not changed despite the distraction of a career which led me to put my initial desire aside. It should have been my most natural ambition. I have always been the storyteller among my friends and family, just like my mother and grandmother were. In the last two decades I have written two novels, more than twenty short stories, two memoirs, and a few poems in both English and Bengali. In addition, I have published five nonfiction books (three as coeditor) and twenty-five articles.

As I approach the end of the seventh decade of my life, I have begun to see a pattern that has been subtly woven through my life. This pattern underlies life's multifaceted events, sometimes magically connected by synchronistic happenings. For example, Martin's brief but significant appearance in my lonely life when I was in my midthirties could easily have been the hint of my future move to Switzerland for nearly a decade where the final chapter of my inner journey back to myself—and my second marriage with Carl—began. More than sixty years ago, my outer journeys from my birthplace in the northeastern corner of India started. I went nine hundred miles west to Calcutta for college and then nine thousand miles further west to the East Coast of America for graduate studies. Although triggered by the necessity of education and adventure, these westward movements paralleled my inner journey of self-exploration and creativity.

Only now I can discern the pattern of my life to be a tapestry woven with three different but equally strong threads, which were spun by emotion, intention, and commitment.

First, my sense of deprivation of Mother's love and my relentless efforts to recreate it by responding to attention paid to me by unsuitable men, brought both intense pleasure and deep pain that also motivated me to search for self-knowledge. Second, my father's affection, support, and encouragement for learning followed by a series of unconventional mentors whose guidance and affection supported my determination, hard work, and commitment led to a creative life in many areas such as academic knowledge, writing, teaching, doing therapy, gardening, cooking, and painting. Third, my strong attraction to a transcendental experience, which was born and nurtured in my childhood exposure to Hindu mythology and rituals, became a centering or holding principle for my life. The first two threads eventually mingled and transformed into this third one leading to a spiritual quest. My spiritual quest was nourished by my analytic practice and teaching, thereby fueling my desire to help others in their journeys and my own writing as an inner preoccupation as well as meditation.

In this spiritual journey, my maternal grandmother's stories of the Hindu gods and goddesses and my paternal family's unconditional love and support were major landmarks. When I chose to study analytical psychology over a promising academic career, the sacrifice was rewarded by the choice. I was guided by the Self, the centering wisdom within us. Jung's theories and concepts helped me understand myself better through my dreams and fantasies by taking me to yet another level of painful journey to my repressed dark side, which paradoxically cast light on the inner connection to the archetypal unconscious. I could return to my nature and culture internally which I had left externally in anger and disappointment. This new process of self-discovery also helped me forgive my mother and my culture despite their rejection of me and other women who dared to go against tradition in order to find themselves.

Carl Jung took me back to my inner home, my fourth home, rendering the outer home irrelevant. Although I am a citizen of the United States of America my emotional and archetypal roots go back to my childhood gods and goddesses whose faithful connection to my psyche act as healing agents to my soul. This healing process deeply connects me to our planet and its survival. I am indebted to my grandmother, who first introduced the stories of the gods to me, and to my country, whose age-old civilization—for better or for worse—created the foundation of my emotional existence and philosophical understanding. One of the dreams in the early stage of my analysis showed buried figurines of Hindu gods and goddesses in the dry river bed which I needed to rescue and reclaim. These gods could offer me ultimate security by connecting me to the archetypal world of the collective unconscious, the source of all healing creativity.

I shall end this epilogue of recapitulation and clarification by reminding the reader of one dream mentioned earlier in this book and by adding another. The dream of the simple woman whose ten fingers have imbedded weapons like the goddess Durga (page 17) was a crucial reminder of my human inheritance of the goddess's eternal power to subdue primitive and demonic energy. However, this powerful inheritance also put me in a double bind. Although I am empowered with a miniscule divine ability, I am also capable of hurting people close to me because the hands studded with the jewelry-like weapons may scratch when I touch their faces. The dream, therefore, is an important reminder of the built-in paradox of our relationship to the divine power.

The last dream I want to share is a dream that has appeared repeatedly in slight variations at different times of my life whenever I found myself overly preoccupied with too many activities and under stress of everyday life.

I am walking slowly uphill with a group of people, going toward higher mountains, sometimes in single file because of the narrow path, eventually leading to a high valley, reaching an emerald glacial lake reflecting the snowy peaks of the surrounding high mountains. The air is still and crisp.

This dream takes me back to a pilgrim center in the Himalayas, which is the source of the Ganges, the holy river of India, and also the abode of the divine couple Shiva and Durga, the goddess of my childhood. Manas Sarovar, "the lake of contemplation," is not only the source of the Ganges but also the source of Brahmaputra, the ferocious river of Assam where I was born and raised. So Manas Sarovar is an apt pilgrimage for me for more than one reason. I always wanted to visit this beautiful lake but never could. Its altitude of over 15,000 feet and its location on the Tibetan range of the Himalayas posed a problem. These days there are pilgrim tours available for healthy travelers. Since my weak heart and my age prevent me from visiting this sacred place where geography and mythology come together in a story, I believe my unconscious sends me this dream repeatedly to offer me the tranquility and peace of a pilgrimage to heal my soul again and again. This dream also points out the importance of nature in our lives, especially if it is mingled with the cultural mythology of human imagination.

The End

anas   One-sixteenth of an old Indian rupee, before the metric system was introduced.

anjali   Offering of flower petals and wood apple leaves (*Bel*) to the god in a ritual of *puja*.

aparajita   A small, beautiful, dark blue flower with a yellow center that blooms on a vine.

arati   A circular motion made with a set of oil lamps by the priest before the image of a deity, usually an integral part of the ritual of worshipping.

Balo Hari, Hari bol   When a dead body is carried to the crematorium the pall bearers repeat these words, hailing Hari, another name for the god Krishna, perhaps to make the final journey of the departed safe.

brata   Literally means vow. A family may make a vow to worship a particular god if a calamity is averted by the grace of the same god. There are several rituals connected to vows in a rural calendar that the women observe by worshipping a particular god in a specific season with a distinct purpose of receiving a blessing, for example, suitable marriages for girls in the family.

dhoti   A long piece of unstitched white cotton about five yards long, with a very thin border of dark color, which is part of the traditional attire for men in many parts of India. This material is wrapped around the waist with folds in the front and the back. The length and the manner of wearing a *dhoti* varies from place to place.

duli   A square boxlike vehicle with a thick wooden pole that goes through the top and is held by two people, on their shoulders, one on each side. The *duli* was used to carry women and children in some rural areas of India, where paved roads for wheeled vehicles were rare, until early in the twentieth century. The use of this vehicle disappeared with the advent of wheeled transport.

Durga   The name literally means "fortress." The goddess (who has one hundred and eighty other names), with weapons in her ten arms, is powerful and was the only divinity who succeeded in subduing the buffalo demon. Consort of the god Shiva, she is worshipped for four days in autumn by Hindu Bengalis with pomp and grandeur. An elaborate mythology tells the story of her birth, her marriage, her four children, and her death due to her father's rejection of her mortal incarnation. She rides a lion.

Ganesh   The elephant-headed god, who is also the oldest son of the goddess Durga. Remover of obstacles in any venture and the keeper of space and time, he is worshipped by business people. Ganesh's animal is a mouse, and he is known to be a scribe, the one who wrote down the *Mahabharata*, the longest epic of the world, as it was dictated by the poet Vedavyasa.

ghee   A clarified butter, which is made by cooking the butter very slowly for a long time so that the milk solids brown and impart a unique flavor to the resulting oil. It is used for some gourmet Indian cooking and in religious rituals to light the fire symbolizing the god of fire.

Gopal   One of the many names of the god Krishna when he was a child. Many male children are named Gopal after the young god.

guchi fish   A kind of tasty freshwater fish that belongs to the shark family.

gulab jamun   A round red sweet made of cheese and thickened milk, deep-fried and dipped in sugar syrup.

ha-du-du   A children's game that is played between two competitive groups. One of the players has to hold his or her breath, saying "ha-du-du," and run to touch a target within that short time before the opposite group can stop her or him.

Hamam soap   A popular brand of bath soap used mostly by women. A preference for this soap, which has a pleasant fragrance, along with Pond's cold cream, is handed down through generations of women in many families.

jewel-boat A large old-fashioned river boat with sleeping space below the deck. Beautiful engraved designs in copper or brass adorned the bow.

kachari bari or *ghar* The outer part of a large village home situated near the entrance, usually used to receive formal guests and nonrelatives for official business. The oldest male member of the family sat there in the morning and afternoon for a few hours to receive visitors.

Kartik The youngest son of the goddess Durga and Shiva. Known for his handsome looks, he stood for sexual love and was usually worshipped by prostitutes. His animal is the peacock.

khichuri A dish made of rice and legumes (often mung beans and lentils), popular among Bengali people, especially on a rainy day. It is served with fried vegetables, fish, and eggs.

Krishna The god of love and an incarnation of Vishnu, one of the Hindu trinity. He is also one of the main characters in the epic *Mahabharata* and worshipped by Hindu women in their household shrines.

Lakshmi Durga's oldest daughter and consort of Vishnu. She embodies wealth, the hearth, and family welfare. Her animal is the owl.

Lakshmi Puja *Puja* literally means the ritual of worshipping a god. Lakshmi Puja takes place three weeks after the big festival of Durga Puja in autumn. Lakshmi is also worshipped by housewives every Thursday in their household shrines by reading from a book that describes the goddess.

loitya A small fish that looks like a river eel. It is eaten widely in rural Bangladesh, often in a dried form.

ludo A board game similar to snakes and ladders, played among four players with two dice and colored discs.

lukluki A tiny tropical berry, pale blue in color, that grows on large bushes and needs to be rolled between the palms to make it soft and edible.

lungi A cylindrical piece of cotton like a long straight skirt worn mostly by rural Muslim Bengali men of poor background. It is also worn inside the house during the hot season for comfort.

mamarbari Literally means "home of mother's brother," but it also refers to the maternal grandparents' home. Typically children prefer visiting this home rather than the home of their paternal grandparents, because in a patrilineal system they are expected to be spoiled and indulged by their maternal grandparents; their paternal grandparents or uncles are expected to discipline the children.

mandap A sacred room separate from the rest of the family home where the deity is housed and worshipped and nobody except the priest and his assistants are allowed to enter.

mela A country fair.

paisa One-sixty-fourth of an old rupee, before the metric system was introduced.

pakoras Small pieces of vegetable dipped in a batter of chickpea flour and deep-fried. A popular snack in India, they are often eaten with hot tea.

pathshala The literal meaning is "place for lesson." Usually it refers to a small makeshift schoolroom in a village where one teacher teaches the alphabet, math, reading, and writing to a handful of young children age five to ten.

petnies Petnies are female ghosts who speak in a nasal tone and reside on the high and leafy branches of big trees. They are white apparitions. Some of them jump on the shoulders of pedestrians and do not let go; a few of them desire to marry humans.

prasad The literal meaning is "divine grace." In worship, *prasad* are the foods (fruits and sweets) that are offered to the gods, and then returned consecrated and distributed among the worshippers.

pronam A gesture of respect by a younger person toward an older relative, made by touching the dust of the elder's feet and then touching one's own head. This custom used to be very common in Bengali culture in the past. Among the modern urban population it is now nearly extinct.

puja The ritual worshipping of deities.

Saraswati   Durga and Shiva's second daughter, who stands for learning, music, and the arts. Students worship her in the month of February every year, and they are exempt from studying during that day. Her animal is a white swan.

Shiva   Durga's husband, who is also one of the Hindu trinity along with Brahma and Vishnu. The name refers to "auspiciousness." He is a multifaceted god who embodies opposites like creation and destruction, and an unconventional god, known for his devoted love for his wife. His animal is a bull.

Shiva Ratri   The literal meaning is "Shiva's night," and it refers to the particular date on which he is worshipped in the middle of the night when there is a new moon. Unmarried young women worship him in hope of being blessed with husbands who, like him, are committed and loving.

rasogolla   A popular Bengali sweet made of homemade cottage cheese shaped into walnut-sized balls and cooked in thin boiling sugar syrup.

rajbhog   The larger version of *rasogollas*.

Rohu fish   A large and costly fish belonging to the perch family, which is considered a delicacy in Bengali kitchens and is known for its ritual importance in a Hindu wedding. A large *Rohu* fish with a gold nose ring may be sent by the groom's family to the prospective bride's family to mark the engagement.

golap jaam   A rare fruit, close to the size of a plum, that has a mild flavor of rose. One does not see this fruit in the market nowadays.

samosas   A savory snack of deep-fried triangles made of dough stuffed with cooked vegetables or ground meat. Samosas are popular all over the Middle East and South Asia and are relished with hot tea or as appetizers before meals.

shenai   A double-reed wind instrument, similar to the oboe, that is played during a wedding ceremony. The tune of the *shenai* carries sweet and sad memories for the bride who leaves her father's home to be part of her husband's.

Vijaya Dashami   The tenth day of the lunar calendar and the fourth or the last day of Durga's worship every autumn in most of Hindu India. This day is marked by a sadness for the worshippers, who say good-bye to Durga and her four children until the next year when the festival takes place again.

ACKNOWLEDGMENTS

I am indebted to my parents, to whom I owe my life, and to Carl Gustav Jung, scientist and artist of the soul, for helping me to understand it. I have been blessed with loving siblings, relatives, good friends, and wise mentors.

I want to thank several individuals whose contributions were invaluable in publishing this book. Apart from being my constant and loving supporter, my husband, Carl von Essen, helped me with the sketches and digital reproduction of the photos. I want to thank C. Scott Walker, cartographer, Harvard University, for doing the map for the book. Jaffray Cuyler had read and made some useful comments at an earlier stage of writing the manuscript. I am grateful to Siobhan Drummond for her skillful editing and patient collaboration with me. Len Cruz of Chiron Publications has believed in the book from the beginning at our first meeting at a congress in Copenhagen. Finally, I want to thank my colleague and friend Viviane Thibaudier for writing the foreword.

www.ingramcontent.com/pod-product-compliance
Lightning Source LLC
Chambersburg PA
CBHW020527270326
41927CB00006B/469